D1527254

SONS OF ADAM,
DAUGHTERS OF EVE

The Peasant Worldview of
the Alto Minho

.

Sons of Adam, Daughters of Eve

The Peasant Worldview of the Alto Minho

JOÃO DE PINA-CABRAL

CLARENDON PRESS · OXFORD

1986

Oxford University Press, Walton Street, Oxford OX2 6DP
Oxford New York Toronto
Delhi Bombay Calcutta Madras Karachi
Kuala Lumpur Singapore Hong Kong Tokyo
Nairobi Dar es Salaam Cape Town
Melbourne Auckland
and associated companies in
Beirut Berlin Ibadan Nicosia

Oxford is a trade mark of Oxford University Press

Published in the United States
by Oxford University Press, New York

British Library Cataloguing in Publication Data

Pina-Cabral, João de
Sons of Adam, daughters of Eve : the peasant
worldview of the alto minho.
1. Peasantry—Portugal 2. Portugal—Social
life and customs
I. Title
305.5'63   HN593.5
ISBN 0-19-823255-1

Library of Congress Cataloging in Publication Data

Pina-Cabral, João de.
Sons of Adam, daughters of Eve.
Bibliography: p.
Includes index.
1. Minho (Portugal)—Social life and customs.
2. Minho (Portugal)—Rural conditions. 3. Peasantry—
Portugal—Minho. I. Title.
DP702.E25P55   1986   946.9'12   85-13577
ISBN 0-19-823255-1

Set by DMB Typesetting, (Oxford)
Printed in Great Britain by
Biddles Ltd, Guildford and King's Lynn

To
Daniel P. de Pina-Cabral
Ana A. de Pina-Cabral
Ruth Rosengarten

PREFACE

In his introduction to *A Portuguese Rural Society* José Cutileiro argues that a social anthropologist who studies his own society is at a disadvantage and that 'in order to observe and describe the life of some of my fellow-countrymen I had, as it were, to impersonate an Oxford anthropologist' (1971: p. vii). Later on, in the 1977 Portuguese edition of the same work, he changed his mind, arguing that, if the methods of social anthropology are to be trusted at all, they are not dependent on the particular person who uses them.

This issue is clearly debatable. My belief, however, is that we have to take for granted that the social anthropologist as a human being has vested interests in the way he presents his data, whatever the conditions under which his fieldwork was carried out. As Maybury-Lewis points out in the introduction to *Akwẽ-Shavante Society* (1974), the social anthropologist himself should have the honesty to point out any factor which may have had a particular influence on his picture or his knowledge of the society he is studying.

In my own case, even though I am by birth and by education Portuguese, I grew up in Africa as an Anglican. In the summer of 1977, when I first started to prepare for fieldwork, the staunchly Catholic world of provincial Portugal represented to me a largely novel experience. I made a point of choosing an area of rural Minho where I had had no previous contacts, in an attempt to obtain greater freedom of movement, at least during the first period of adaptation to, and discovery of, the field. The suggestion of the borough of Ponte da Barca came from Manuel Villaverde Cabral, then spending a sabbatical year in Oxford. My acquaintance with local society was facilitated by D. Eurico Nogueira, Archbishop of Braga, who gave me letters of introduction to two local priests. I take this opportunity to thank him for his kindness, both then and later.

It took me three months to be accepted by the residents of Paço, where I eventually took up residence. These were three very difficult months. It was only later, however, that I became aware of a problem which I had not predicted and which eventually proved extremely difficult to overcome. This was the progressive discovery of my identity as a member of the urban élite. This membership gave me both status and an informal kind of power: privileges which I did not at all welcome, particularly as I came to realize that they were hindrances in my relations with the peasantry. Throughout the fieldwork I had to contend with the expectations, prejudices, and biases of townsfolk and peasants alike, both of whom imputed to me beliefs, habits, and attitudes which, in most cases, I did not hold.

At the time, this struggle was largely unstated and unconscious. It was only in the process of writing up the material that I became aware of how important my personal experience of the conflict between the bourgeoisie and the peasantry had been for my understanding of local society. I believe my perception of the struggle was increased by my being a native Portuguese. Fewer expectations would have been placed on a foreigner, particularly one who did not speak Portuguese fluently.

This study was written as a D.Phil. thesis for the Institute of Social Anthropology of Oxford University. The thesis was examined in March 1982. To John K. Campbell, who supervised my work, I owe an immense debt of gratitude. I am also grateful to Rodney Needham, whose passion for perfection instilled in me renewed enthusiasm at a difficult moment in the process of completing the thesis; and to Peter Rivière and Julian A. Pitt-Rivers, my examiners, who encouraged me to continue the work and to publish the results.

Back in Lisbon, from 1982 to 1984, I continued to visit the fieldwork area in regular short trips, while radically revising the text of the thesis; in some instances I even changed my mind. Unable to thank all who helped and encouraged me throughout these seven long years, I have to limit myself to those whose generosity was particularly outstanding: Hermínio Martins, Manuel Villaverde Cabral, Renée Hirschon, Rui G. Feijó, and, in Ponte de Barca, António José da Costa and his household, Alzira das Dores e Silva and her household, the late António da Silva Oliveira, his wife and children, Father Fernando Sá and Father José Cerqueira Carneiro.

I make acknowledgement for the use I have made of parts of my own articles to the Editors of the *Journal of the Anthropological Society of Oxford, Análise Social, Estudos Contemporâneous* and to Croom Helm. Much detail omitted in this book is recorded in these articles.

I am grateful to the British Council and to the Philip Bagby Trust (Oxford) for their funding of the early stages of the thesis. In Lisbon, the Instituto de Ciências Sociais provided the indispensable conditions for the transformation of the thesis into a book. Just as the book went to press, I was appointed to a Research Fellowship at the University of

Southampton funded by the Calouste Gulbenkian Foundation, which it is hoped will allow me to continue to develop the arguments expounded in the present work. I am equally indebted to these institutions.

Finally, there are those whom I cannot thank enough and to whom I dedicate this work, my father, my mother, and my wife.

CONTENTS

Contents

LIST OF PLATES

LIST OF FIGURES

LIST OF TABLES

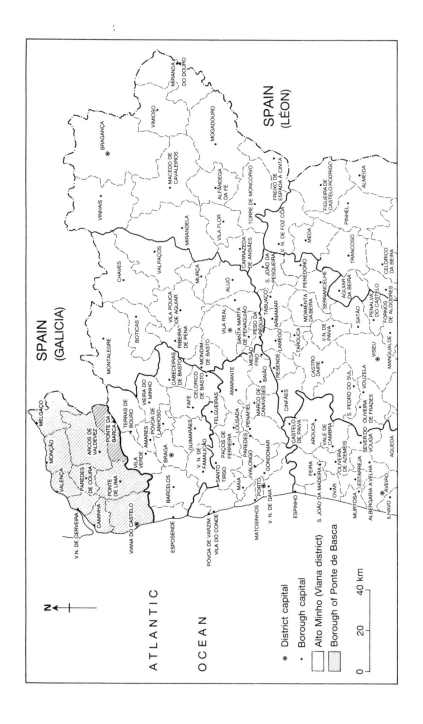

ATLANTIC

OCEAN

SPAIN
(GALICIA)

SPAIN
(LÉON)

N

0   20   40 km

⊙ District capital
• Borough capital
▢ Alto Minho (Viana district)
▨ Borough of Ponte de Basca

I

Introduction

Long ago [man] ceased merely to live, and began to think how he lived; he ceased merely to feel life; he conceived it. Out of all phenomena contributing to life he formed a concept of life, fertility, prosperity, vitality. He realised that there was something which distinguished the animate from the inanimate, and this something he called life.

A. M. Hocart, *Kings and Councillors*

1. The setting

I

The River Lima runs westwards from the Spanish province of Orense to the Atlantic coast, which it meets at Viana do Castelo, the capital city of one of the districts of the Portuguese province of Minho. Further along the southern bank of the Lima are two small towns, Ponte de Lima and Ponte da Barca, whose names refer to the bridges (*pontes*) crossing the river at the points where the road which follows it meets the major ancient routes south to north from Braga (the ecclesiastical and economic capital of Minho) to the River Minho on the northern-most border of the country. Paço de S. Miguel and Couto de S. Fins, whose residents are the subjects of this study, are two riverside parishes of the small borough of Ponte da Barca, which is situated on the southern bank of the river about forty kilometres from the sea.[1]

The north-eastern part of Minho, where Ponte da Barca lies, is usually referred to as the Alto Minho, as opposed to the lower and flatter areas of this province. It is a humid and on the whole fertile region which, apart from the most mountainous stretches, has a fairly temperate

[1] As a means of stressing the fact that these parishes are studied here as samples of peasant life in the Alto Minho and not for any specific characteristics which might distinguish them from others, as well as a means of protecting the subjects of this study, I have chosen to give the two parishes pseudonyms. The name Paço was chosen because of the importance in this parish's history of the House of Paço to which I will refer later. The names of the boroughs and districts are the correct ones. Most names of residents of the two parishes are pseudonyms.

climate with average rainfall just below 2,000 mm and an average temperature of 13° C to 14° C ranging between a minimum of 4° C to 5° C in January to a maximum of 27° C to 28° C in July.[2] Paço and Couto, therefore, have fairly warm and dry summers and very humid, wet, and moderately cold winters. The situation of these parishes on the southern bank of the river renders the climate rather less temperate than that of neighbouring ones on the northern bank. This is aggravated by the contours of the terrain. From Pegadinha, on the south of Paço (517 m altitude), to the river (14 m altitude) the land rises approximately 500 m within a distance of barely 4 km. This means that Paço and Couto are like two north-facing amphitheatres where the terraces remind one of small rows of seats, with the river, the main road, and the churches forming the stage.

II

Minho as a whole has a cultural identity which distinguishes it clearly from the other Portuguese provinces. This is particularly pronounced in the Alto Minho. Although this study deals in particular with the two parishes where I took up residence in 1978-80 for two periods of eight months each, its conclusions are on the whole valid for most of the Alto Minho. When, in the course of this work, I refer to *minhoto* peasants or to *minhoto* culture, I have in mind in particular the Alto Minho. These two parishes were chosen not because they presented any specific identifying features, but precisely because they were like most of the other parishes in this region, in their accessibility to the road, proximity to a town, and consequent openness to urban influence. The more isolated, mountain parishes of the borough, such as Ermida, have a different and more picturesque character. One such parish was Vilarinho das Furnas, which Jorge Dias described in his now famous work (Dias, 1981) and which now lies under a dam. These communities, however, are very unlike those of the common *minhoto* parishes, and even Soajo, on the northern bank of the Lima, which was described by Cailler-Boisvert, is in many ways atypical (Cailler-Boisvert, 1966). Her articles, however, are the ethnographic accounts whose subject is geographically nearest to the material presented here.[3]

---

[2] Average rainfall, 1979: Viana observatory: 1712.1 mm, Braga observatory: 1818.1 mm. From *Anuário Estatístico*, 1979.

[3] Unfortunately, the differences between northern and southern Portugal are such that José Cutileiro's *A Portuguese Rural Society* (1971) is not a natural companion to this study. A far closer example is provided by Carmelo Lisón's work in Galicia (1971a; 1971b; 1973; 1974; 1976).

Rural parishes are grouped around a small town (*vila*) and together they form a borough (*concelho*). These towns are the seat of the local representatives of the central administration, and of large business firms. Similarly, the locally elected administrative body of greatest significance, the municipality (*Câmara*), is found here, as well as the hospital, the health centre, the social security centre (*Casa do Povo*), the law courts, and the large shops. It is also here that the fairs (*feiras*) are held. The town, which is normally rather sleepy but livens up on market days, is the centre for the borough's élite, the provincial bourgeoisie, which is eager to distinguish itself from the rest of the population, the peasantry, which it looks down upon as backward and uneducated.

Most peasants live in hamlets (*lugares*) scattered across the hillsides, which are composed of from five to eighty households (*casas*), and which possess a definite social identity. Hamlets are associated with specific stretches of land, whether or not all of this land is owned by hamlet residents. There is no local conception of a social group independent of its geographic setting, so that when a *minhoto* speaks of his hamlet, parish or borough, he has both the people and the land in mind (cf. Pitt-Rivers, 1971: 7). A number of hamlets, in turn, are centred around a cemetery and a church to form a parish. Under the name *freguesia*, the parish is the smallest administrative unit which the government recognizes and it elects a Parish Council (*Junta*) which represents its interests; under the name *paróquia*, the parish is the smallest ecclesiastical unit to which a priest is appointed and elects a Church Committee to represent its interests (*Comissão Fabriqueira*).

Both the parish and the hamlet are primarily conceived of as aggregates of households—the *casas de vizinhos*. The word *casa* may refer both to a household and to any building inhabited. Similarly, the word *vizinho* has two related but none the less distinct meanings: when used to refer to individuals, it has much the same meaning as the English 'neighbour'; when *vizinho* is used—often in the plural—to refer to a household, however, it applies only to those households which own land and reside permanently in a parish or hamlet (cf. Serrão, 1965: s.v. *vizinho*). This practice not only stresses the association of the household with the land but also implicitly denies the rights of residence to landless people who do not form households in the sense of *casas de vizinhos*, for these necessarily require a direct and permanent link with the land. The double meanings of these central terms *casa* and *vizinho* reflect an ambivalent attitude to landless people. The *minhoto* peasant's concern with equality of status, which will be discussed below, excludes landless labourers as a group, although it does not exclude them as individuals.

For as long as we know, the *minhoto* peasantry has not been a uniform group. There have always been considerable differences in wealth between *jornaleiros* (landless people), *caseiros* (share-croppers), and *lavradores* (owner-farmers). Larger landowners rarely work the land and tend to live in the towns rather than in rural areas. Those who do live in rural parishes usually inhabit large houses in a *quinta* (large farm). In this region of Portugal, wealthy landowners who identify themselves with the provincial bourgeoisie do not call themselves *lavradores* but *proprietários* (literally, owners).

In spite of their differences all of the three types of peasants to which I have referred participate in a common identity by opposition to the provincial bourgeoisie. They dress and behave alike, they speak with the same accent, they share roughly the same attitudes. The population of the borough, therefore, is clearly divided into two status groups: the bourgeoisie and the peasantry.[4]

The primary aim of this study is to describe analytically the modes of thought and perception of the world of the *minhoto* peasants—hereafter referred to as 'the peasant worldview'. In doing this, I am trying to place this worldview in its historical, sociological and economic context, and I am searching for the underlying principles which unify it both in a diachronic and synchronic sense.

My use of the term 'worldview' was suggested by Daryll Forde's early definition in *African Worlds*, as consisting of 'the dominant beliefs and attitudes of one people concerning the place of Man in Nature and in Society, not only as revealed in formal and informal expressions of belief but also as implicit in customs and ethical prescriptions in both ritual and secular contexts' (1954: p. vii). Generally speaking, the long but erratic history of the term shows two tendencies which I specifically attempted to avoid: the temptation to use the term exclusively in the context of religious ideas, and the incapacity to relate it to the process of socio-economic change (v. Kearney, 1975 and Kiernan, 1981). Similarly, Berger and Luckman's use of the notion of 'worldview' is too restricted for my purposes; my own usage is closer to their alternative concept of

---

[4] Weber defines 'status' as 'an effective claim to social esteem in terms of positive or negative privileges' and 'status group' as 'a plurality of persons who, within a larger group, successfully claim a) a special esteem and possibly also b) status monopolies' (1978, I: 305-6).

'everything that passes for "knowledge" in society' (1966: 26–7). Anthropological literature provides us with an array of terms which might be used to cover much the same object of study. I chose 'worldview' as an alternative to 'culture', which would be too inclusive; to 'ideology' which tends to imply falseness; and to 'cosmology' or 'folk model' which overstress the systematic and codified aspects of everyday perception of the world.

In regard to the most important issues which have accompanied the history of the concept of worldview—those raised by the notions of space, time, causality, and self—my approach is not systematic. Rather, the ethnographic illustrations of these issues become clear in the course of this study, an essential factor of which is the problem of rationality— itself an old companion to the concept of worldview.

III

The organization of this study was motivated by the search for an underlying cultural coherence. After a general introduction, I first look at the symbolic features of the elementary social unit, the household, and its formation. I then proceed to examine relations within the household, mainly those between the sexes, and attitudes to human reproduction. This is followed by a description of various manifestations of an experience of community between parish members, and of co-operation between households and between humans and divine beings. This leads to a discussion of 'envy' as the perceived source of social conflict and inequality, and of the means by which it is counteracted, mainly through the offices of priests and 'white witches'. The study concludes with a description of burials, an analysis of attitudes to death as expressed in various forms of worship centred around death, and with the realization that the opposition between life and death—a profound desire for life in its widest possible sense—is the ultimate concern of the peasants of the Alto Minho.

2. The history

I

The historical roots of the present-day division of the land into parishes are to be found in the Roman occupation of the Iberian peninsula. The first Romans reported to have reached the River Lima were the soldiers of Decimus Junus Brutus in 137 BC, but full control of this region finally took place only during the Pax Augusta (Reis, 1978). The Romans curbed the war-like nature of the Celtic population and encouraged settlement in the more fertile and hitherto unexploited valleys (Carvalho, 1956). Agriculture was organized within the regime of the *villa*. A Roman settler would be given a stretch of land where he would organize and manage production, usually with the aid of a foreman. Due to the hilly nature of the terrain in this region, most of the land of the villa was divided into discontinuous plots which were worked by semi-free labourers (Saraiva, 1978; Sampaio, 1979).

The villas were positioned at strategic points near rivers and roads. Paço and Couto may have originated in this way. The Roman burial site which was found near the church in Paço favours this interpretation, particularly as it is near the very ancient House of Paço, one of the noblest houses of this region (Costa, 1868, I: 208). The word *paço*, Sampaio argues, derives from *pallatium* which, in this region, designated the house of the lord of the villa (1979: 68–9). This would have meant that the road which follows the left bank of the river passed outside its door. In Roman times, this particular stretch of the road linked two major military and civil routes: that which extended from Braga to Tuy and another from Braga to Monção. This second road crosses the river at the spot where, in the fifteenth century, the town of Ponte da Barca rose. During the same period, a bridge was built where previously a barge had crossed the river. This bridge gave the name to the town and later the borough: Ponte da Barca – literally, 'bridge of the barge'.

In 411 the region was invaded by barbarian hordes, the Sueves. These were followed by the Visigoths in 585, who, in general terms, continued the Roman system of exploitation of the land. Throughout the last centuries of the Roman occupation, most of the local population had been converted to Christianity. By the sixth century, when the Sueves and, shortly after, the Visigoths were converted to orthodox Christianity from Arianism (550-60 and 589, respectively), a new and revitalized ecclesiastical organization had taken root. I shall quote Saraiva's summary of this process:

The parishes substituted the *villas* as civic units and the moral headship of the communities passed from the hands of the *dominus*, to those of the parish priest. This evolution is at the root of the word *freguesia*, the term which progressively came to designate the new units of population and neighbourhood. The worker who, from the point of view of the villa, was a serf; from an ecclesiastical viewpoint was a son: *filie ecclesiae* (Saraiva, 1978: 22).

The Muslim invasion in the eighth century was not felt strongly in this area and Christianity did not suffer greatly. Although the city of Braga had been taken in 716, by 868 the Christians had recovered it. To this day, 'the Moors' remain strongly present in the popular mind and mythology, but in fact the influence of Islamic culture was minimal. This may help to explain some of the distinct ethnographic differences between northern and southern Portugal and particularly the preservation of the peculiarly north-western sexual division of labour which had already puzzled the Roman invaders.

By the Middle Ages, the discontinuous plots attached to the Roman villa had become fully independent agricultural enterprises. This is the origin of the various old farms (*quintas*) which, in both Paço and Couto, control the best stretches of land and which were until very recently owned by members of the rural aristocracy.

The more isolated populations always remained largely outside the control of the noble landowners. These mountain villages maintained systems of co-operation which some authors claim to be very ancient.[5] To some extent this is the case with the hilltop hamlets in Paço and Couto, where the land has always been owned by the residents and where some hamlet-wide systems of co-operation survived up to the time of the Second World War.

Large stretches of land were put under the control of war-lords by the medieval kings and called *Terras* (literally, lands). Paço and Couto belonged to the Terra da Nóbrega which, with a few alterations, became the borough of Ponte da Barca in the mid-nineteenth century. The earliest references to Paço and Couto as parishes are found in a list of the taxes, written before the middle of 1097, which each church had to pay to the Archbishop of Braga (Costa, 1959: 61). The dedication of Paço to St Michael indicates that the church was originally attached to a seigneurial home and we know in fact that its *padroado* (the right to appoint the priest) was still in lay hands in the twelfth century (Costa, 1959: 135; Oliveira, 1950: 64–5). The church of Couto received its patron, S. Fins, at a later date, perhaps when a monastery was created there by Augustinian canons. In 1180, Afonso Henriques (the first king of Portugal) confirmed that the parish was a *couto* of the monastery which meant that it was managed entirely by the monastery, without royal interference. The monastery was abolished in 1434 (Costa, 1959: 197).

[5] Arguments in favour of this view: e.g. Saraiva, 1978: 235–6; Dias, 1981: 19. For a cogent argument against the 'communitarian' interpretation: Costa, 1959: 235–6.

II

Largely due to the geological constraints of the hilly terrain and to the characteristically dense population, land has traditionally been much divided in Minho. In the seventeenth and eighteenth centuries the overwhelming majority of the land was exploited in plots less than half a hectare in size (1.20 acres) (Oliveira, 1980). Thus, the big landowners of Minho were usually owners of a large number of very small plots.

Tenancy was held mostly under emphyteusis, a system of Roman law which divides the tenure of the land into two categories of rights; that of the owner, who receives an annual rent, and that of the perpetual tenant, who has power over the land to use it in whatever way he wishes. The *ancien régime* system of exacting rent came to an end with the set of laws passed by the elected parliament (*cortes*) of 1821-3 and with the laws written by the liberal minister Mouzinho da Silveira in 1832. These abolished the tithe and most other seigneurial and ecclesiastical dues, they favoured the purchase of full rights to the property by the tenant, abolished the system of tax-collectors and finally in 1863 abolished entailed interests. The intention of these reforms was to open the way for the development of capitalist agriculture, a purpose never fully achieved.

From the beginning of the seventeenth century a new agricultural system, which was dependent on the use of new vegetable and cereal crop species, had been developing in this region. Maize, which by the turn of the seventeenth century had become a major crop in the humid region of Minho, has a productivity three to four times higher than that of wheat or rye, the cereals which had previously been cultivated there. Yields of fifty to one, and even up to three times that amount, are common and maize is better suited to the climatic and geological conditions of Minho than is wheat or rye. This meant that a greater amount of land could be cultivated profitably and it is possible that even in the eighteenth century maize had contributed to demographic growth. Finally, owing to its reliability, maize put an end to the periodic famines which had previously been so frequent (Braudel, 1967: 108-13; A. Oliveira, 1974: 252-3).

Maize required irrigation. In Minho large-scale waterworks are not usually necessary as irrigation is easily achieved by redirecting the small streams which run down the hills or by digging out horizontal wells from the sides of the hills (the *minas*). Water nevertheless remains scarce and the issue of rights to it, in a region where there are so many small sources, becomes extremely complex. To this day water rights are one of the most frequently encountered reasons for legal disputes.

By considerably reducing the area of marsh and uncultivated land, the introduction of maize is largely responsible for the decline of free-range and transhumant cattle-breeding and the development of stable cattle-breeding. The by-products of maize compensate for the reduction in pastures, as the stalks, the leaves, and the male flowers on top (the latter two being picked even before the grain is harvested), as well as the grain itself, are used to feed the animals. Furthermore, a new system of crop rotation, and the fact that maize does not exhaust the soil as much as wheat or rye, meant that fields could be cultivated every year. Typically, from October to March or April, the fields are used to cultivate fodder for the cattle or other 'novelties'[6] such as beetroot, parsnips, lupins, and other leguminous plants which enrich the soil and prevent its exhaustion. Bean plants grow up the maize stalks, thus producing one of the farmer's most important staple foods. Increased cereal production, therefore, was achieved without a significant reduction of cattle-breeding.

At the same time that maize was being introduced, another change was also taking place. Vines were no longer being grown on the ground, where they occupied much-needed space, but instead trees were being planted along the edges of the fields and the vines were trained along them. This meant that they did not occupy space and that the produce of the trees (often edible chestnuts) could also be utilized. At a later stage, vines started being grown on pergolas around the edges of the fields. When these are on flat ground, leguminous plants are grown under them; alternatively they are placed over the terraces dividing the fields, which would otherwise be wasted. The increased need for fertilizers was usually answered by cleaning the scrubland and using the bushes as beds for cattle stables to produce manure. By the early twentieth century, however, artificial fertilizers were being used in Minho (Halpern Pereira, 1971: 103).

Other important species such as pine trees, olive trees and potatoes were new features of the landscape throughout the eighteenth and nineteenth centuries (Taborda de Morais, 1940: 97-138). As the raising of goats decreased, the area dedicated to pinewoods increased considerably and these now cover many of the less profitable hilltop lands, thus providing sources of long-term income for the peasants. The complex

---

[6] *Novidades*, a word used to describe species which, in the seventeenth century, were indeed new.

articulation of stock-breeding in stables, together with intense agriculture in small scattered and irrigated plots, is what is usually referred to as mixed farming—*policultura*—the system that still dominates the rural areas of Minho. The result is an intense utilization of the land where even the smallest plateau or terrace in the hills can be put to use.

Throughout the nineteenth century there was a conscious effort on behalf of the *minhoto* farmers to diversify production. The common conception of nineteenth-century peasant agriculture as a subsistence agriculture is incompatible with this effort, as well as with the well developed inter-regional and international commerce in cattle, wine, and fruit, and finally with the existence of large towns and cities in the north-west, the economies of which were dependent on rural production (cf. Halpern Pereira, 1971).

The development of mixed farming in Minho may be understood as a response to two contradictory pulls being made on the farmer: the existence of a market economy and of a reasonably widespread system of exchange which makes it possible for the farmer to produce a surplus; and a concomitant unwillingness to rely on the market system for the most essential requirements. Mixed farming represented a form of protection against market fluctuation in prices and against climatic variability. By diversifying production, the farmer assured himself that if one of his products did not fare well during a certain year, he could be recompensed by profits on other products: as a man in Paço once said to me, 'When God gives maize, he does not give wine.'

Finally, the variety of products meant that although, strictly speaking, agriculture was not of a subsistence type, the household was not dependent on purchased commodities since it produced most of its essential subsistence requirements. As Andrew Pearce has pointed out, 'the schematic answer to why the subsistence orientation of family productive units should survive is simple enough: the peasant does not perceive the existence of a secure system of distribution of goods and facilities for family livelihood based on money-exchange, and his perception generally corresponds to the real situation' (1971: 72-3). The peasant's justified suspicion of the market system means that a subsistence orientation has survived until today.

In spite of the relative prosperity of the rural areas during the 1860s, male emigration continued throughout the nineteenth century. Emigration was not a new phenomenon in the area and dates back to the fifteenth century at least. In the eighteenth century rural poverty had led to male emigration to Brazil on a large scale: José Fernando da Silva, writing about the navigability of the River Lima towards the end of the reign of José I (1750-77), includes a description of the town and borough of Ponte da Barca. He comments on the fertility of the region but complains about the poor living conditions in the rural areas and the serious exploitation of small farmers. As a result of this, he argues, the young men leave and only the aged remain behind.

When, in the 1890s, commerce in agricultural products collapsed in the face of competition by other more efficient producers, the country found itself in a position of economic bankruptcy and this rural recession is clearly reflected in the emigration figures. Until 1868-9 emigration had remained fairly stable, even decreasing slightly, but from that date onwards it started to rise, reaching peaks in 1888, 1895, and again in 1912 when the national figures were almost four times what they had been in 1888 (see Figure 1). Confronted with the economic recession, shortage of land, and an increased penetration of state bureaucracy, the peasant was forced to emigrate. Emigration was seen by the participants

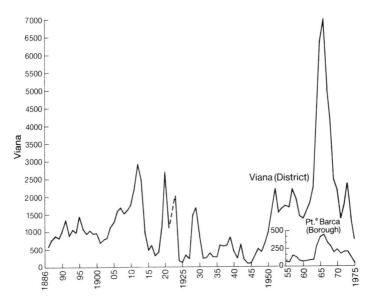

Figure 1. Number of legal emigrants per annum in the borough of Ponte da Barca (1955-75) and the district of Viana (1886-1975). The scale for Ponte da Barca is twice the size of that for Viana. *Source*: Anuários Demográficos, Instituto Nacional de Estatística, Lisbon, 1951-79.

as a last resort in the attempt to avoid indebtedness, the subsequent expropriation of land, and rural proletarianization.

During the First World War, owing to the difficulty of travel, emigration figures dropped drastically, only to rise again after 1918. They are erratic during the 1930s and 1940s, again due to external circumstances. At home this led to an increased shortage of land and more rural impoverishment. The wave of emigration (mostly to Brazil) in the 1930s left many women without their husbands. For the most part these men neither sent any remittances nor returned. This behaviour is an anomaly and is locally interpreted to mean that their economic failure in Brazil prevented them from doing either. The decade of the 1940s is still remembered as a period of hunger and even starvation, when poor women were often forced to sell their bodies to obtain bread during the winter months. Rural proletarianization increased and the proceeds of agricultural wage labour were extremely low. As rural employment was seasonal, extreme hunger was common among the *jornaleiros*, the landless labourers.

After the end of the Second World War emigration figures returned to the pre-1914 level. At this stage, however, peasants tended to emigrate to Europe and North America and no longer to Brazil. Suddenly, as the western European economies prospered, we find an unprecedented rise in the number of emigrants. At its peak, in 1966, legal emigration for the whole of Portugal reached the extraordinary figure of 120,239. If we take into account the fact that the estimated percentage of clandestine emigrants to France ranged from 44 per cent in 1960 to 61 per cent in 1970, we can see how the figures for legal emigrants, high as they were, hide the real magnitude of the phenomenon (Serrão, 1974: 63). For a country with a population of under nine million the impact of this trend on the rural areas, from which most emigrants came, can readily be understood. Between 1961 and 1970, 13.4 per cent of the population recorded by the 1960 census in the district of Viana had emigrated legally, and in the borough of Ponte da Barca the number of legal emigrants corresponded to 15.3 per cent of the total 1960 population.

Post-war emigration exhibits characteristics which explain why the exodus was so great and which differentiate it clearly from previous trends. The percentage of clandestine emigrants was very high. Poor peasants, who previously had not been able to afford the journey to Brazil, could now emigrate: any landless labourer who was courageous enough—for the hardships were great—could pack his satchel and go to

France.[7] Young men conscripted into the army, which in the 1960s meant going to fight in Africa, could escape without too much difficulty; the expenses involved in the trip, high as they were, were within the reach of most peasants and, even if a migrant did not manage to make much money abroad, it was always easy to return. Finally, although very few succeeded in making a fortune, the salaries which were paid to migrants were comparatively high by Portuguese standards.[8]

Remittances from emigrants had an almost immediate impact on the north-western rural economy. Land prices rose sharply and emigrants began buying back the land. A wealthy peasant farmer in Paço classified for me the great changes in the ownership of land which have taken place within the past two decades in the following terms: 'Now, things are as in the times of Afonso Henriques, of the *Reconquista* from the Moors, the share-croppers are buying back the land.'

Landlords were, on the whole, interested in selling land for two reasons. First, the exploitation of the land in the traditional way had become unprofitable both in terms of competition from technically more advanced agriculture and in terms of the rise in labour costs. Secondly, in the seventies in particular, the demand for land was so intense that prices rose sharply. Wealthier peasants demanded the right to own land and were willing to sacrifice their savings in order to do so. The landlords, therefore, were easily persuaded to yield control over land which was not very profitable economically, but which was now worth great sums of money.

At the same time, the peasants started buying houses and renovating their old ones. This brought a great deal of wealth to the rural areas as it fostered the development of a local building industry, which then employed many young people who were in search of paid labour in the non-agricultural sector. Concomitantly, remittances from emigrants paid for a small but substantial development in agricultural techniques.

The sociological effects of this emigration were also considerable. First, it significantly improved rural standards of living. The difference between the three traditional strata of the peasantry—landless labourers, share-croppers and tenant farmers, and owner farmers—progressively

[7] In fact, they often still had to pay the *passadores* who organized their clandestine travel. The amounts, however, were comparatively smaller. For a description of one of these truly epic journeys, see Viegas Guerreiro (1981: 283-99).

[8] In 1967 the average hourly wage of a worker in Portugal was a sixth to a third of that in the five European countries studied by Xavier Pintado (1967: 57-89).

diminished. Nowadays there are very few day labourers, since most of them either emigrated and brought back some wealth with which they bought land, or took up jobs as paid workers in the building industry. It may be remarked that the increasing economic well-being of rural Alto Minho was not accompanied as a rule by a significant development of industrial activities apart from building.

In 1974-6, due to the widespread recession and as a means of mini-mizing the growing problem of unemployment, France, Germany, and Canada closed their borders to new emigrants. In Paço and Couto this did not cause an immediate local crisis; some young men went to Venezuela, others were employed by the building industry which was still being boosted by emigrant remittances. Since 1980, however, remittances have started to decrease rapidly as most of the emigrants of the 1960s have returned or settled abroad. Consequently, new oppor-tunities for the employment of the young are becoming scarcer.

Emigration brought about radical changes in peasant society. The resultant economic well-being was accompanied by a weakening of the subsistence sector and the peasant is today dependent on purchased commodities. Furthermore, although standards of living have risen, the technical development of agriculture has not kept up with consumer demands, with the result that peasant families have become dependent on alternative sources of income. At present, the region is entering a crisis: agricultural work functions as a means of hiding a serious unemployment problem, but the standards of living of the rural popu-lation are once again decreasing rapidly.

III

At the time of my fieldwork the figures of the 1970 Portuguese census were not available (definitive figures have never been published). As an attempt to overcome this serious gap in our knowledge, a household census of both parishes was carried out in Paço in 1979 and in Couto in 1979-80. In 1982, the official provisory figures for the 1981 census were published and they proved to be significantly comparable to our unofficial figures.

Although, due to its larger size, Paço has a higher number of house-holds than Couto, the growth patterns of both parishes are very similar (see Figure 2). There was a slow growth which was interrupted in the 1890s and again in the 1930s. Since 1950 there has been a steady decline which reflects the emigrational exodus.

Table I.

'Present' population		
	1979-1980	1981[9]
District of Viana		255,614
Borough of Ponte da Barca		13,999
Paço	1,106	1,114
Couto	618	646
'Present' households		
	1979-1980	1981
District of Viana		70,840
Borough of Ponte da Barca		3,949
Paço	281	291
Couto	176	183

From 1930 to 1950, the demographic growth rates[10] are positive in both parishes, accompanying the general trend for both the district and the borough (cf. Table II). From 1950 to 1960, the growth rate is negative in the parishes and in the borough; the mild growth at district level reflects the development of the city of Viana. From 1960 to 1970, the decrease in the population is felt at all levels. In Paço it is weaker, reflecting the deeper attachment to the land of its inhabitants. By contrast, Couto systematically shows the greatest population decrease. Finally, from 1970 to 1981, the decrease is again milder. Until 1974, the emigrationary trend of the previous decade continues; after that, however, and especially after 1976, emigration practically finishes. The district of Viana has a positive growth rate for the decade, once again reflecting urban and not rural growth.

In 1795, Paço had 160 households and 573 inhabitants, while Couto had 116 households and 348 inhabitants (Cruz, 1970: AP. II); nearly two centuries later, in 1979, these numbers had not doubled. The reasons for this slow rate of growth are to be found in emigration and not in birth or death rates. This becomes clear once we compare the

---

[9] The 1981 census figures refer only to 'present' population, that is, the households and inhabitants who were in residence at the time of the census.

[10] These demographic growth rates were worked out on the basis of the formula $r = (\sqrt[m]{\frac{Xn}{Xt}} - 1)\,100$: where r = growth rate; m = number of intervening years; Xn = the population in the last year of the series; and Xt = the population in the first year (Floud, 1979: 93-7). Sources: Portuguese censuses, 1930-81, 'present' population.

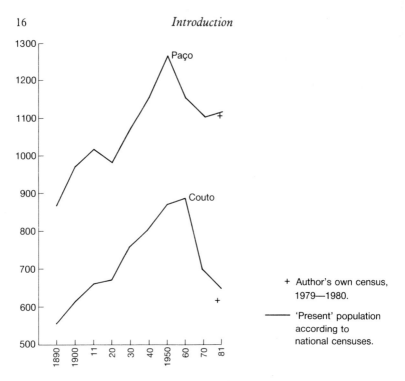

Figure 2. Population of Paço and Couto. *Source*: Recenseamentos gerais da População, 1890–1981. Instituto Nacional de Estatística, Lisbon.

Table II.   Demographic growth rates (per cent per annum, see note 10)

Years	1930-50	1950-60	1960-70	1970-81
Viana, district	+0.67	+0.03	−0.93	+0.17
Ponte da Barca, borough	+0.64	−0.16	−1.16	−0.27
Paço, parish	+0.84	−0.96	−0.41	+0.08
Couto, parish	+0.68	−1.01	−1.27	−0.62

evolution of population numbers with the emigration numbers: the periods of crisis in the 1890s and in the 1930s and the exodus of the 1960s are all reflected in the demographic growth (see Figures 1 and 2).

3. Aspects of the economy

I

As Portuguese agrarian economists have argued, the articulation between the agricultural and the industrial sectors of the Portuguese
economy would appear to be negative if it were not for the fact that the
agricultural sector has functioned as a producer and reproducer of the
labour force. This is true not only for the Portuguese industrial sector
but also, via the process of emigration, for the countries which received
Portuguese workers. Furthermore, during periods of recession, the
Portuguese agricultural sector has reabsorbed some of the excess
workers, a conclusion corroborated by the variation in emigration
figures cited above. The currency remittances sent back home by
emigrants have allowed both for an accelleration of industrialization
through the purchase of equipment abroad, and for the satisfaction of
the growing demand for food products of the urban population,
through the purchase of food from foreign countries. Thus, the low
levels of productivity of Portuguese agriculture, as well as its articulation with the capitalist sector of the Portuguese economy, can be understood only if we take into account Portugal's peripheral position in the
world economy (cf. Barros and Ribeiro Mendes, 1982: 3-4).

II

The investment of the emigrant's currency remittances, as well as the
development of the capitalist sector of the economy in the 1960s and
early 1970s, brought about a more extensive penetration of capitalist
activities into the rural areas. Nevertheless, the extreme subdivision of
the land, and the failure by the government to rationalize the
commercialization of agricultural products and to provide technical
support and investment for rural development on a significant scale,
hindered the creation of a fully mechanized, capitalized agriculture.
Some development did take place, however, and a certain amount of
small-scale mechanization is nowadays in evidence (cf. Cabral, 1983).
The main effect of this mechanization has been to reduce the labour
requirements of peasants who own more land than they can cultivate
and who were finding it difficult to pay for manual labour since they
could not compete with the capitalist sector for wages.

Following a typically peasant strategy, emigrants invested a very large portion of their savings in the purchase of land (cf. Mendras, 1967: 107). Land prices rose steeply, but production was not significantly increased. Agriculture remained, in the majority of cases, economically a fairly unrewarding activity. An increasing amount of land, therefore, is being left fallow each year, through lack of interest on the part of the owners. While, on the one hand, peasant agriculture was reinforced by an investment of emigrant remittances which allowed it to survive, on the other hand it stopped being the peasant's primary source of income. (This is particularly the case if we take into account long-term family strategies.) Economically speaking, then, peasant life is not viable today. Yet, socially speaking, it is still the only way of assuring the individual of a kind of social security and belonging from which he cannot afford to abdicate.

In spite of these changes, the term 'peasant' is still apposite in describing the residents of Paço and Couto as a whole, for the majority remain agricultural producers who extract from land they control the greater part of their subsistence needs. Even those residents engaged permanently in wage-earning are seldom completely landless. Whether they own the land or rent it a minimum of agriculture is considered a necessity for a proper family life and the whole household is seen as a joint productive enterprise. When a man is out working for a wage, the rest of the household tills the land. This co-ordination is conceived of as an economic spreading of the household rather than as an aggregate of separate economic activities, as would be the case in urban society. The concept of a 'job', a wage-earning activity which is independent from family life, is foreign to these people. This explains why, even though nowadays most of the household's income is usually derived from non-agricultural sources, the individual still conceives of himself as a peasant.

Table III indicates the dominant economic activities of all residents of Paço and Couto who were over 18 in 1979-80. From it we can see that 75.7 per cent of the adult population of Paço, and 68.38 per cent of Couto, are engaged in agricultural activities. The majority of them are self-employed agricultural workers (farmers) who fit the traditional image of the peasant; the rest are agricultural wage-earners. The numbers of the latter have been so drastically reduced over the past decades that nowadays they represent only 8.72 per cent of the adult population of Paço and 7.71 per cent of that of Couto.

Among the farmers (self-employed agricultural workers), the percentage of women is high (68.6 per cent in Paço and 74.15 per cent in

Table III. Types of economic activities of the adult population*

	Males	Females	Total
Paço			
Self-employed:			
Agricultural	135	295	430
Non-agricultural	27	9	36
Wage-earner (blue collar):			
Agricultural	12	44	56
Non-agricultural	53	—	53
Wage-earner (white collar)	6	2	8
Pensioner	24	24	48
Other †	8	3	11
Couto			
Self-employed:			
Agricultural	61	175	236
Non-agricultural	29	5	34
Wage-earner (blue collar):			
Agricultural	12	18	30
Non-agricultural	26	3	29
Wage-earner (white collar)	10	1	11
Pensioner	14	17	31
Other †	13	5	17

* Born before 1961.
† Handicapped, students, and profession unknown.

Couto). Some of these women are the wives of emigrants who remained behind to look after the household's agricultural activities. The predominance of female farmers, however, remains evident even when we allow for the number of male households heads who have emigrated (46 in Paço and 25 in Couto). This reflects the practice of combining wage-earning by the males with the household's agricultural activities. Finally, the predominance of females over males (females make up 58.72 per cent of the total adult population of Paço and 57.58 per cent of Couto) once again reflects the tendency for men to leave the parish while women remain.

Another important category is that of self-employed, non-agricultural workers. This includes cattle-dealers, shop-keepers, and the owners of small industries such as building and timber concerns, power-driven mills for maize and oil, and distilleries. By local standards all of these are fairly wealthy men, many of whom acquired abroad the capital necessary to start their businesses. Except for a stone-grinding plant owned by a man from Paço, all of them are small businesses. This category also includes three seamstresses, one shoemaker, two tailors, two taxi-drivers, one barber, and one basket-maker, who practise their trades at home without any considerable capital investment. To these we can also add State employees and office clerks: three primary school-teachers, two policemen, one forest guard, one river guard and a number of office clerks who work in the town but reside in their parishes of origin. Finally, there are a number of artisans such as builders, carpenters, stone-masons, and metal-workers. Overall, the percentage of adults engaged permanently on these non-agricultural tasks does not rise above 15.1 per cent of the same sample in Paço and 19.02 per cent in Couto.

Ironically, however, by far the most important economic activity after agriculture—and in terms of overall household income certainly the most significant—is emigration. We do not possess official numbers for legal emigration at parish level (for legal emigration at borough and district levels, see Figure 1). But in order to give some idea of the extent of the phenomenon, we shall consider a sample of all the people be-tween the ages of 15 and 30 (in 1979 in Paço and 1979-80 in Couto) whose households of origin are still in Paço and Couto (the 'youth sample'). Although this sample is quite obviously incomplete, it will certainly provide an idea of the rate of emigration during the period be-tween 1963 and 1978. Since 1976 there has been an attempt by most receiving nations to stop emigration and even, in the case of France, to pay emigrants to return to Portugal. In 1979-80 the only place still receiving a substantial number of emigrants was Venezuela. This means that the youth sample chosen here is already less extreme than it would have been had it not included 1977 and 1978.

The number of young emigrants as a proportion of the sample of young persons is 37.5 per cent for Paço and 33.33 per cent for Couto. Of all the young migrants, 32.62 per cent in Paço and 33.33 per cent in Couto were women, which is a smaller percentage than that found by Serrão for the whole country in the 1951-60 period, which was 38.1 per cent (1974: 123). This indicates that the preference for male emigration was still evident even during the exodus of the 1960s and early 1970s. Finally, this sample includes both emigrants to foreign countries and youths who left to work in the big Portuguese cities. The percentage of the former over the total number of young migrants, however, is approximately 80 per cent in both parishes.

Most emigrants went to France. Germany, Venezuela, Canada, Andorra, Australia, and Brazil are the other important receiving countries in decreasing order of importance. From the data available it is impossible to establish precisely how many emigrants eventually return to their parishes of origin. Judging by the number of men in the 50 to 60 age group who are returned emigrants, it would appear that this percentage over the last two decades has been reasonably high in relation to previous trends of emigration. The rate of return also varies considerably depending on the period of migration and which receiving countries are chosen.

III

The extremely small farm plots are perhaps the most distinctive feature of *minhoto* agriculture. The terrain being very hilly and formed by wide, V-shaped valleys, most agriculture has to take place on small terraces on the hillsides. Already in the seventeenth century, Aurélio de Oliveira judged that most of the land held by tenants of the Abbey of Tibães was in plots of under half a hectare (1.24 acres, 5,000 square metres) (1974: 12). Be this as it may, M. Halpern Pereira argues that until 1870 'the division of the property was not viewed as a serious obstacle to regional development' (1971: 183, note 92) and Minho was referred to as an example to be imitated by other regions of the country. Later, however, the problem became increasingly acute, although in 1949, in the district of Viana, the average size of a landholding remained half a hectare. This has to be seen in context, however, since, as Cunhal argues in his famous *Questão Agrária*, average numbers are not highly significant. Although each plot is very small, a farmer usually cultivates a number of plots, and a landlord owns many. The size of plots, therefore, has to be compared with the overall size of the farms. Table IV indicates how the farms in the district of Viana were distributed according to size in 1979.[11]

What this means is that, over 90 per cent of all farms are smaller than 4 ha (9.88 acres). The problems which such division of the land can bring about will become obvious when we realize that 26.39 per cent of the farms in Viana in 1968 were composed of more than ten unconnected plots: not only do most people till very little land, but the terrain

---

[11] In 1949, in Viana, 36.36 per cent of the farms were less than ½ ha in areas; 60.85 per cent were between ½ ha and 3 ha; 2.37 per cent between 3 ha and 5 ha; 0.51 per cent were more than 5 ha. These percentages were worked out on the basis of the numbers cited by Cunhal (n.d.: 236).

Table IV. Size of farms in the district
of Viana, 1979

Under 1 ha (< 2.47 acres)	57.77%
From 1 ha to 4 ha (9.88 acres)	32.99%
From 4 ha to 20 ha (49.42 acres)	6.89%
From 20 ha to 50 ha (123.55 acres)	0.26%
Over 50 ha	0.08%

Source: *Anuário Estatístico*, 1979, Instituto
Nacional de Estatística.

itself is much divided. In 1968, in Ponte da Barca, an inland and therefore hillier borough of the district of Viana, 29.84 per cent of the farms
were composed of more than ten scattered plots (Instituto Nacional de
Estatística, 1968). In fact, the division of the terrain in these hillier
regions of the district is such that, in Paço and Couto, fields range between 0.1 ha (0.24 acres) and 0.5 ha (1.23 acres). Moreover, in the upper
parts of these parishes, where land is even more rugged, each of these
fields is usually divided into three or four terraces. In the mountain
parishes on the eastern side of the borough, a field measuring 0.03 ha
(0.074 acres) is called *um campo de carro* because it requires an ox-cart
full of manure to fertilize it, and it is considered a prize possession.

Such great subdivision of the terrain is certainly uneconomic, not
only because of the land taken up by paths and hedges and because of
the length of time required to reach different plots of the same farm, but
also because it prevents the use of complex agricultural machinery and
a consequent adoption of modern agricultural methods. However, this
subdivision of the terrain is to a certain extent consistent with the mixed
farming system described above. Each household has a group of plots
scattered around the parish, usually within walking distance of the
house, though sometimes even across parish boundaries. When the
fields are too far away they are usually rented out to local people. Different types of land have different uses: vegetable patches; maize fields
surrounded by pergolas for vines (irrigated land); rye fields (dry land);
land where one collects scrub for the cattle beds; woods; and plots with
chestnut, walnut, olive, or fruit trees (these are often also planted along
the edges of the fields). If a household does not own one of these types
of land—especially the more essential ones such as maize fields with
vine pergolas and vegetable patches—they will rent what they require
from an emigrant or from someone with unused land.

Some landless or nearly landless households establish contracts of *parceria* (share-cropping) with wealthier landlords. Though most tenants paid half of the yearly product, until the early 1970s it was still common to find contracts under which the tenant paid two-thirds of the yearly product of the land. Large landlords had a number of share-croppers (*caseiros*) working on their land and their agricultural affairs were managed by a wealthier peasant, the *feitor* (foreman). As the land is progressively bought by returned emigrants from absentee landlords, *caseiros* who work only rented land tend to disappear. Nowadays in Paço there are only eight *caseiros* and in Couto thirty-three.

The major products at present are maize, rye, beans, potatoes, wine, olive oil, and cattle fodder and most households produce some quantity of all of these. Similarly, middle and wealthy households own at least one cow and often a pair, which are used for milk, traction, and breeding. Finally, many households keep pigs to be slaughtered in November or December to provide a major source of protein during the winter months. In the past, fewer households managed to keep pigs.

The agricultural year is punctuated by a succession of religious feasts which represent the season and its occupations. At Easter the land is ploughed, manure is spread, and maize is sown; potatoes are also planted. The period around the night of St John (23 June) is the second most active of the year: rye is threshed, the potatoes unearthed, and the vines first sprayed with insecticide. The middle of summer is not very eventful agriculturally except for the continued and regular spraying of the vines. This is the time when most *festas* are celebrated and emigrants return on holidays.

The feast of St Michael (27 September) is the time for harvesting the maize and the grapes, planting grass for cattle fodder, and removing the maize cobs from their leafy coverings. This is the period of greatest labour involvement. 'The St. Martin', in late November and early December, is the season for killing the pigs, gathering the chestnuts and walnuts, sowing the rye and starting to drink the new wine. Finally, after Christmas, scrub is gathered for the cattle beds and vines are pruned.

IV

The products which the household does not require for its subsistence may be sold immediately or stored for a limited period to be sold later, when prices have recovered from the slump caused by harvest abundance. Larger and wealthier households own *espigueiros* (maize granaries) which are a source of pride and prestige. Storage is a problem, however, for most products do not easily survive well until the end of the next agricultural year. This is the case with the two major crops, maize and the local home-made wine, *vinho verde* (green wine), with its low alcoholic content.

There are different ways of selling the various types of crops. In the case of chestnuts and walnuts, middlemen from the cities come with trucks and give a small percentage to a local shop-keeper who helps them in their rounds of the households. Most business deals, however, are carried out at the *feiras* (fairs). Even when the produce is not actually taken, it is here that contacts are made, and prices standardized, the acquisition of this valuable information being one of the major reasons for attendance; here also the household buys most of the commodities it requires. Finally, the fair is used as an opportunity for meeting people from other parts of the borough and contacting doctors, lawyers and officials: as Lisón puts it, 'the fair is a window to the world' (1971b: 53).

Fairs were instituted by the monarchs as free markets during the Middle Ages; many were granted as part of the borough charters but often the king would issue a special decree for their institution. In these decrees, special privileges and liberties were bestowed that freed the participants from the constraints of feudal by-laws and hindrances; they were called 'the peace of the fair'.

The fair of Ponte de Lima was instituted as early as 1125, the fair of the district capital, Viana do Casteldo, dating only from 1342. It appears that fairs began to decline in the middle of the sixteenth century from their medieval importance and magnitude. V. Rau must be partially correct when she argues that permanent commercial houses took much of their business (in Serrão, 1965: s.v. *feira*). It must be remembered, however, that these shops do most of their business on fair days and that the fair remains a major local institution, most households sending at least one member of the head couple and often both.

Ponte da Barca, in the eighteenth century, had a monthly fair on the first and second days of each month. At the beginning of the nineteenth century these were changed to the 2nd and 22nd. At present the fair is held twice a month on Wednesdays, alternating with the fair of the neighbouring borough of Arcos de Valdeve. This alternation is an interesting example of the co-ordination between boroughs which occurs over the whole of the district of Viana. It concerns more the travelling salesmen, who go from fair to fair selling their wares (suits, shoes, gold and silver ornaments, pottery, medicine and pseudomedicine, cassettes, belts, etc.) than the peasant himself, whose range is rather more limited. Attendance at fairs depends on the kind of business one wants to carry out and for a more important deal or for a wider choice of commodities one chooses a larger fair. In the case of Ponte da Barca and Arcos, this would be the fair of Ponte de Lima (held on alternate Mondays). It is interesting to note that there seems to be a hierarchy of importance between fairs and that there are distinct classes of fairs, the weekly (or fortnightly), the monthly, and the annual.

In the weekly class, the most important fair in the district is that of the capital, Viana, held on Fridays. An even larger fair is that of Braga, the capital of the neighbouring district, held on Tuesdays. There are no other fairs of the weekly class on these two week days in the district of Viana: they would not be able to compete. The fairs of Barcelos on Thursdays and of Ponte de Lima on Mondays are somewhat less important than the two former ones and are directed at the population of different regions.

Most other borough capitals hold their weekly or fortnightly fairs independently of one another, for they do not compete for customers. There are a few exceptions, however, such as Vila Praia de Âncora, a town which is not a borough capital, and whose fair on Sundays coincides with that of its borough capital (Caminha). This may be explained by the unusual situation of a town not being a borough capital.

There is a monthly fair in the district for every two days of the month. Bigger centres such as Valença and Monção, for example, coordinate monthly with weekly fairs. None of these monthly fairs, however, coincide. The big annual fairs are attached to *festas* of a patron saint. They are held mostly at borough level and do not coincide with others in the district.

V

The ownership of land remains a very important index of wealth and prestige in local society. In the absence of a land cadastre, however, it has been impossible to carry out a detailed study of land ownership. This difficulty is increased by the subdivision of the land and the existence of many different types of land which are variously valued. Furthermore, alternative sources of income have become too important to be disregarded in an assessment of economic differentiation. When I compiled the household census of Paço and Couto, I asked the informants to specify the relation of each household to what they thought would be the average situation in the parish. They usually took a very

short time to master this technique of description. There was the problem of distinguishing between economic power and standards of living,
which in many cases were not correlated. Whenever the question arose,
I asked the informants to pay attention to economic power rather than
to standards of living. I also acquired information on the size of
agricultural production above subsistence requirements, on non-
agricultural occupations, on government pensions and subsidies, and in
many cases on unusually large savings due to emigration.

This information was provided in most cases by one informant for
each hamlet, and it was later cross-checked and added to by comments
from other informants and by my personal observations. Overall, the
assessment of relative wealth thus obtained provides us with an impres-
sionistic but nevertheless fairly reliable picture of economic differentiation and inequality in Paço and Couto.

I have divided the households into three basic groups, which were
then each divided into two, thus giving rise to six sub-groups: the Very
Rich, the Rich, the Upper Middle, the Lower Middle, the Poor and the
Very Poor (Table V). The sub-group of the Very Poor is composed of
people who do not own any land and often live below subsistence level,
that is, they barely manage to survive. The majority of these people
work as day labourers, share-croppers of small farms, or as blue-collar
wage-earners. The pay for agricultural day labour is still very low: in
Paço and Couto, in the summer of 1979, it was 150$00 a day (approxi-
mately £1.50 at the time).[12] The pay for non-agricultural labour,
however, is higher. In their old age these people used to be destitute.
Nowadays, the government provides through the Casa do Povo an
old-age pension amounting to 1,100$00 per month in 1979 (approxi-
mately £11 at the time). This has greatly improved their lot. The
category of the Very Poor represents 15.35 per cent of the households of
Paço and 25 per cent of Couto. Finally, in both parishes, 23.25 per cent
of these households are headed by single mothers.

The Poor sub-group is formed by households which, on the whole,
just manage to carry out subsistence agriculture, often owning some
land and possibly even getting a modicum of cash from the sale of their
produce. Their cash income, however, often derives from the cattle they
raise for cattle-dealers. Their younger people usually work as blue-
collar wage-earners and many of them emigrate. Most of these house-

---

[12] In these two parishes men and women have traditionally been paid the same for un-
skilled agricultural work. This is not the case in other parishes. Men are often paid more
because most skilled work is carried out by them.

Table V. Percentages of wealth sub-groups in the total number of households

	Paço		Couto	
	Number	Percentage	Number	Percentage
The Very Rich	2	0.71	2	1.16
The Rich	7	2.50	2	1.16
The Upper Middle	76	27.14	25	14.53
The Lower Middle	78	27.85	45	26.16
The Poor	74	26.42	55	31.97
The Very Poor	43	15.35	43	25.00
?	1		—	
Total	281		172	

holds complement their agricultural enterprises by some rented land and by day labour in the peak season. They represent 26.42 per cent of the households of Paço and 31.97 per cent of Couto.

The Lower Middle sub-group consists of households who live reasonably above subsistence level. Mostly they own their own land and whatever rented land they take on is seldom vital for their subsistence. They do not work as day labourers under normal circumstances and many of them are engaged in small businesses and non-agricultural activities. In the lower parts of the parishes one finds among this sub-group a certain number of high-school students, which indicates that there is money available to invest in the child's education. This sub-group represents 27.85 per cent of the households of Paço and 26.16 per cent of Couto.

The households of the Upper Middle sub-group have considerable economic ease; usually they own more land than they alone can work and are thus forced to hire day labourers and to rent out fields to others. The owners of larger businesses (oil and wine presses, timber-yards, large shops, and workshops) form part of this sub-group. Much of the agricultural production of these households is aimed specifically at the market, as their subsistence needs are usually considerably less than their total production. They represent 27.14 per cent of the households of Paço and 14.53 per cent of Couto.

The Rich sub-group consists of seven households in Paço and two in Couto who own a great deal of land, as well as the most profitable local businesses. Their houses are modern, they usually have cars, and they rent out a considerable proportion of their land. They form 2.50 per cent of the households of Paço and 1.16 per cent of those of Couto.

The Very Rich are two households in Paço and two in Couto (0.71 per cent and 1.16 per cent respectively). They are exceptionally rich people, much of their land lying outside their parish of residence. Three of these households owe their exceptional wealth to the successful investment of earnings from abroad. They emigrated before the Second World War and returned to their parishes of birth when most people were leaving in the late 1950s and early 1960s.

VI

Paço and Couto are, in many respects, closely interlinked within the context of the borough of Ponte da Barca as a whole. In the Middle Ages, the monastery of Couto owned land in Paço and still today the two parishes are economically connected: the residents of Paço make many of their purchases in Couto and the residents of one parish provide business for the small industries of the other. Socially too the two parishes are close to each other: for example, they have shared a priest for the past few decades.

None the less, the comparison of the percentage of the households in each sub-group suggests that Couto is a parish of extremes of wealth, while Paço is one where the middle group predominates and where, as a result, the feeling of parish unity and the preservation of typically peasant attitudes are more evident (see Figure 3). Furthermore, the data presented earlier indicated that, although the differences between the two parishes are never large, they are nevertheless consistent. For example, while 75.7 per cent of the adult population of Paço was engaged in agriculture, in Couto the percentage is only 68.38 per cent. In Paço 15.1 per cent of all adults are engaged in non-agricultural activities, while in Couto the percentage is 19.02 per cent. Finally, the emigration figures provided by the 'youth sample' are deceptive, for they do not take into account population reduction: there are more young emigrants in Paço (37.5 per cent of the youth sample) than in Couto (33.33 per cent) because in the latter there has been a stronger trend towards family emigration and a smaller percentage of returning migrants. Since these families severed their ties with the parish, their young members could not be included in the sample. This argument is supported by the fact that the population of Couto has decreased more rapidly since 1950 than that of Paço (see Figure 2 and Table II).

The major key to the understanding of the differences between these two parishes lies in the ownership of land. Couto is a parish of poor people, where the land has been owned by relatively wealthy and predominantly absentee landlords, while Paço is on the whole a parish where, although the best land was owned by absentee landlords, many peasant households managed to own some land of their own. This argument, which is fully subscribed to by the residents of both parishes, is also supported by the discovery that, while in Paço there are only eight full-time share-cropping households, in Couto there are thirty-three. Before the 1950s Couto also had a higher percentage of illegitimate births which, in this region, as we shall see, is related to landlessness.

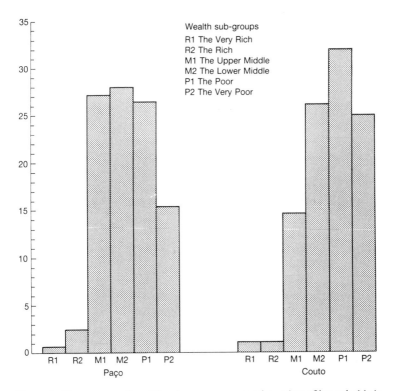

Figure 3. Percentages of wealth sub-groups over total number of households in each parish.

Indeed, once again, this is the explanation given by parish residents for this widely recognized difference between the two parishes. Couto, therefore, was a parish where fewer people owned land and where rural poverty was more evident, and this is reflected in higher mortgage and illegitimacy rates.

With the advent of post-war emigration, the exodus increased, population decreased, and more people had recourse to non-agricultural means of earning a living. The final result is that there has been a greater penetration of urban values into Couto. A striking example of this is the explanation given by the people for the fact that the shops in Couto (a smaller parish) are larger, better stocked, and more prosperous than those of Paço: indeed, most of the residents of this parish prefer to buy their commodities in Couto and at the fair, where their neighbours cannot easily keep watch over them. Residents of Couto have no such compunction. The reason for this secretiveness is that, for the residents of Paço, a household which cannot produce enough for its subsistence loses prestige. Furthermore, for them, a household which engages in the consumption of 'unnecessary luxury' is improvident and its members should not be trusted.

4. Peasant and bourgeois

I

Cultural differentiation at parish level, however, must be seen within the context of Alto Minho society as a whole. Due to the extent and rapidity of cultural change over the past decades, cultural differentiation may at first appear to be random. Nevertheless, closer inspection reveals that this is not so and that we require a conceptual framework within which both cultural differentiation and change may be located. Broadly speaking, *minhoto* society can be divided into two types of cultural areas: urban and rural. Within urban areas, the dominant worldview is that of the bourgeoisie, while within rural areas it is that of the peasantry. Bourgeoisie and peasantry are the two most significant status groups of local society. Within rural areas we also find beggars, gypsies, members of the urban élite who live in the countryside, and mobile landless labourers, but all of these are quantitatively and qualitatively insignificant in relation to the peasantry. Similarly, within the urban areas, we find a remainder of the old rural aristocracy, the beginnings of a proletariat, and even some peasants, but again these are not numerically or culturally significant in relation to the bourgeoisie.

Earlier on, I justified my use of the term 'peasant' to qualify the inhabitants of Paço and Couto by arguing that the majority are 'agricultural producers who extract from land they control the greater part of their subsistence needs'. Yet this definition is at once too inclusive and too exclusive: it excludes peasant merchants and artisans, emigrants and semi-proletarians, and at the same time it includes people who live in the countryside but are clearly members of the urban élite, the *proprietários*. Cultural terms must be included in a definition of peasantry. As Redfield, for example, points out, its cultural subordination to an urban gentry is as central a factor in defining a peasantry, as is its economic subordination (1960, II: 20). The choice of the term 'worldview' favours the awareness that in regard to peasant modes of thought and perception of the world, we are not dealing with a fully separate and independent cultural framework, but rather with part of a complex cultural tradition. Similarly, the choice of the Weberian term 'status group' reflects both the concern with a cultural perspective and the need to define the peasantry and the bourgeoisie by their mutual relation.[13]

The relationship between the urban élite and the peasantry is not symmetrical. On the contrary, as will be demonstrated later (chapter V, sect. 17), the bourgeoisie and the ecclesiastical hierarchy allied to it are the intermediaries through which the cultural hegemony of what Redfield calls the 'great tradition' operates. This control over the local use of the *ciência*, the *cultura*, and the *religião*, invests the provincial bourgeoisie with technical, ideological and spiritual power over the 'uneducated' peasantry. In the past, this control had been in the hands of the rural aristocracy but during the nineteenth century the provincial bourgeoisie took over this role as mediator, and therefore manipulator, of the 'great tradition'.

The belief in its own cultural inferiority is an important aspect of peasant culture and behaviour today (see chapter III, sect. 9. V). The Alto Minho, then, is an example of the situation typified by Redfield when he argues that 'every peasant finds his self-respect, his contentment, qualified by the knowledge that he is poorer and ruder than the gentry, those people of the towns' (1960, II: 75). This is not to say that

[13] An analysis of peasant behaviour in class terms would tend to minimize the significance of cognitive aspects in determining social action. As Weber has argued, 'the factor that creates "class" is unambiguously economic interest' (1978, II: 928). Although economic interest is widely varied within the peasantry, which includes both wealthy landowners and extremely poor share-croppers, peasants do not recognize status differentiation among themselves and, more importantly, they share a common worldview.

the peasant worldview has had no influence on the bourgeois worldview, for the contrary is often demonstrably the case. Neither does it imply a confusion between the worldview of the provincial bourgeoisie and the 'great tradition'. The bourgeoisie of the small provincial towns is a mere link in a chain which finds its origins in the great scientific, cultural, and religious metropolises of the world.

II

Everyday cultural life in a *minhoto* hamlet is diverse and mobile. People disagree and change their minds, learn new things and forget old ones, so there is a sense in which statements of the kind 'the people of this hamlet think this or that . . .' are nonsensical. Yet a detailed study of this cultural life will demonstrate that everyone's thought relates to particular concepts and images. Natives may accept these, they may argue against them, they may manipulate them for their own benefit, they may even be crushed by them with a mute acceptance of the very principles of their personal destruction. In relation to these concepts and images, one may then say that 'the people of this hamlet think this or that . . .' Albeit from a rather different theoretical background, Redfield expresses the same idea when he says that 'the social structure of a small community is a set of limiting conditions within which the conduct of individuals takes place, it is a system of ethical direction, a set of signposts to the good and virtuous life' (1960, I: 46).

This 'more or less coherent view of the good life' is not something which the natives can consciously describe. The researcher has to explore the most diverse aspects of the culture before he begins to form an image which may hypothetically approach the shared core of the vague images which exist largely subconsciously in the mind of each and every member of the social group in question. Throughout this study I have attempted to develop such an image of 'the good life' as applicable to the peasant population of the Alto Minho. In more abstract rephrasing, at the centre of this worldview I encountered a particular ideal image of the elementary social unit, its reproduction, and its participation and integration into the social whole. The term 'reproduction' must be understood in its widest sense for it refers to the process of acquisition of the material, biological, and ideological conditions for the projection of the elementary social unit through time. To summarize my findings: the elementary social unit is the agricultural household (*casa*) which is essentially, but not exclusively, composed of the head-couple and their offspring. The household finds its identity in the unity of commensality, residence, management, and property; it produces its own food on land which it controls; and it is ideally independent of external food sources. This direct link to the land is the essential condition for full participation in this peasant society and the proper tending of the land, and not genealogical position, is given as the justification for the head couple's headship. Fertility, wealth, and physical well-being are essential for the survival of the *casa*, but so is an orderly social life, and this requires control of fertility, acquisitiveness and one's bodily desires. To control these the society uses a body of religious as well as secular symbolism which reproduces and reinforces the ideals attached to inter-household relations. These operate on the basis of an identity of status between all the landed households; thus, they are ideally based on equality, symmetrical reciprocity, and friendship. To this complex of images I have given the shorthand title of 'the subsistence prototype' because central to it is the conception that the household survives by its own means.

The concept of subsistence prototype should be distinguished from its close neighbour the 'subsistence ethic', as propounded by James C. Scott (1976). The latter is certainly a very rich construct, for it specifies that which is specifically characteristic of peasant economic behaviour: the need to be safe from hunger and never to fall below the level of subsistence—what Scott calls the 'safety-first principle'. This, he argues, is manifested in two ideological devices: the insistence on *reciprocity* and the villager's *right to subsistence*. On the basis of these principles he constructs a phenomenological theory of peasant exploitation which appears to have great explanatory value as far as peasant revolt is concerned. Personally, I would not follow him in depreciating the value of a substantivist theory of exploitation, as will be obvious later: both have their place at different theoretical moments.

The concept of the subsistence ethic is, therefore, perfectly compatible with that of the subsistence prototype, but they should not be confused: the subsistence prototype is a wider-ranging concept than that of the subsistence ethic; and I do not claim for the subsistence prototype any automatic descriptive validity beyond that of the specific *minhoto* data which I analyse here. If, as I maintain, cultural life is centred on an image of the elementary social unit and of its means of reproduction and relation to other social units—the basic cultural prototype—that image would generate its own moral economy. In this particular case, it would indicate a *specific manifestation* of the principle of reciprocity, as I shall argue later, as well as a *specific manifestation* of the right to subsistence.

One potential criticism of the concept of the basic cultural prototype is that it postulates a static core to a culture, which would only postpone the problems of explaining cultural diachrony, displacing them from the culture's (or worldview's) surface level to its deeper levels. The answer to such a criticism is that basic cultural prototypes cannot be conceived of as static, but as permanently re-created in the process of cultural interchange between the members of the social group who themselves (as individuals, as groups, and as one group) are continuously placed in the dialectic between action and cognition. This approach is akin to Bourdieu's, and it could even be argued that these prototypes might be thought of as part of the *habitus*.[14] Bourdieu's verbosity, however, in my opinion, hides a lack of central coherence which makes his terminology a very treacherous tool for anyone else to use, and the reliance on the ambiguous term *disposition* weakens it by rendering it universally applicable, thereby reducing its descriptive value.

III

Although this study is primarily concerned with the peasant worldview, I shall nevertheless have to refer to the relationship between this world-view and that of the urban élite, since to isolate it would be to ignore one of the most important characteristics of peasant thought today. The postulation of a basic cultural prototype for the bourgeoisie, such as the one proposed above for the peasantry, would demand as lengthy a study of the urban strata. I shall limit myself here, therefore, to pointing out the clearest differences between the bourgeois worldview and that of the peasantry, thereby necessarily underestimating the internal differen-tiation of urban society.

The bourgeois worldview is based on a conception of the nuclear family and of individual participation in the cash economy as typified by the sale of labour for a salary. In this, it is distinct from the peasant worldview and its central notion of *casa*. Individuals and their families are ranked separately according to status differences. The bourgeois does not divide society into large status blocks as does the peasant; rather he sees society in terms of a continuum of prestige. His own status is a matter of permanent doubt, which explains his concern with

---

[14] 'Systèmes de *dispositions* durables et transposables, structures structurées predisposées à fonctionner comme structures structurantes' (Bourdieu, 1980: 88).

'appearance' (cf. Lefebvre, 1971: 177 ff). A peasant's social standing is based on a safe and visible economic asset—his land—while the bourgeois's social standing is based on often invisible and ultimately perishable assets. At the same time, peasants are loath to demonstrate differences of wealth among themselves, owing to their preference for a definition of social relationships as communal. For the bourgeois, social relationships are typically thought of as associative and a strong emphasis is placed on the external demonstration of economic differentiation (Weber, 1978, I: 40-2).

If we were to choose a concept which typifies the bourgeois worldview as that of subsistence typifies the peasant worldview, it would be the concept of salary. Typically, the bourgeois of today is a man who depends on a smaller or greater salary and whose personal life (the life of consumption) is separate from and unrelated to his 'job' (the life of production).

The old household enterprise (*a casa comercial*) which was run at family level is progressively being abandoned for a conception of the enterprise as 'business' (*a empresa*) which separates it from the *família*. Nowadays, fewer people own their own businesses, and those who do are modelling themselves increasingly on the image of the manager (*gestor*) rather than the traditional image of the 'boss' (*o patrão*). This bureaucratic conception of productive activities is taking the upper hand both for the increasingly large number of civil servants and for those employed by the public sector.

The townsman of the Alto Minho is not typically an enterprising 'accumulator of profit' who is willing to run risks in order to increase his economic power. He is dominated by reproductive rather than productive concerns. His accumulation of 'savings' (*poupanças*) is not a means of increasing profit but an attempt to safeguard his present level of consumption. Being an employee, he typically detaches himself from responsibility for the process of production, which explains the institutionalization of sick leave and the low productivity levels of which large enterprises and the State so bitterly complain.

The constant references to 'good deals' (*arranjos, negócios*), so common a feature of bourgeois conversation, are in many ways misleading. Typically, these 'deals' lead to the acquisition of consumer and not production goods. The townsman, as opposed to the peasant, measures himself and others by the capacity for consumption, as his central concern is not the accumulation of profit but the maximization of consumption.

IV

The division of *minhoto* society into two cultural types is not absolute. Nevertheless, while it may be found that many local residents, at times, make statements which could be classified as belonging to one world-view or the other, the worldviews themselves remain largely irreconcilable. Confronted with two alternative 'social definitions of reality', the individual chooses one or the other according to different situations and audiences, and according to his own individual history and interests.

The peasantry and the bourgeoisie have always been in close contact. With increased penetration into the rural areas of the institutions of the modern state, of capitalist economy, and of the media, this has been intensified: individual members of one status group often utilize their knowledge of the worldview of the other status group. But, while bourgeois values are increasingly present and intrusive in all areas of society, peasant values are undergoing a process of decline. It is therefore to be expected that cultural conflict should be stronger among peasants.

In an increasing number of situations rural dwellers are finding it necessary to have recourse to urban conceptions, values, and definitions. Yet, at the same time, the conditions for the reproduction of the subsistence prototype are still present. The economic marginalization of peasant agriculture in the 1970s did not imply its social and cognitive marginalization: to have land and to work it remain the ultimate means of obtaining both social security and prestige. Thus, in economic terms, the land alone no longer ensures subsistence, offering merely a basis upon which families can operate their strategies of economic maximization within a world which is increasingly non-agricultural. Cognitively speaking, however, the conceptions of subsistence and the agricultural household (*casa*) have survived.

II

Household and family

Historically, the concept of the family had several meanings, and it is only useful if its particular meaning is always clearly defined.

Max Weber, *Economy and Society*

5. The concept of *casa*

I

There are four Portuguese terms which may all be translated as 'household' in English: *casa* (literally, house); *lar* (literally, hearth); *fogo* (literally, fire); *família* (literally, family). As in Galicia (Lisón Tolosana, 1971b: 377-80), the term which is most commonly used by the rural population of Minho is *casa*. The bourgeoisie, however, use the term *família* far more frequently. Such a shift in terminology is not due merely to differences in language use; it is rather a manifestation of a real divergence between the two social groups.

For both the bourgeoisie and the peasantry, the household is the elementary social unit. The basic constitution of this group is the same in both instances: a married couple and their children. But, as will become apparent throughout this study, what at first appear to be minor shifts in conception between one worldview and the other turn out to be largely irreconcilable differences, once we begin to analyse the conceptual implications and the assumptions underlying the apparent community of language between the bourgeoisie and the peasantry.

The preference for the use of the term *família* to describe the household among the bourgeoisie reflects the fact that, for the urban population, the nuclear family *is* the household, and other persons living with the *família* are seen largely as extrinsic to it even when they are related by ties of kinship to the head couple. For the peasants, on the other hand, these co-residents are full members of the household. The choice of the word *casa* (house) reflects this conception, as it stresses the spatial unity of the members rather than the kinship relations among them (cf. Du Boulay, 1974: 18). The *casa* is a compound of land, buildings, animals, people, absent relatives, and even the dead of the household (cf. Cátedra Tomás, 1979: 37).

The bourgeois urban dwellers, who limit the elementary social unit to the nuclear family, perceive the existence of a wide rift between the realm of the economic and the realm of the familial. For the peasant such a split makes no sense: the *casa* is not only a unit of reproduction and consumption, it is also a unit of production and property. The spheres of the economic and the familial, which for the bourgeoisie are antonymical and almost irreconcilable, are inseparable for the rural *minhoto*. Thus, the very conception of the elementary social unit contains in itself an ideal image of the basic principles of social action.

These differences are clearly discernible when we compare the use of space in the houses of the two social groups. A peasant household is centred around the kitchen, and in particular around the fireplace or the iron stove which today provides heat for cooking and warmth in the houses of the richer peasants. Except for the biggest room (the *sala*), which is used only on ceremonial occasions, all the other rooms are small and only used for sleeping in. The living quarters are usually situated above the cellar and the stables. The norm is for the house to be built on a terrace, so that both the lower and upper storeys have direct access to the outside. Around the house there is a cleared area where there are always chicken-coops, pig-pens, sheds for the storage of agricultural implements, ox-carts, and produce, and an *espigueiro* (maize granary). The beautiful egg-shaped haystack and the threshing-floor (*eira*) are also prominent, as are piles of wood left out to dry or to age. Most of this yard, except for the threshing-floor, is often covered with pergolas where vines are grown. Whenever possible, the vegetable patch where the women grow all kinds of *verduras* (literally, greens) is just beyond this cleared area.

The bourgeois home is very differently organized. Typically it is an urban home, where there are no agricultural implements, and where, instead of cleared ground, there is a garden in which flowers are grown. The centre of these houses is the dining-room, where the most valuable objects are displayed and where the man of the house sits, eats, and, nowadays, watches television. The kitchen is smaller and the men seldom enter it. It is in the dining-room that visitors are received rather than in the kitchen. Furthermore, the other rooms in the house tend to be larger and to be used for purposes other than sleeping.

II

The importance of the kitchen in a peasant home is not only related to practical needs. It is around the kitchen that life is organized, and it is in the kitchen that the fireplace is found.

So far we have dealt with the most common names used to refer to the household. But there are two other names which are important even though they are less commonly used: *lar* (hearth, home) and *fogo* (fire; nowadays mostly used in the plural). The symbolism implicit in these terms is not purely circumstantial, as indeed the fireplace forms the sacred core of the peasant household. The particular way in which this is expressed may change from place to place, but its underlying features are the same for all *minhoto* peasants: fire is endowed with a purificatory power which makes it the symbol of the sacred character of the household.

A profound relationship is held to exist between the members of a household and the fire around which they are united. The residents of Paço and Couto believe that one should not take fire out of a house where there is a dead person. Should that happen, the soul of the dead man would follow the light and be incapable of finding its way back.

All year round there are festivities centred around the ritual utilization of fire. The Eve of St John's (23 June), the best known of these, is celebrated by each household, each parish, each borough, and even each district (cf. Caro Baroja, 1979; Lisón Tolosana, 1971a: chapter 6). In the major cities of the north-west (Porto, Braga, and Viana do Castelo) the Eve of St John's brings most of the population into the streets in an expression of convivial fraternity. The most important event of this night is the kindling of bonfires in the yard of each household, in an area of cleared ground in each hamlet, and in the central square of each parish and each of the town's neighbourhoods (*bairros*).

For the residents of Paço and Couto, the Eve of St John's is *a noite de feitiço* (the night of sorcery) or *a noite das bruxas* (the night of the witches). Jumping over the fire, as well as the utilization of various strong-smelling herbs and plants, accompanied by much riotous behaviour and great hilarity, are seen as efficient means of counteracting the forces of evil which may attack the household and its members during the following year.

The ritual use of fire is also a major feature of the Eve of St Sebastian's (19-20 January), the Eve of St Martin's (11 November), and Christmas Eve. 'Hunger, plague and war' (i.e., hunger, epidemic disease, and military conscription for the young men) will not enter households where a fire has been lit on St Sebastian's Eve. Similarly, during the Eve of St Martin's, chestnuts and potatoes are cooked in their jackets on the open fire and a great deal of new wine is drunk by all but the poorest households. The symbolic meaning of wine cannot be overlooked in this context. Wine is the symbol of the pride and worth of the males of the household, which is offered to anyone who visits the *casa*. It is considered extremely shameful for a household to run out of wine. The Eve of St Martin's, therefore, marks the success of the household in reproducing itself in terms both of food and social standing for yet another year.

Finally, on the day before Christmas Eve, no work is done. The women spend the day cooking and preparing the relishes which are served throughout the night, and the men spend it cutting wood for the fire. This time, however, the fire is in the fireplace, but it is no ordinary fire, for it must be so big 'that you have to turn away'. Behind the fire a log is left which has to burn slowly until the day of Kings (5 January) and is then stored away. This is called *o canhoto dos trovões* (the thick log of thunder) (cf. Carré Alvarellos, 1965: 116). It is believed that if you set a piece of this log on fire whenever there is a thunderstorm during the following year, the house will not be struck by lightening.

On all of these occasions fire is used as a means of reproducing the welfare of the household and its security. The household is protected from evil forces: bad weather, sorcery and witchcraft, and 'hunger, plague and war'. Fire, then, is a source of power which, by means of these rituals, the household appropriates. This power, however, is indiscriminate. It can be used for both good and evil. It is significant that the periodic fires which burn down enormous expanses of the country's forests are seldom blamed on the dryness of the summer season, on the widespread use of fireworks, or on the inefficiency of forestry policy. Rather, they are usually blamed on things taken as symbols of the antisocial forces which besiege society, that is 'the communists', the greedy acquisitiveness of wood merchants, or the jealousy of neighbours.

It is in the symbolism of purgatory that the most widespread associations of fire become explicit. In purgatory, fire is a purificatory agent. The roadside tableaux which depict the souls in purgatory burning for their sins (the *alminhas*), constantly remind the *minhotos* of the sufferings which souls have to undergo in order to be purified. The ritual jumping over the fire on the Eves of St John's and St Sebastian's is also a form of purification; people are cleansing themselves of the evil forces which besiege the group. On these nights people do not dare the powers of fire; rather they utilize them to their best advantage, partaking in their purificatory powers.

The use of fire as a purificatory agent is again encountered in a very common practice attached to childbirth. It is considered absolutely essential that as soon as the umbilical cord is severed, it should be thrown into the household fire and allowed to burn completely. Should the umbilical cord be lost, it is feared that the baby will grow up to be a robber. The final link between the baby and his or her (truly antisocial) origins—the umbilical cord—can be destroyed safely only by the cleansing power of fire. Moreover, the fire used for this ritual cannot be any fire; it must be the fire which is at the centre of the household in which the baby is born and will be reared—the hearth which symbolizes the unity of the household.

There are many other rituals and interdictions attached to the protection of the mother and child during childbirth and pregnancy. While some, like the one described above, apply only to the mother and child, others must be observed by all members of the household. These will be discussed below. For the present discussion, what is relevant is that these interdictions are applicable only to people 'who live in the same household: those who eat together'. Commensality is the criterion for deciding who is responsible for the reproduction of the household in its widest sense.

While doing fieldwork I was repeatedly reminded that the ultimate determining factor for the existence of a household was commensality—'those who eat together' (*os que comem juntos*). The elementary social unit finds its definition in the consubstantiality (Pitt-Rivers, 1973: 92-4) which results from the partaking of the 'daily bread' produced on the household's land itself. The household in the Alto Minho is based on a unity of production, management, property, and residence, but all of these are symbolized by the unity of commensality.

III

All consumption in a peasant household takes place around the fire, and all food is cooked on the hearth. The symbolic relationship between fire, commensality, the reproduction of the household, and the position of women in the home is clearly underlined in the bread-making process which, due to its heavily marked symbolism, may readily be called a ritual.

Food can be 'pure', healthy, and socially beneficial, but it can also be misused and made 'impure' when its consumption is motivated by gluttony or greed—when it is out of measure. The very term to refer to people who are considered unduly acquisitive and who cheat in their various dealings is *comedor* (literally, eater). The metaphor that gives rise to this expression is based on the assumption that people steal because they are greedy—they cannot control their affects.[1] When they use this expression, the locals refer to the person's uncontrollable craving for food.

Bread, however, is a very special kind of food, for it is the food *par excellence*, the very source of life. From the ritual of the Holy Communion to its simple consumption at home, bread is used as a symbol of community created through the unity of commensality: a form of commensality which sustains life, both physically and spiritually. The analogy between the Host and the household's 'daily bread' does not escape the locals, who indeed express it when they argue that *o pão é sagrado* (bread is sacred).

The traditional household bread (*broa*) is made of coarse wholemeal maize flour. Until very recently, bread-making was one of the major duties of the housewife in all households. This is still the practice in many of them, although nowadays the bakers of the town send small vans selling 'white' wheat bread through the rural areas. There is a certain status value attached to the use of this bread. The members of many households are becoming increasingly concerned with stressing the pride derived from being able to spend cash, rather than the pride derived from being self-sufficient. The wealthy households which own sufficient land, however (even those who have also accumulated money from emigration), tend to compromise. They use the maize bread for their daily consumption and as a complement to the 'white' bread which is given to visitors.

This 'bread' (for the dough, the flour, the grain, and even the maize plant in the fields are called by the word for bread—*pão*) ought to have been recently reaped, freshly ground, and produced by the household. It would be seen as somewhat absurd to buy flour for bread-making, and the taste of old maize is often disparaged. The household should not be dependent on others for its most important foodstuff, that which symbolizes its continued capacity for subsistence, nor should it be in short supply. It is significant that, although maize has stopped being the

---

[1] I use the term 'affect' as a reference to the work of Norbert Elias (e.g. 1978: 221 ff.) to mean 'the emotion that lies behind action' (Chambers, s.v.).

most important crop—for it is not as marketable as wine nor does it any longer form the basis of everyday diet—its cognitive priority has been preserved. Land assessors (*louvados*), for example, when they establish the value of a piece of land, start by finding the basic price per square metre on the basis of the land's productiveness in terms of maize and only then do they vary it according to the field's other features, such as wine and olive oil production, nearness to roads, facility for construction, water, etc.

In all peasant kitchens the *maceira* is a prominent piece of furniture. It is here that the bread is kneaded and left to rise. The *maceira* is a small table with raised edges which form oblique angles to the table, which is covered with a wooden lid. This lid is removed only for breadmaking. Although hygiene in a medical sense may not be a matter of concern, in the case of all foodstuffs, and particularly bread, freedom from contagion is. Thus, for instance, the *maceira* is always washed with boiling water before the start of the bread-making process. This is because mice (or rats) and spiders may have got inside and left *peçonha* (poison or pestilence). The use of this term does not imply the belief that spiders, mice, or rats are poisonous. Rather, it implies a fear of contagion. These are animals which live in the household but do not belong to it and are destructive of the household's products. As such they come to characterize the threat which internal forces of destruction represent to the unity and reproduction of the household.

The term *puro*—pure—is the one used locally to refer to products freshly produced by the household and protected from impurities or contagion. This once again demonstrates that the material subsistence of the members of the household is better provided for by the recent products of the household, those which have come directly from the household's own land. The 'purity' of these foodstuffs lies in the fact that they reinforce the worldview's most basic classifications.

The most important concern in the bread-making process is that the bread should rise. When a new household is formed, the wife brings a piece of uncooked dough from her mother's home, which is then mixed with the newly kneaded flour to make it rise. Yeast is not used. The flour is mixed with water, and then carefully kneaded, after which it is put on the left side of the *maceira* and left to rise with a cross marked on top of it. A small bottle with a little vinegar in it is stuck into the dough on its right side. Having asked what this was, I was told that without it the bread would not rise. Alternatively one can put the trousers or the hat of the male head of the household on the right side of the *maceira*.

Should the dough still not rise, the household head himself may be asked to sit on the *maceira*'s lid for a while to make the bread rise. Although the people are not capable of talking analytically about this practice, its sexual symbolism is as clear to them as it is to us. I asked one of my friends why she used vinegar and she replied that this was done 'because vinegar is rough and coarse [*áspero e rude*] like a man.'

Should the dough still not rise, this is because a spider or a *rato* (rat or mouse) is thought to have passed beneath it. In this case, only a piece of burning wood from the hearth is able to purify the bread. The under-part of the *maceira* is carefully branded with fire. Once more we witness the household fire being used for purificatory purposes. In this particular case it purifies the symbol of the household's capacity for reproduction: the bread.

The process of the symbolic integration of the male and female aspects, which is central to the breadmaking process, represents the very nature of the household and its process of biological reproduction. This is evinced by the fact that the stress is not laid on the baking of the bread but rather on the swelling of the kneaded dough. Once the dough has risen, then it is 'alive' and will be usable as the basis of the household's unity of commensality. Thus the rising of bread and pregnancy are analogically related.

However, while the basis of pregnancy is sexual intercourse which, even in the context of the household, is seen as impure and animal-like, the basis of the bread-making process is a *pure* co-ordination of male and female principles (as the stress on purificatory practices demonstrates). The husband is symbolically related to this process through the roughness of the vinegar and in some instances may even participate personally by sitting on the *maceira*: the wife participates via the piece of uncooked dough and by her labour, for she cooks the bread. It must be reiterated that not only are hats and trousers specifically 'male' objects, but also that vinegar is associated with maleness. This is both because it is 'rough and coarse' and because it is made of wine, an eminently 'male' product of the household.

We are justified, therefore, in claiming that the symbolism implicit in the bread-making ritual is sexual. Yet the unavoidable impurity in which the biological reproduction of the household takes place—the sexual act, and the corruption in the bellies of women—is carefully eradicated from this ritual: the bread will rise only *if* the *maceira* is completely clear of impure, animal contagion. Similarly, not only is a cross marked on the bread as it rises, but also the piece of uncooked dough, which is put aside before the bread is baked for the next batch of bread, is also kept in 'pure' conditions and marked with the sign of the cross.

In *The Myth of the Eternal Return* (1954), Mircea Eliade points to the existence in what he calls 'ancient cultures' of rituals which repeat the act of creation, i.e., cosmogonic rituals. In his opinion these serve the function of negating history, for they create an eternal return to the mythical starting-point. This idea seems particularly apposite here since it allows us to perceive the existence of a relationship between the ritual practices of a social group and its mythology.

In the Alto Minho, the significance of the biblical myth of the creation of the world and its re-enactment in the structure of the week is reduced when compared to the myth of Adam and Eve. But there is in Christian mythology a second creation, one which both mirrors and opposes the first: the birth of Jesus Christ. Theologically speaking, this was when the new Adam was born. In terms of the *minhotos*, it was also at that moment that their society was created for, above all, they see themselves as Christians.

The great importance of the Virgin is dependent on her maternity. The Virgin did not conceive on her own; she gave birth after being visited by the Holy Spirit. The conception of Christ involved a combination of male (divine) and female (the Virgin) elements, but it was *not* sexual in that it was stripped of all 'impurity'. As in the case of bread-making, the pregnancy of the Virgin is socially beneficial in the highest degree, for it reflects a form of reproduction which is 'pure'—one which overcomes the stain of original sin. Thus, the practices described above can be seen to form what Eliade would call a cosmogonic ritual. In its 'purity', the reproduction of the household as symbolized in the ritual of bread-making can be seen to mirror the 'ideal' act of reproduction, the mythical conception of Jesus Christ. In demonstrating this connection I am not attempting to show how the conception of Christ suffuses bread-making with meaning, but rather how bread-making participates in the symbolic relevance of the conception of Christ, for the residents of Paço and Couto.

IV

The rapid socio-economic change since the 1960s has certainly influenced people's view of the *casa*. No better indicator of these changes can be found than the actual houses which people build.

Until the 1950s, a returning emigrant or a successful local entrepreneur invested most of his money in land and in building or refurbishing his house. As a rule, and depending of course on the amount of money the particular person had managed to amass, these houses were more comfortable and more ostentatious than those they had inhabited before they left. However, they remained basically peasant homes: they were still clearly agricultural establishments, facing the yard where all the agricultural implements were kept. Most importantly, they were still centred around the kitchen. Although the kitchen may now have included a modern iron stove, the fireplace was still maintained, and the bread was still cooked in the oven which would be built on the wall next to the hearth. The sitting-room, a cold and musty place, was used only on ceremonial occasions such as Easter, when the priest came to bless the house, or upon the marriage of a daughter. It would also be here that the returned emigrant would lie, surrounded by wailing women, on his last day at home, before being taken to the cemetery.

During the 1960s and the early 1970s, however, a new and clearly distinguishable type of house evolved. These houses are widely known as *casas de emigrante*, for they were built mainly by returned emigrants, although the style was adopted for most of the houses built during this period. Three main features distinguish them from the previous type of house. The most marked of these is their architectural style and colour. They often have decorative references to the urban architectural styles of the countries where the emigrants had worked, even if the basic rectangular plan with two floors remains traditional. They have 'modern'-looking verandas with iron railings, steeply pitched roofs, often covered in black tiles, and front doors with panes of coloured glass. To these, the emigrants add their local feeling for brilliant colour. Each house combines at least three colours, the range being unlimited. Furthermore, no house is complete without coloured flowerpots and garden gnomes and one or two panels of painted tiles depicting a patron saint or a religious scene. These self-consciously 'urban' houses symbolize freedom from the constraints of the monotonous, difficult, and 'dirty' toil of the land. In this, they have the same meaning at the stands (*andores*) which are used to carry the saints during the processions at *festas* and which are completely covered in mutlicoloured shiny paper. Like their showy foreign cars, the houses represent the emigrants' claim to 'urbanity'.

The second feature of these houses also illustrates this point. While the earlier houses were clearly agricultural establishments, these are seldom suitable for a peasant life-style. Whenever possible they are built facing the road rather than the yard, and instead of a cellar or a tool-shed they are bound to have a garage.

Finally, these houses only rarely have a hearth. The chimneys and the kitchens are smaller and the latter do not readily lend themselves to being used as the main room. They have no bread-ovens, and generally the stoves are run on gas rather than wood, for wood is 'too dirty'. There is always a refrigerator, a television, and a radio.

Had their owners fully intended to lead a peasant life-style on their return, these houses would have been incongruous. They were built as outward manifestations of the rapid rise in standards of living which took place during the period. The recourse to symbols of 'urbanity' must not be seen as an abandonment of peasant values, but rather as representing the continued persistence of the peasant identification of better standards of living with urban, bourgeois, values. This is clearly discernible when we consider the trend since approximately 1976. In 1974/5, the European emigrationary trends which had characterized the previous decade were suddenly arrested when the economies of France and Germany started to feel the recession. It was no longer easy to earn money abroad and, the recession being felt even more strongly at home after 1979/80, the importance of agriculture as a basic insurance of subsistence again increased. For both the returned emigrant and the locally employed semi-proletarian, the work of the land became once more an essential aspect of overall economic policy. This change is reflected in the physical manifestation of the *casa*: secondary kitchens (with all the 'traditional' peasant facilities) were built anew or added to the old ones; 'garages' returned to their traditional definition as *lojas* where products are stored, wine is made, implements are repaired, and cattle are kept; sheds were built to surround the house; and even the taste for bright colours increasingly gave way to more practical, sober tones.

6. The composition of the household

I

Most households, whether peasant or urban, are centred around a married couple. Because productive activities take place at the level of the household in peasant society, and because of the conception of the *casa* as attached to a unity of production and property management, the executive powers of the peasant head couple are more clearly delineated.

Thus, even when two couples live in the same household, there is always a consensus among the neighbours and the members of the household as to who 'rules' the house—*quem são os donos da casa*. Furthermore, there is never more than one 'young couple' in the house. Two married siblings cannot live in the same household, for it is believed that the conflict between them would be too disruptive.

So far I have been referring to the head couple rather than to the 'household head'. This is because, with the exception of widows and unmarried people, the headship is not consigned to one person, but is held jointly by a couple. Two expressions are used to refer to this couple—*os donos da casa* and *o patrão e a patroa*. In this instance, the meaning of the word *donos* is more akin to that of 'lord' than that of 'owner'. The implications of private property in 'owner' are not present in this expression, where the stress is on executive rights (much like the Latin *dominus*) rather than on ultimate private ownership. The expression *o chefe da casa* (literally, the chief of the household) is used mostly in urban circles, where it tends to reflect the male dominance which is characteristic of the bourgeois home.

The generalizing of facilities for paid employment at local level during the second half of this century, which meant an increased break in the household's unity of production, did not automatically alter the head couple's position. The situation in relation to the household of members who are locally employed in the capitalist sector outside the household is not radically different from that of emigrants, an old feature of this society. Conceptual priority is given to the household as the basis for subsistence and the extra-household economic activities are seen as supportive of it and optional. This attitude explains why, in order to understand peasant economic behaviour, we have to look for household strategies and not individual ones. What has altered the position of the head couple, is the changed relative importance of the extra-household earnings of the young. This affects not so much the household's unity of production as its unity of property.

It is worth noting at this point that the conception of property to which I refer here is by no means the same as the notion of private property which has come to be enshrined in the Portuguese legal system. The members of a borough, a parish, or a hamlet feel that they have exclusive rights over the decisions which concern the land of the borough, parish, or hamlet, even though the legal ownership of that land is not necessarily in the hands of local residents. This is a kind of property claim. Similarly, the members of a household feel that they jointly own certain tracts of land, buildings, animals, etc., even though not all members have the same rights to legal ownership. This is true in at least two senses: first, resident servants, relatives, or friends are considered members of the household even though they have no individual rights of inheritance; second, property brought by different spouses is never fully agglomerated. The latter is particularly noticeable in cases of widowhood and remarriage, where there were children from the first marriage. Although in formal terms the specifications of the Civil Code are followed, there is a clearly manifested desire to allow the surviving spouse to remain with that particular part of the common property brought by him or her at marriage or subsequently through inheritance.

As the relative importance of agriculture decreased within the general household budget during the 1960s and 1970s, young people felt that their parents' claim to incorporate all pre-marital earnings into the common property of the household was unjust. Although there seems to be a general agreement that the things purchased with these extra-agricultural earnings of the children should not enter the division of the household for the purposes of inheritance, young people felt that this practice prevented them from saving.

At the basis of the problem lies the very notion of *salário* (salary or wage). If one's reference point is the subsistence prototype, this notion makes little sense. The labour of the members of the household belongs to the household, and production is carried out at the level of the household. The 'products' of the labour, therefore, belong to the household and are to be used for its benefit, which, of course, also means the upkeep of the members. But a 'salary' is not a 'product', and here lies the difficulty. 'Old-fashioned' parents, as they are referred to locally, adopt the interpretation of 'salary' as a form of 'product' and see it therefore as belonging to the household, which may or may not use it for the benefit of one of its members. Young people see this otherwise: their private labour yielded a payment and whatever remains of this after discounting the costs of their personal upkeep belongs to the wage-earner himself.

In the eyes of the older generation, any property that a child who leaves the parental household at marriage takes with him or her is a boon to the household of destination at the cost of the household of origin. Younger people, however, have been influenced by bourgeois, individualist mores: for them, it is unjust that their personal earnings (or the interest yielded by these until such time as the parental household is divided) should benefit their parents' household and not themselves.

While older parents think in terms of justice at the level of the household, the younger people think in terms of justice at the level of the individual.

In practice it appears that, while the majority of female children entrust their parents with their earnings (or at least a great part of it), most male children avoid doing so and often entrust friends of the family, relatives, or even the priest with their savings. One often hears male children complaining that they do not gain any benefits from the way the money which they entrusted to their parents was used. I have never heard these complaints voiced by female children whose attachment to the parental household is usually stronger and who often marry uxorilocally,[2] thus benefiting directly from the investment of their money in increasing the economic success of the household as a whole.

II

In criticizing Lévi-Strauss's conception of marriage, Octavio Paz argues that what ultimately characterizes marriage is that it is a 'mediation between renunciation and promiscuity . . . thus creating a closed and legal environment in which erotic play can develop' (1970: 127). This statement provides a clue to the understanding of marriage as it is seen by the peasants of the Alto Minho. Marriage and the household assume a sacred character precisely because they mediate between the evil of sex and the necessary reproduction of the group. Divinity and perfect sanctity are beyond the reach of ordinary human beings. Nevertheless, within the household, and via the sacrament of marriage, the ideal of purity in reproduction is achieved. It is in this context that the ritual of bread-making, which was described above, assumes its cosmogonic significance.

All true marriages have to be celebrated by a Christian wedding. Civil weddings are typically called 'cow's weddings' for, in the peasant's view, they merely license cohabitation. A household must be a unified entity with a prolonged temporal existence. Divorce and remarriage, which civil weddings allow, negate its wholeness, as they permit the repeated breakdown of the relationship which is most central to the household. In opposition to what appears to be the case in north-eastern Portugal (O'Neill, 1982), in Paço and Couto the horizontal relations in the

[2] For the use of this term see Carrasco (1963: 133–4) and Casselberry and Valavanes (1976: 215–26). By 'uxorilocality' I understand the residence of a married couple in the household of the wife's parents. By 'uxorivicinality' I understand the residence of a married couple in the vicinity of the wife's parents, by opposition to the vicinity of the husband's parents.

household, that is, those between the members of the head couple, are by no means subsidiary or even merely less significant than the vertical relations, that is, those which unite parents with their offspring.

A clear statement of the view that marriage is a relationship which should last eternally is found in the practice of burying couples in the same grave (usually the grave of the wife's family). A woman once explained to me with earnest satisfaction that, at the recent burial of her father, as it was discovered that her mother's coffin could accommodate his on top, it was placed there gently so that they could *ficar juntinhos*, lie cosily together.

A further reason for the distaste for civil weddings is that they do not create a sacred relationship between the partners. The restriction of a person's sexual activity to one constant partner does not make sex any less polluting. The symbolic processes which are implicit in Christian rituals are essential for the effectiveness of the mediation which marriage effects between the evil of sex and the desirability of the reproduction of the household. Therefore, even when a civil wedding leads both to a permanent, exclusive sexual relationship between two partners and to the creation of a household, it is still not the means to a fully acceptable reproduction of the social order.

Weddings are events at which social differentiation is openly declared. In opposition to most other ceremonies, and particularly funerals, at weddings individuals are allowed openly to challenge the assumption that all peasants are 'equal' and the corresponding practice of underplaying social and economic differentiation within the peasant community. It seems that this attitude already obtained before the 1950s (e.g. Valle, 1965).

Weddings have been partly transformed by being associated with the return of emigrants. As many young men emigrate before they get married, most weddings take place in August when they return. By having ostentatious weddings, emigrants accomplish two ends simultaneously: the need to advertise their economic power both upon their return from emigration and at the beginning of their conjugal life. In order to do this, young people have started to acquire consumer goods as status symbols. This is because consumer goods are identified with the bourgeoisie which, in the eyes of the rural population, is characterized by wealth and economic power.

Weddings are always at the expense of the bride's parents and take place in their home, or at least in the bride's parish of residence. In order to marry off a daughter 'decently', a man has to use up a considerable amount of his savings.

As they described their daughters' weddings to me, time and again informants recounted amazing tales of overspending. They described superb food which was so abundant that (and this seems to be the central phrase, constantly repeated) 'we even had to throw cakes and relishes to the dogs.' There was always such a surfeit of food 'that we could have lived off it for a whole year.'

For a wedding, all the cars are taken out of their garages and sheds, and new dresses and jackets are worn with an exuberant, competitive delight. The honour of driving the couple is much sought after among the groom's friends, not so much because of the personal preference that this might be supposed to imply, but because the young couple will invariably choose from among their neighbours, relatives, and friends the one with the best and most showy car.

Weddings occasion overspending for everyone, a tendency which is particularly marked in the hamlets which lie nearest to the river (the 'lower half', where there has been more cultural and economic communication with the urban centres). After the wedding, the guests discreetly compare the presents, trying to decide whose was most generous. But not everyone is concerned with outdoing everyone else. This applies both to guests and to hosts. In Paço it is commonly accepted that no one can 'do better' than the richest local landowner (a man of peasant extraction). The wedding of his eldest daughter, which took place more than twenty years ago, is still remembered as an event unsurpassed in grandeur. This does not worry most people. The members of each household are predominantly concerned with outdoing those whom they classify in the same category as themselves.

This selective competitiveness also explains the ambiguous attitudes of those who remained behind towards returned emigrants. On the one hand, they complain of the emigrants' arrogant and self-assertive behaviour. On the other hand, emigrants are expected, and indeed encouraged to indulge in a spending spree. People need to know who the emigrant's competitors are and what his new position will be. Worse then accepting defeat is not knowing whether one has been defeated or not.

A household which is known to be wealthy and yet does not want to spend its money on a daughter's wedding never outlives the harm that this does to its reputation. Similarly, people who live above their means and at their daughter's wedding prove to be incapable of making a good show, will also be denigrated. *Vizinhos* are always eager to exaggerate such failures. The assessment of the failure or success of a wedding, however, also depends on the relation of the guest to the couple. On the whole, the guests on the groom's side are less outspoken about the success of the wedding. There is a certain underlying competition between the parties and, although the groom's friends and relatives like to say that the marriage was a success, they are unlikely to admit that it was more successful than the weddings of the groom's sisters.

Today, as in the past, most marriages are the result of an agreement between the parents and the children. As a rule they are preceded by a *namoro* (courtship), which is a socially recognized relationship between two young people. Usually the couple meet at a *festa*, a fair, or around the churchyard on a Sunday. A boy and girl who are interested in each other may then dance or chat semi-privately for a while. Shortly after this meeting, the boy comes to visit the girl at the door of her home and, if her parents do not strongly oppose his presence, this becomes a regular activity on Sundays and feast days. It is then said that they are *conversados* (literally, they have spoken). Indeed, publicly, talking is the main activity which is associated with courtship. This ideal of pre-marital sexual continence, however, is not taken too seriously. Unmarried women are free to move around the fields and often do so on their own. Opportunities for private meetings between lovers are easily arranged. It is believed that very few women are virgins at marriage.

III

Normative statements concerning household composition are notably difficult to elicit from the parishioners of Paço and Couto. Value judgements and statements concerning ideal conditions are, of course, encountered, but informants are eager to show that these do not strictly correspond to practice. Indeed, the individual *minhoto* perceives the composition of his household as resulting from a series of strategic decisions, rather than as an adjustment to normative principles. We are thus encouraged to look for a statistical model in order to describe the dominant strategies and the factors which determine their variations. It will be argued that the relation between land and household, the cognitive significance of which has already been pointed out, manifests itself in yet another form. Household composition strategies appear to be closely linked to economic differentiation within peasant society and more specifically to land ownership.

Unfortunately, the lack of a land cadastre, the extreme subdivision of the land, and the extensive variation in type of land, have made it

impossible to establish a relation between land and household composition. But even if we did possess a uniform comparative standard for
assessing land values—a practical impossibility—this relation would still
be difficult to establish, for the legal ownership of the land would not be
an adequate indicator. What affects household composition is not legal
ownership of the land *per se*, but rather the right to manage production
on a particular stretch of land, and the certainty of benefiting from a
sufficient amount of the produce of the land to reward the labour on
average, that is, a permanent control over a viable agricultural enterprise. This difference is especially significant when we consider that the
land worked by a household often belongs to emigrant relatives or is
held under such conditions of tenure as to assure the farmer and his
family of subsistence, even after a poor agricultural year.

Two comparisons may help us bypass these problems. First,
household composition in Paço and Couto can be compared, as we
know that in Paço there are more people who own the land they work,
and that the residents are more deeply attached to a peasant way of life.
Second, household composition can be related to the wealth groups which
have been established on the basis of the household census (see chapter 3,
section V).

70.71 per cent of the households of both parishes together are composed of a nuclear family (NF), that is, a couple or a widow(er) with or
without children; 21.50 per cent are composed of extended families
(EF), that is, a nuclear family plus one or more members, 1.46 per cent
of these comprising an unrelated member, often a servant; finally, 7.72
per cent are households headed by single people (SH).[3]

Unless one controls the family developmental cycle, the economic differentiation within the parish, and the differences between the two
parishes studied, these percentages bare little significance. Unfortunately, we are dealing with very low numbers—295 households in Paço
and 184 in Couto, and at times even fewer, as we lack some data in relation to a number of households. This means that it is not possible to
interrelate more than two variables, as the samples would otherwise
cease to be representative. This problem is insoluble since a detailed
census, such as the one carried out for the purposes of this analysis,
could not practically be effected for a whole borough; furthermore,
analyses of an intermediate range must be avoided as they would

[3] I have not had recourse to a typology of households such as that elaborated by the
Cambridge group (cf. Laslett, 1972: 31), as it would be too complex for the purposes of
the present analysis. Unless otherwise stated, all these figures refer to 1979–80.

destroy the variation between parishes which is so important, as the comparison between Paço and Couto will demonstrate.

IV

Households headed by unmarried people (SH) must be considered separately from others, for they cannot properly be called *casas* and correspond to a situation where the accepted standards have not been followed. 28.41 per cent of all the households in the lower wealth subgroup (P_2) in Paço and Couto together are headed by unmarried people. This percentage decreases progressively as we climb the stratification scale: 4.54 per cent in sub-group P_1, 3.03 per cent in sub-group M_2. In the upper echelons only two cases were encountered: the household of the priest (M_1); and that of the aged, single descendant of an old aristocratic house (R_1). Both of these cases must be considered independently.

The association between poverty and households headed by single people is not contradicted by the fact that, at present, Paço has approximately the same percentage of households of this type as Couto (7.80 per cent and 7.60 per cent, respectively). This is an ironic result of the surge in emigration of the 1960s and early 1970s. Couto has, and always has had, a greater number of landless people, who, lacking the security provided by the land and the agricultural household to entice them back, were less likely to return to their parish of origin. This explains why the population of Couto has decreased at a faster rate than that of Paço (see chapter I, sect. 2.III).

Landlessness, households headed by single people, and illegitimacy are interrelated phenomena. Some parishes of the borough suffer from the reputation of being *putanheiras* (literally, full of whores)—Couto is one of them. Invariably, these are poorer parishes, where a great deal of land is owned by absentee landlords and where the rate of illegitimacy is higher. The term *putanheira* presupposes a moral explanation for illegitimacy: in the peasant worldview, illegitimacy is perceived as being antisocial, even though in the Alto Minho it does not correspond to any form of open ostracization or diminution of civil rights. Landlessness is associated with illegitimacy not only at intra-parish level but also at the level of individual household composition: even today 68.97 per cent of all households which include illegitimate offspring belong to the lowest wealth echelon (P_2), and 17.24 per cent to the one immediately above (P_1).

The landless peasantry of these parishes approximates very closely the model of Laslett's 'bastardy prone sub-society':

a series of bastard-producing women, living in the same locality, whose activities persisted over several generations, and who tended to be related by kinship or marriage. Many of the women were credited not with one illegitimate birth only, but with several. (1980: 217)

Furthermore, it is interesting to note that the periods during which illegitimacy reached its peak over the past century (the 1890s and the 1930s, see Figure 4) bear out Laslett's conclusion that illegitimacy rose 'when proletarianization was on the increase and when obstacles may have been placed in the way of proletarian marriage' (1980: 226).

Caseiros, share-croppers who work the land of absentee landlords, bequeath the right to work this land and to inhabit the house which is attached to it to the married child who remains at home, usually a daughter. As they own little land of their own, the other daughters find it difficult to marry locally. The same happens with owner-farmers whose land is not sufficient to distribute to all the children. Their daughters either go to the cities to work as housemaids or remain at home, unmarried (*solteironas*). Over the past twenty years, female emigration and the emergence of alternative sources of income have contributed towards a change in these patterns. However, one still finds today cases of adult men and women who remain at home working under the headship of a married sibling (cf. Bourdieu, 1962).

Women who are completely landless are in a still less enviable position than the daughters of *caseiros*. Until the 1960s, not only were they likely to fail to find husbands, but also they did not have the security of an agricultural household, since their mothers themselves had often been unmarried. They did not own houses and were forced to live in temporary, makeshift lodgings such as barns, stables, and rented houses. Since they were paid for their work on a daily basis and their employment was therefore seasonal, they often found it necessary to have sexual relations with wealthy farmers as a means of acquiring food and other necessities during the winter months.[4] Hence, the fathers of their children were often their employers, or other wealthy peasants in the vicinity. Sometimes such relationships could be profitable. Camilo Castelo Branco, a nineteenth-century novelist, provides an illustration:

[4] Contrary to Laslett's opinion (1980: 56), this was the explanation given by informants for the majority of cases studied directly (cf. Furtado Coelho, 1861: 2).

'Brazilians'—money lenders who returned from Brazil after having closed their shops in that far-off land—dishonour girls, and then give them dowries (*dotes*) the contents of which are already pre-established by accepted usage; the contenders to the hand of the girls who receive these dowries, dispute by means of cudgel-fights for the legitimate enjoyment of the girl who is now able to become a bride (1885: 70–1)

What horrified Camilo was that these girls had failed to find husbands not because they were not virgins, but because they had no land. Once endowed, many men would be willing to marry them. For the peasant who, contrary to bourgeois practice, does not draw a strict frontier between the realm of the family and that of the economy, the penetration of economic logic into a sexual and familial question is perfectly acceptable.

Camilo, quoting Oliveira Martins, says of *minhoto* peasants that 'many, many girls who are not virgins get married, and this, though it is common knowledge, is not considered scandalous' (Castelo Branco, 1885: 70–1). Then, as today, pre-marital pregnancies were frequent. If a girl's parents are reasonably wealthy, her lover is usually easily convinced to marry her. In cases where the lover refuses to do so, an abortion is usually procured. If the affair has become public knowledge, however, the girl's marriageability will have decreased and she may have to lower her expectations. Her parents may be forced to give her a reasonably good advance on her inheritance at the time of marriage. The residents of Paço and Couto are adamant, however, about the fact that unmarried couples should not form a household. Local residents do not object to sexual intercourse between unmarried people, but the creation of a household which is not based on a sacrament of marriage is considered to be an offence to the whole hamlet.

This explains why, of all the households headed by single people in both parishes, only two are headed by an unmarried couple. It is furthermore significant that both of these should be in Couto, a parish where fewer people manage to enact the type of household composition which ideally matches the conception of the *casa* as expressed in the subsistence prototype. These couples are criticized, but the neighbours do not have the necessary moral weight to prevent their occurrence.

In Paço, however, the *vizinhos* of most hamlets do have such power. I shall quote only one example: in the mid-1970s, a married man who had been having an affair openly with a single woman for quite some time, decided to abandon the house of his quarrelsome wife in order to sleep at his lover's home. As soon as his intentions were known, the hamlet *vizinhos*, who until then had sympathized with him, turned violently against the adulterous couple. They were stoned out of the hamlet, never to return.

Even today, landless women who become pregnant find it difficult to marry and they do not always receive help from their lovers in bringing up the child. Those who do not succeed in marrying bring up their children in their mothers' homes. Their sons are likely to emigrate and seldom return to the parish; their daughters follow their mothers' life-style and one finds cases of women today whose grandmothers too were unmarried mothers.

Illegitimacy was very common until the 1950s, but it is now disappearing. Nevertheless, today, 8.33 per cent of all households in Couto, and 3.73 per cent in Paço, are headed by unmarried mothers. From 1860 to 1940 (at which time illegitimacy rates started to decrease) the percentages of illegitimate baptisms per decade oscillated between 14.3 per cent and 22.5 per cent in Couto and between 5.8 per cent and 12.5 per cent in Paço, (see Figure 4).

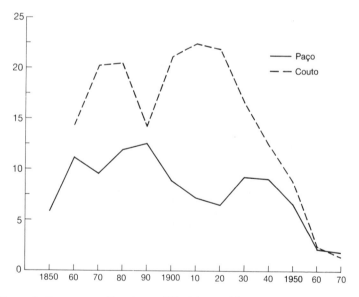

Figure 4. Percentage of baptisms of illegitimate children per decade in the two parishes. *Source*: Parish Registers.

Since the 1960s landless peasants have been able to find alternative sources of income and could therefore marry. Concomitantly, returned emigrants started to buy up the land of the absentee landlords, and people who had previously been landless were no longer so. This had the effect of practically ending illegitimacy. The percentage of baptisms of illegitimate children in both parishes together in the 1970s was 1.56.

Unmarried mothers, whose sexuality has not been redeemed by marriage, are not feared or ostracized because of their 'illegitimate motherhood', but are despised and considered somewhat impure. It is often said of their offspring that 'they are brought up like little goats,' thus stressing their animal-like nature.

Individually, unmarried mothers are considered inferior; but, as a group, landless peasants are all inferior, for they cannot be said to form *casas*. For there to be a household there has to be a stable relationship between a group of people, a building, and land. Landless peasants are seen as mobile and are deprecatingly called *cabaneiros*. Literally, this word refers to a person who dwells in a hut, a temporary house; figuratively, however, the term is far richer in meaning. Having asked a wealthy peasant what it meant, I received the following answer: 'A *cabaneiro* is a puny person, who cannot deal with anything; a "dead" person who belongs to the Do-Not-Bother Company Ltd. Such a person is a cul-de-sac.' Landless people do not have a strong link to the land. They are, therefore, conceptually excluded from the peasant society proper.

Unmarried mothers, then, are more resented than pitied, for they are blamed for what is considered to be loose sexual behaviour. Furthermore, there is a feeling that whoever does not have land, does not deserve to have it.

V

Even among those households who succeed in forming *casas*, there is a positive correlation between household composition and wealth. There are more extended family households (EF) both in Paço in opposition to Couto, and in the higher echelons in opposition to the lower.

Among the extended family households, we find seven which include members who are not related to the head couple. Five include servants, and two a friend or neighbour. The occurrence of these households, in contradistinction to households headed by unmarried people (SH), is associated with the higher economic echelons. They represent 1.2 per cent of all households in sub-group M_2, 3.70 per cent in M_1, and 33.33

per cent in $R_{1/2}$. Furthermore, there are no cases of households including servants in Couto.

The reason for this is largely classificatory. The informants of this
parish differed from those of Paço in classifying a worker who is permanently employed as a *jornaleiro permanente* (permanent day-labourer,
sic), rather than as a servant (*criado*). In this way, they conceive of this
person as extrinsic to the household, in opposition to the informants of
Paço, for whom servants have much the same status as an apprentice in
the medieval household of a craftsman. A similar attitude is evinced in
relation to resident friends or neighbours. Both instances encountered
in Paço are old women who were accepted into the household on condition that their property be left to the household at death. Again, in
Couto we find no such case.

If we now compare the occurrence of nuclear family households (NF)
with that of extended family households (EF) in both parishes, we
discover that Paço has a higher percentage of the latter (see Table VI).

Table VI.

Household composition	Paço		Couto	
	Numbers	Percentage	Numbers	Percentage
Extended family	74	27.21	28	16.87
Nuclear family	198	72.79	138	83.13

A similar result is obtained when we compare household composition
with the wealth sub-groups. In order to make the samples more
representative, we will compare the lowest echelons with the highest.
(Even then the sample for the highest echelons in Couto is not sufficiently representative, see Table VII).

We can, therefore, conclude that the occurrence of extended family
households (EF) is higher both among the higher wealth sub-groups,
and in Paço in opposition to Couto. Nevertheless, in one aspect, these
percentages are still misleading—as Meyer Fortes already pointed out in
1949 (Fortes, 1970: 7-8). In order to understand the real meaning of
household composition, we have to take into account the family

Table VII.

Wealth sub-groups	Household composition	Paço		Couto	
		Numbers	Percentage	Number	Percentage
P_2 P_1 M_2	Extended family	45	24.76	22	16.30
	Nuclear family	137	75.27	113	83.70
M_1	Extended family	29	32.22	6	19.35
$R_{1/2}$	Nuclear family	61	67.78	25	80.65

developmental cycle. As in these parishes it is usually the youngest married daughter who succeeds the parents in the headship of the household, there will necessarily be long periods during which the household will have a nuclear family composition, without invalidating the existence of a type of household composition strategy which favours the extended family household. By controlling the age of the household head we can, therefore, develop a clearer picture of the occurrence of such a strategy in the course of the developmental cycle.[5]

The data presented in Figures 5a and 5b allow us to conclude that at least 50 per cent of all households in Paço and 33.33 per cent in Couto go through one or more periods of the developmental cycle in which their composition corresponds to an extended family situation.

There is a higher incidence of this situation at three moments of the cycle: the periods when the youngest member of the head couple is 25 to 35, 50 to 54, and 70 to 74 years of age. In the first of these moments, that which lasts longest and in which the percentage of extended family

[5] I have made my computations in terms of the *younger member of the head couple*. This is one of the possible ways of approaching the household developmental cycle. I have chosen it because it is more meaningful in terms of the age of child-bearing and of final inheritance (for both spouses must inherit before full economic independence is achieved). It also gives a better indication of the time-span of headship since, if widowhood occurs too early in the life of the surviving spouse, he or she will remain in power for longer than would otherwise be expected of a widow or widower. Finally, considering the strong tendency to practice uxorilocality, the age of the wife, who is nowadays, as a rule, the younger spouse, seems more important.

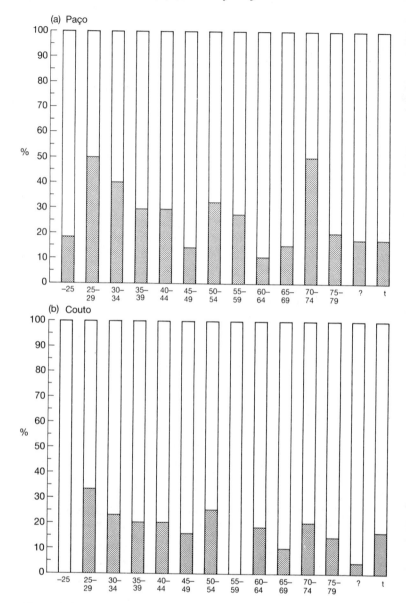

Figure 5. Percentage of extended family households per age group (excluding households headed by single people). (a) Paço (b) Couto. See Appendix 1.

households is highest, the households are comprised of a young couple and its children accompanied by siblings of the household heads and/or members of the ascendant generation (mother or father, generally widowed, and aunt or uncle, generally single). As the latter die of old age, the occurrence of extended family households decreases.

The 50 to 54 age group witnesses again a rise in this type of household. This time, however, its composition is different: it is now a young married couple who live under the headship of the parental head couple. The high percentage in this age-group corresponds to the marriage of the first daughter, and that in the 70 to 74 age group to the marriage of the daughter who will eventually inherit the headship. Finally, the higher incidence of extended family households in the 70 to 74 age-group is also explained by reference to the situation where a widow lives with the grandchildren or with these and a married daughter, who does not take over the headship formally because her husband is working abroad. Thus, in interpreting these figures, and particularly as far as the age groups above 50 are concerned, we must take emigration into account. Many of the young couples who would otherwise be living with their old parents live abroad. They nevertheless remain profoundly attached to the household.

VI

The division of households in Paço and Couto into three types (SH, EF, and NF) should not be understood to indicate three types of strategies of household composition. The correlation between wealth, particularly as expressed in the ownership of land, and household composition is so marked that it must be taken to mean that the existence of households headed by single people (SH) corresponds to a negative strategy: those who are landless cannot form a *casa*. Only those who own land can create *casas*, thus living up to the ideal expressed in the subsistence prototype, which is shared by all.

A similar explanation can be given to the relative occurrence of extended family and nuclear family households. It is the differential ownership of land which, in the last instance, explains the adoption of different strategic attitudes. The contrast between the two parishes, however, must equally be taken into account. Paço is not only a parish where a larger number of people own the land they work; it is also a parish where the values of the peasant worldview are more deeply entrenched and more strictly followed. Thus, even within the same economic echelons, the percentage of extended family households is higher in Paço.

In the Alto Minho, the strategic attitude which corresponds to a higher incidence of extended family households is attached to a peasant type of identification with the land and the agricultural household. The strategic nature of household composition is the very reason why this relationship was not included by me in the drawing up of the subsistence prototype. The association between the *casa* and the extended family composition strategy is the result of the enactment of the values expressed in the prototype: it does not have the ideological weight of a culturally shared ideal. It is a strategic tendency which results from a series of decisions which, at a conscious level, are presented as independent and unrelated. It corresponds to a great concern for the survival of the household as a whole and of its land as a unit. By means of the common residence of as many people as is practically possible under the headship of one couple, the amount of land worked is increased and, concomitantly, the moral weight of the *casa* as a recognized social unit with its own identity is reinforced.

The logic of this strategy must also be understood at an individual level: a member of a large and wealthy household, whose membership assures him of support and subsistence in case alternative sources of income should fail (either through old age or through unemployment in the capitalist sector), will not be eager to abandon the household or to break its power and prestige. So long as the household owns land, its members are interested in remaining together.

This tendency, however, is not taken to its logical conclusion, that is, the situation where various married siblings live together with their nuclear families. Not only is there no case in either parish of the cohabitation of two couples of the same generation, but such a situation would be considered perfectly unacceptable. What characterizes the household is its unity; the possibility of conflict for the headship or, even worse, a duality of headship, is as aberrant to the *minhoto* as the break in the reproductive unity of the household which it would represent. It is significant that, although unmarried siblings of the head couple are fully entitled to be members of the household, their illegitimate offspring are not, and I encountered no instance in Paço or Couto of such an occurrence.

We are, then, confronted by a single logic of strategy which may be expressed positively or negatively. On the one hand, there is the pole corresponding to the situation which favours the appearance of extended family households. This is the *positive strategy*, reflecting an attempt by the members to prolong the existence of the household as a social entity and to preserve the unity of specific stretches of land which are associated with the household. In kinship terms, it is a centripetal strategy which leads to the maintenance of close ties between the descendants of the *casa*, as expressed in the marriage of cousins (so as to bring back into the household fields which had been lost through inheritance).[6] Furthermore, as the *casa* is defined in non-kinship terms, it readily integrates servants or even friends. This strategy leads to a maximum social presence for the household *and* for each of its members. As was argued above, parish and hamlet membership are essentially defined in terms of participation in a *casa*. This is a strategy of maximization of citizenship in peasant society.

On the other hand, there is the *negative strategy*: that which is adhered to by the *jornaleiros* and the poorer *caseiros*, which leads to a high percentage of households headed by unmarried people (SH) and the infrequent occurrence of extended family households. Their lack of land means that they cannot be assured of subsistence and therefore landless peasants seldom even marry (marriage makes little sense for the *minhoto* peasant if it is not associated with a household). Illegitimacy is high and matrifocal families with a reduced male presence are common, for the husbands and male children who emigrate often fail to find an incentive to return. Marriage too is less stable. Those who manage to buy land and create a landed household tend to play down their kinship links. This is a centrifugal and negative strategic position, to which people have recourse who are forced to do so by circumstances outside their control.

Between these two poles, there exists a continuum of variations. The wealthier a family, the more likely it is to create an extended family household. For those who have some, but not much land, the individual interest in household membership is not sufficient for them to resist the natural centrifugal tendency. This explains why there are more nuclear family households in these intermediary groups.

Finally, in Couto, where fewer households achieve the type of social presence which results from extended family composition, and where more people depend on non-agricultural incomes or on land which they do not hold securely, the ideal of the subsistence prototype tends to weaken and there is less insistence by the residents as a group on

---

[6] Unfortunately, it was not possible to collect data concerning the precise relation between spouses for a sufficiently representative number of people.

conformity to the principles which shape the peasant worldview. In this way, we can understand why the residents of Paço adhere more closely to this worldview and are less susceptible to the penetration of a new kind of household composition strategy: that which results from a bourgeois worldview and from urban, non-agricultural conditions of existence.

7. Inheritance and wealth

I

The conceptual guidelines given by the residents of Paço and Couto concerning household composition tend to relate to the inheritance and succession of the headship of the household. The conceptual priority given to this moment of the household developmental cycle is in itself significant since, as was argued above, it is in the persons of the head couple that the various forms of unity which define the household are embodied.

In the first place, it is emphatically stated that, be it male or female, an only child must always remain at home. This is equivalent to saying that parents and children should do all they can to prevent the household as an independent social unit from disappearing.

Another often repeated statement is that, if the household owns only one building fit for human habitation, it should be left to a daughter. Various reasons are given to justify this, the most common being that a daughter can easily co-operate with her mother, while a daughter-in-law 'is never as good as a daughter' to her husband's mother. This, in turn, is explained by reference to women's inherent quarrelsomeness. The conflict-laden nature of this relationship cannot be denied, as the cases of virilocality encountered demonstrated. A more satisfactory explanation may be found, however, in the close identification of women with the home.

While women are anchored to the household, men are free to move about. The incoming daughter-in-law is a competitor who cannot be kept at a distance, as the field of action of women is rather more limited than that of men. Similarly, the mother-in-law constantly suspects the daughter-in-law of keeping an allegiance to her natal household and of being more interested in her private fortune than in the improvement of her new household. Furthermore, since women identify themselves strongly with their natal households, the mother-in-law is very often justified in her suspicions.

Finally, although it is stated that all children have equal rights of inheritance, parents should favour that child which 'looks after them in their old age', by giving him or her a greater share as a compensation for the effort. As this is the child who succeeds to the headship of the old household, this means that, in the process of inheritance, the original household is favoured over the households of the other children (be they newly founded or old).

Considering the emphasis on the social identity of the household, one might have expected to find a system of inheritance which prevented its breaking up, such as the ones described by Lisón Tolosana for neighbouring Galicia (1971b). In Paço and Couto, however, such an issue cannot be approached in prescriptive terms. In fact, the residents claim that 'all children are equal' in their parents' eyes and that all have the right to inherit. However, as is so often the case with such statements of equality in Minho, this does not mean that they will inherit the same amount and the same things. The concern with reproducing the social identity of the household, in practical terms, means that not all children can take the same, particularly when the parental household is not very wealthy. The rise in the standard of living of the past few decades, and emigrant remittances have softened this conflict temporarily, as they meant that many young couples could set up households which, had they relied completely on an agricultural income, would not have been economically feasible. Nevertheless, a close watch on various actual processes of inheritance revealed that the tendency to favour the successor to the headship has survived. Following Bourdieu, it can be claimed that

the objective adjustment of the dispositions and structures ensures that there is a conformity to the demands and objective urgencies which owes nothing to the norm or the conscious conformity to a norm, as well as an apparent finality which does not at all imply the conscious positioning of the objectively attained ends (1980: 245).

As has been repeatedly argued, the land and the household are strongly identified, so much so that it is the work of the land which is seen to justify the headship. Thus, when it is felt that the head couple is no longer capable of looking after the land to its best advantage, pressure begins to mount for them to *dar a partilhas*, that is, assess and divide the land, and, subsequently, yield the headship. The *vizinhos* are ready to criticize couples whose 'thirst for power' is such that they are willing to sacrifice the land, and therefore the household, in order to keep the headship for a few more years.

Legally, each spouse has the right to dispose freely of one-third of the half of the property that belongs to him or her.[7] When *ante mortem* inheritance is practised, the old head couple or the surviving spouse usually keeps control over this third. Local residents say that 'whoever gives away his property before death, deserves to be beaten up,' meaning that parents should never lose control over at least this third of the property, and that they should use it as a means of ensuring their security after retirement and for their old age. This part of the property is usually left to the child who succeeds to the headship of the household. A large number of old people (according to the notary public of Ponte da Barca approximately 60 per cent of those who make a will) still feel that the child who cares for them in their old age (*que os aturou*) ought to benefit most.

II

The process of inheritance begins to gain momentum from the time of the marriage of the head couple's first child. After marriage, most couples take up residence at the house of the bride's parents. There are primarily three reasons for this. First, women are more attached to the household and the land, while men are more mobile. Couples feel that their daughters have a greater allegiance to their households than sons. Second, women are seen as far less protected than men. They are thought to be more subject to risks. For this reason parents prefer to have their daughters at their side. Third, the locals are very strongly aware of the demographic imbalance between the sexes in favour of women. It is more difficult to marry off a daughter than a son. By taking in the young couple, the parents are reducing the economic pressure on the couple during the first years of marriage and are therefore facilitating the marriage of their daughters.

At present, most weddings are accompanied by very small transfers of wealth. During the years preceding the wedding, the bride and her mother collect a trousseau (*enxoval*) which consists of prestigious household goods. The family of the groom, in turn, is supposed to buy new clothing for the groom and, if they are *orgulhosos* (literally, proud; in fact this expression generally means that they are wealthy), they give the couple a piece of furniture, usually a double bed.

---

[7] During the period of fieldwork (1978) the Civil Code was altered in relation to matters of inheritance. Among other things, the new legislation gives equal rights of inheritance to the surviving spouse and the children, as well as to legitimate and illegitimate children (Decreto-Lei n° 496/77 de 25 de Nov.).

A person's *dote* is a very important consideration when choosing a marriage partner. This term as used at present in these riverside parishes has come to refer to an expectation of eventual inheritance. Thus, a spouse's *dote* is the amount of property which he or she will *eventually* contribute towards the common fund of the household. It must be understood that, while the word *dote* is correctly translated into English as 'dowry', and while there have been areas in Portugal where the practice of giving a dowry to a daughter on marriage has been common, in these parishes, at present, the term *dote* has come to be equivalent to inherited property. When a woman from Paço or Couto says that a certain young person has a 'good *dote*', she means that when the young person's parents divide their household's property for the purposes of inheritance, the young man or woman will receive a large amount of property by local standards. As a household's property is usually divided when one of the spouses dies or when they both reach old age, most couples only come into the full possession of their *dote* quite a few years after their marriage. In order to raise their child's marriageability, however, wealthy parents sometimes promise to give part of the *dote* to their son or daughter on marriage. This often consists of a plot which produces maize and wine, but it may also be money or a house. Although it is entrusted to the young couple on marriage, this part of the *dote* given in advance is taken into account for the purposes of inheritance when the parental household's property comes to be divided. Therefore, and since it may also be given to a son, I suggest that the *dote* in this context is more constructively approached as a form of 'diverging devolution', as Goody would have it (e.g., 1973: 1 ff.), rather than as a form of 'dowry' in particular.

When the part of the *dote* given in advance is a field, it is managed together with the land of the parental household where the young couple take up residence (usually the wife's). Some of its proceeds, however, are handed over to the young couple who, in this way, are allowed a modicum of economic independence. This part of the *dote* given in advance is seen as compensation for the child's work for the parental household, and is given only if all of the child's work or earnings previous to the marriage have been handed over to his or her parents. As few male children still do this today, the practice is disappearing in the case of men. In the case of daughters, *dotes* given in advance are sometimes still offered by particularly wealthy parents.

As two married siblings cannot live in the same household, when the younger daughters reach marrying age, the elder usually finds a house in the vicinity of the parental home. The youngest married daughter is the one who, as a rule, remains at home looking after the parents during their old age. This practice of uxorilocality attached to female succession to headship may explain why, in the last decade of the nineteenth century, the average ages of marriage per decade of men and women were so similar. In the 1880s, the average age of marriage of women was even higher than that of men in both parishes (see Table VIII). In the past, local residents argue, two young people could get married only when they inherited property from their parents or when the retirement of one of the parental couples was imminent. As this was usually the bride's, her age of marriage was necessarily high.

At the same time, this meant that many people had to remain single. Fewer marriages, therefore, took place in the late nineteenth century than they do today. Although the number of households in the two parishes taken together increased by only 19.3 per cent between 1890 and 1979, the number of weddings per year in the 1970s was 106.4 per cent higher than in the 1880s.

Table VIII. Average age of marriage per decade

Decades	Paço		Couto	
	Males	Females	Males	Females
1860	—	—	30.47	29.32
1870	—	—	31.12	29.00
1880	27.06	27.30	29.94	32.68
1890	27.95	26.26	29.12	28.12
1900	26.66	25.40	27.21	25.03
1910*	—	—	—	—
1920	27.56	26.95	28.40	25.43
1930	26.83	26.04	27.00	25.68
1940	27.58	27.16	24.52	23.65
1950	26.93	25.06	27.07	24.20
1960	27.75	24.69	27.42	23.16
1970-7	25.43	23.17	26.02	23.09

* The figures for the revolutionary years which succeeded the Republican Revolution of 1910 are incomplete and in some years totally lacking.

Source: Parish records of Paço and Couto. Marriages which involved widows or widowers were excluded.

The figures in Table VIII, which were taken from parish records, must be regarded with caution for, even though marriages which involved widows or widowers were excluded, the sample is not big enough to absorb idiosyncratic cases. The general trend since the 1890s has been a decrease in marrying age for both men and women, but the differences between the two parishes are significant. Since the 1920s, in Paço, the marrying age of men has been closer to that of women than in Couto. This, once more, reflects the predominance in Paço of peasant values and life-style. In a parish such as Couto, where young couples rely less on the succession to headship and more on wages, earned mostly by men, there is less motivation for the late marriage of women. This hypothesis is further substantiated by the fact that, while in Paço the average marrying age of women fell below 25 only during the 1960s, in Couto this had already happened during the 1940s.

The average male marrying age decreased significantly only in the 1970s. The investment of the considerable earnings of those who had left in the 1960s created new opportunities for local paid employment. This allowed many couples to get married earlier, for they were no longer as dependent on inheritance. Moreover, neolocal residence became more viable as it was now easier to build a new house or to renovate an old one.

Uxorilocality and uxorilateral succession to headship—which, I repeat, in Paço and Couto are tendencies and by no means norms—are reflected in the process of division of the land of the household. Not all landed property is alike. The household is named after the plot of land on which it is built. It is closely identified with this plot as well as the other household plots which adjoin it and which often form with it a conceptual unit, sometimes even having a generic name. These are all plots of arable land; forest land is less closely associated with the household. When one hears of first cousins getting married 'in order to put together land' (*para juntar terras*)—which, according to local residents, often happens—this is invariably an attempt to reunite the unit of closely related plots which had been associated with their grandparents' household.

In following the process of *partilhas* of various landed households, I discovered that there was an unstated attempt to keep these plots together and, furthermore, to give them to the child who would predictably succeed to the headship. Concomitantly, arable land was divided among all children, male and female, but sons received a greater part of their share in land which was further from the house and in forest land.

The explanation for this, in one instance where it was avowed, was that in any case the son would be more likely to settle uxorilocally in another hamlet. Once more we find that women are associated more closely with the household and that, therefore, they are favoured as the guardians of the identity of the household—in the case in point, as expressed though the plots of arable land on which the household is built and after which it is named.

III

When a married daughter has to leave the parental home so as to allow a younger sister to marry, she usually finds a house in the vicinity. In many cases, the girl's parental household yields land or even some disused buildings for the young couple to build upon or renovate. These are advanced under the same terms as the *dote* discussed above; often they had already been promised at the time of the marriage.

Thus, there is a continuity between uxorilocality and uxorivicinality which explains why even the daughters who do not succeed to the headship tend to be favoured over sons at the time of inheritance. Simultaneously, the practice of uxorivicinality gives rise to the creation of localized kin groups which are centred around a group of sisters. The members of these households receive the same nickname—often the personal name of the sisters' mother—and co-operate closely in all matters. The link between their households is the household of origin. The ties, which are still very close during the life of the widowed member of the retired head couple, are weakened during the span in which the siblings are household heads, and, finally, they tend to disappear at their death. Indeed, the tendency is for households headed by cousins not to keep up special relationships of co-operation and mutual help.

This pattern, of course, applies only to landed households who manage to enforce the positive strategy delineated above. The negative strategy, followed by those who have no land, and which is associated with a high occurrence of households headed by single people, does not give rise to such kin groups. Various factors contribute to this: first, there is a high personal mobility, for people are not held down by property; second, due to the high incidence of illegitimacy, people often have only half the kinship links; third, there are no shared lands or buildings to remind people of their common origin; and finally, due to the loss of prestige which is associated with illegitimacy and with belonging to a landless household, a certain genealogical amnesia is apparent. Even nicknames seem to be less extensively used.

Once again, between these two extremes, we find a whole range of variations. But in all cases, the localized kin group formed by the households of siblings living in the same hamlet does not survive the death of the siblings. Kinship relations in the Alto Minho are less intense than in the south of the peninsula (cf. Pitt-Rivers, 1971 or Cutileiro, 1971). As a matter of fact, neighbourly relations tend to assume a greater practical meaning, while kinship relations outside the sibling group are put to use mostly on ceremonial occasions.

Each wedding establishes an alliance between two households which will eventually, but not immediately, give rise to a new household. During this period of gestation, the new couple has to be attached to a parental household, either through succession to headship or through residence within its sphere of influence. As a rule, the bride's parental household prevails, for often the groom's parental household is not particularly interested in this new burden. A certain competition between parental households is nevertheless visible in cases where the groom's parents want the couple to live with them or near them. This may happen for a variety of reasons: when the groom is an only child; when his elder sisters are living abroad or virilocally; or when the new couple represents a capital of prestige for the old household (for example, when they are educated, or particularly successful at some non-agricultural venture). The net result is that the alliance between households which each new household represents is always balanced in favour of one of the partners. This imbalance can be minimized by hamlet endogamy and by the marriage of cousins—as indeed often happens—but it can never be fully resolved.

A large number of residents of each hamlet are more or less distant kinsmen. Considering that hamlets seldom exceed seventy households, hamlet endogamy is rather high: in 27.48 per cent of all weddings celebrated in Paço between 1941 and 1977, both spouses were residents of the same hamlet. The barrier between neighbour and kinsman, between 'kith and kin' is, under these conditions, necessarily vague (cf. Pitt-Rivers, 1973: 90). Neighbourly relations in these hamlets are neither those of kinsmen nor, strictly speaking, of friends (even though the terminology of 'friendship' is widely used); they might be situated in an intermediary position as they share features of both of these.

It is also significant that, apart from the sibling group, kinsmen are by no means favoured over unrelated people in terms of neighbourly relations when it comes to everyday social intercourse. Such an attitude is perfectly consistent with the egalitarian definition of neighbourly relations, an integral part of the subsistence prototype. As marriages usually unite people who belong to the same wealth group, the kinsmen in one's neighbourhood tend to belong to one's own wealth group. Should neighbourly relations favour these households, this would be seen as discrimination against the poorer households. This would not appeal to anyone, for it would hamper the development of relations of 'friendship' between wealthy and poor households, which will be described below and which are so important for both, providing the wealthy with much-needed labour, and the poor with 'favours' from the rich.

IV

It is a locally acknowledged fact that daughters of wealthy couples seldom lack suitors, for young men are interested in girls who will inherit a sizeable amount of property. This concern with a girl's 'good *dote*' is clear evidence of something of which the *minhoto* peasants are perfectly well aware: above all, marriage is a question of wealth. In order to marry, you need an income. Local people are adamant that, until the 1960s, when it became possible to live independently of the land, 'those who had no dowry, money for expenses, and a house, did not get married' (*Quem não tinha dote, despezas e casa, não casava*). Furthermore, wealthy heirs marry the daughters of wealthy men: the sons of people in the middle wealth group find their wives among the daughters of people in this same wealth group; and still today, landless people find it difficult to marry at all.

In 1881 Oliveira Martins wrote about the women of Minho: 'When they marry, they know the value of the dowry which they receive, and the marriages are like a business deal which they personally debate and arrange' (1925: 186). Similarly, in his study of Galicia, Lisón Tolosana discusses the economic significance of marriage in the following terms: 'I have described the principal traditional techniques used to find a wife; all of them have the same end in view: to find acceptable matches. Now, the acceptability is invariably defined by an economic calculation' (1976: 179).

Even among the residents of the 'lower half' of Couto, who have been most influenced by urban values, the bourgeois idealization of the romantic marriage which is the meeting of two souls before the meeting of two purses, is only half-heartedly acknowledged. Parents want their children, male or female, to marry into a household which is wealthier than their own; at the same time they discourage marriages into poorer households. The net result of this strategy is that wealth reproduces itself over the generations, and that a household's eventual wealth is highly dependent on the wealth of the natal households of both spouses.

In practice, since most marriages are uxorilocal, at least in the beginning, a couple has greater interest invested in the marriage of a daughter than in that of a son. At the same time, through emigration, a man can raise his fortune in a way which is not usually available to women. Thus, the importance of the wealth of the natal household of the wife is greater than that of the husband. On the whole, in rural Minho, while men are the ones who acquire wealth, it is women who preserve it.

In order to show how wealth reproduces itself through generations, the case histories of three families will be examined briefly: a wealthy peasant family; one of average wealth; and a landless peasant family.

The Gomes family

The first Gomes in Paço was a man who came from another region of Minho in the nineteenth century to work as a foreman for an absentee landlord and who, eventually, bought most of his master's land. He married a woman from a wealthy household in Couto and was appointed parish administrator (*regedor*), a position which, at the time, denoted considerable respectability locally.

He had three sons, one of whom was a priest, another inherited his house, and the third married locally and established himself in the neighbourhood. The son who inherited the headship of the household became President of the Parish Council of Paço, as did his own son in later years. The latter's son-in-law (great-grandson-in-law of the original Gomes) is the present President.

Gomes' third son had four daughters and one son. The son emigrated, and the daughters all married well. The descendants of these women form the core of the upper stratum of Paço and one of them was President of the Parish Council for a considerable period.

The story of this family reveals certain interesting points. First, various members of this family hold administrative positions at parish level. In particular, the role of President of the Parish Council has assumed great importance. The Council is responsible for mediating with the authorities on local matters. Until very recently the position was not remunerated; it is nevertheless very much sought after, because the President and the Secretary of the Council can use these positions to distribute (or withhold) low-level patronage. At the same time, by dealing with the authorities, they develop their own connections in the town. In order to be elected President, wealth, prestige, and the ability to mobilize supporters are required, and these are acquired by being a member of an old and established household.

Second, there are a few priests, school-teachers and university graduates in this family. Only wealthy households can afford to invest in educating their children. This education, in its turn, is not only a means to higher status and to better paid positions in the town, but it also provides access to positions in the State bureaucracy.

Third, whenever there was a daughter, it was she, and not her brothers, who inherited the parental home and most of the wealth. Sons marry wealthy heiresses, obtain university degrees, or emigrate. Once they leave the parental home they may return to visit, but they lose their rights of permanent residence there. All of the households at present established in Paço which inherited wealth from the original Gomes are planning to leave the headship to a daughter.

Finally, all the thirteen marriages contracted by the descendants of Gomes involved spouses whose households of origin belonged either to the Rich or to the Upper Middle wealth sub-groups ($R_{1/2}$, M_1—see chapter I sect. 3.I). It is interesting to note that all the children of the last generation of head couples (four households) who are at present married, have followed the same pattern of marrying into wealthy households, even though the emigration of the 1960s and 1970s has made differences between economic strata less clear-cut than in the past.

The Calões

The first person to be called a *Calão* was João Souza, a cattle dealer who managed to earn some money through his business. He was nicknamed *o calão* because he was reported to be a *calaceiro* (a person who cheats). He must have been rather successful, for his only son managed to give a house to each of his four daughters. This son tried his luck in Brazil, but is reported to have returned with little more than he had taken with him.

Calão's only grandson married into a family from the Lower Middle wealth sub-group (M_2) in a parish across the river, and has practically lost contact with his family. All of Calão's four granddaughters married men from households of the same wealth sub-group in Paço and Couto, as did their daughters in turn.

Once again it is always daughters who have inherited the parental households and remained attached to the land. Many of the men emigrated, and most are engaged in non-agricultural professions. There is in the family a large number of entrepreneurs, and two of Calão's great-grandsons have risen to the Upper Middle wealth sub-group as a result of their entrepreneurial activities. The family's upward mobility is directly related to its exploitation of new economic activities which have developed over the past decades.

Finally, there is no priest in the family; no one has a university degree; and no man has been elected as a member of the Parish Council.

Os da Pobre

A Pobre (the poor woman) arrived in Couto on 21 December 1901. She was pregnant and is known to have come from the region of Famalicão. Nothing else is known of her past. We know the date of her arrival because she asked a local wealthy peasant (a descendant of Gomes) if she could sleep in his stable. During the early hours of the following day, she gave birth to a child whom she called Ana. She remained there, working as a day-labourer for the household that had given her shelter.

Ten years later she gave birth to a son, Manuel. Finally in 1916, she had another daughter, Teresa. It is reported that the father of these children belonged to the household for which she worked, but this is not certain.

The three children were brought up in the stable. The son left the parish at an early age. Eventually he managed to get work at a dam-building site a few kilometers away from the parish. He succeeded in getting married to a poor woman. They never owned any land, and they lived exclusively on his earnings. They had five children, all of whom have left the borough. While it is known that some of these emigrated to France, the whereabouts of the others are not known.

The younger daughter of the *Pobre*, Teresa, stayed on in Couto, also as an agricultural day-labourer working mainly for the same household which had employed her mother, and living in the same stable. There, in 1938, she gave birth to an illegitimate son, José da Pobre. This boy, from a very early age, was a companion to his aunt Ana, who is said to be barren (for she had no children), and who took to the road as a beggar. When he was about fifteen years old, this boy emigrated clandestinely to France and then to Germany where he managed to accumulate some savings. He returned to Couto and married a woman who belonged to a household in the Lower Middle wealth sub-group. This woman had been engaged to another man, who left her shortly before the planned wedding. Local gossip maintains that she was pregnant; in any event it is accepted by all that her affair with her previous boy-friend had been public knowledge and that her parents were anxious for her to get married as soon thereafter as possible. The marriage with José was organized to cover up the parents' humiliation and, according to his own mother, he accepted it because the bride received an especially good *dote*, which included a house. He then left his mother and aunt in this house, and emigrated to Germany with his wife. He returns regularly to Couto, for he is building an enormous mansion there, in which he has already installed two refrigerators and two television sets, even though the house has not yet been completed.

This case history clearly underlines the condition of landless peasants who are forced to follow the negative strategy. Due to their poverty, the women do not succeed in getting married for, as the priest once put it, *estão so a juntar pobresas*—they and their husbands would only be joining their respective poverties. However, these women are interested in having children, who can then work and beg, while later they support, or at least financially assist, their mothers.

Finally, the particular characteristics of the marriage of José show how poor men have very few opportunities for arranging advantageous marriages. In order to make an economically successful match José had to accept a woman who found it difficult to marry a man of her own wealth group. However, we must not forget that, in the first place, he was eligible only because, through emigration, he had managed to save some money. Most men in his position leave the parish at a very early age and never return.

V

The relationship between the positive strategy and the process of socio-economic alteration of the past few decades still requires some clarification. It is particularly important to establish the effect of the exodus of the 1960s upon household composition. Following a Le Playsian line of argument, Jorge Dias in 1961 and again Cailler-Boisvert in 1968, argued that, in Minho, there is a disappearance of households composed of extended families which is accompanied by a tendency to favour the creation of nuclear family households (Dias, 1961; Cailler-Boisvert, 1968: 95). The data here presented suggest that this hypothesis is incorrectly stated.

The comparison of the household composition in the 'upper half' (*meia de cima*) of both parishes with that of the 'lower half' (*meia de baixo*) will throw further light upon this point. This division of parishes into upper and lower, which is encountered throughout the whole of

Minho, corresponds to considerable socio-economic differences. The hamlets in the 'upper halves' are invariably poorer and more isolated, there are fewer occasions for non-agricultural employment, and the *vizinhos* are less influenced by urban *mores* and consumerist tastes.

The most noticeable difference between the two 'halves' is the higher percentage of households headed by single people (SH) in the 'lower halves' (see Table IX (*a*)). This is due to the fact that the large farms which employ landless labourers are placed in the lower halves, where the land is less hilly and the plots are larger. In the upper halves, the land is more evenly distributed, which means that a greater number of people manage to form *casas*. However, once we distinguish between the *casas* which are composed of extended families and those which are composed of nuclear families (Table IX (*b*)), we realize that, although the percentage of extended family households is higher in the 'upper halves', it is only minimally so. Considering that the 'lower halves' are far more exposed to urban influence and are economically more integrated into the capitalist sector of the economy, we can then conclude that a new strategic logic reflecting these influences is not apparent.

The impact of emigration upon household composition must be taken into account. The male head of the household is considered to be a

Table IX. Composition of households in 'upper' and 'lower' halves of Paço and Couto

	Lower Halves		Upper Halves	
	Numbers	Percentage	Numbers	Percentage
(a) All Households				
Casas proper	245	90.41	198	94.74
SH households*	26	9.59	11	5.26
Total	271		209	
(b) *Casas*				
NF households*	195	79.59	157	79.29
EF households*	50	20.41	41	20.71
Total	245		198	

* SH households: households headed by single people; EF households: households composed by extended families; NF households: households composed by nuclear families.

Source: Census carried out for the purposes of this study, 1979–80.

'resident' of his household even though he may be away for lengthy periods; similarly, a young married couple living abroad must be seen as 'resident' in the household with which it keeps close ties. In fact, even while away, a young couple is always more closely related to one of the parental households rather than to the other. While previously they may have lived uxorilocally or uxorivicinally, they are now living neolocally. But that is not quite how they see it: for them, the relationship with the parental household persists (cf. Davis, 1977: 175). The head couple of the parental household has power of attorney for the couple's bank account and represents it in all business deals. During the 1970s, it was the fathers-in-law of emigrants who looked after the construction of most emigrants' houses, who bought land for them, and who, often enough, brought up their children. So long as the emigrant couple is abroad, the relationship is not severed, and, at times, it is preserved even after the death of the original household heads, the brother-in-law stepping into the father-in-law's shoes.

Thus, the strategy of maximizing the presence of the household in peasant society (in this case, positively expressed) survived the exodus of the 1960s and early 1970s. Interestingly enough, even the tendency towards uxorilocality and uxorivicinality has persisted. This process parallels that by which the emphasis on subsistence in agriculture has survived in spite of a growing dependence on non-agricultural incomes (see chapter I, sect. 3.II). Family dispersal through emigration has reinforced the positive strategy, for emigrants who want to return are profoundly dependent upon their original household, and they will strive to preserve its identity and wholeness.

The dissemination of a household composition strategy which favoured the nuclear family would necessarily imply a worldview which understated the importance of the link to the land and the social security resulting from membership in a peasant society. But Paço and Couto remain essentially peasant parishes. The progressive growth of a semi-proletariat is counterbalanced by a decrease in the number of landless peasants. The emigrant or semi-proletarian who buys land with his earnings or refuses to sell that which he has, requires the institution of the *casa* in order to keep that land. The continued attachment to the land therefore, presupposes a continued attachment to the positive strategy of household composition.

The sudden halt to emigration in 1974–6 and the intensification of the unemployment problem in the capitalist sector of the economy has brought about a further strengthening of this attachment to the conception of the *casa* and the positive strategy of household composition. Agriculture has become a form of under-employment for many people who are waiting for a job and the security provided by the parental household is once again indispensable for young couples.

III

Men, women, and sexuality

The continuation of the household through time is dependent upon human reproduction. But, for the *minhotos*, human reproduction is a sensitive issue as it draws humans nearer to their antisocial aspect, their physical or animal nature. Furthermore, unchecked, human sexuality would lead to reproduction outside the boundaries of the household, which would prevent the very reproduction of the *casa* as the elementary social unit. The power over human biological reproduction has to be transferred from women to men and women within the household. The residents of Paço and Couto argue that 'marriage is for women', meaning that it is women who benefit most from it; but this is true only because of the sanctions the society imposes on women. Marriage is a necessary support of the *casa* and of the power of men. In a society such as this one, where women have such a central social and economic role, their natural control over biological reproduction presents a real threat to the social structure. Any interpretation of the local conceptions of sexuality, gender roles, and human reproduction must take this into account.

8. Gender roles

I

Once, I asked an old woman of Paço what the main differences between men and women were. She laughed at me, replying that these were obvious. The next time I met her, however, having understood that the question had not been asked in jest, she treated me to a full version of the myth of Adam and Eve, which she ended thus:

It was then that our [women's] unhappy lot began. That was the start of the world. That was also the source of death; till then, nobody died. It was then that everything began.

In her eyes, this myth demonstrates that women have always been morally weak while men, who know what is right, are controlled and tempted by women into evil acts. In the context of the Alto Minho, this story assumes a specific meaning, for it reflects a constant conflict and ambiguity in gender roles: women, while being morally weaker, are exceptionally powerful as they are the corner-stones of the household. The conflict between the sexes is nevertheless somewhat reduced by the sexual division of labour. As the same old woman went on to explain, 'men and women have different *superioridades* (areas of superiority): men go out to work, women stay at home.'

Each spouse is in charge of a particular aspect of the household's management. Men look after the cattle, the fruit trees, the vines, the olive trees, and the pine woods; women are more concerned with the pigs and the poultry, the maize, the beans, the potatoes, the pumpkins, and the kitchen garden. While women are mostly in charge of housekeeping, men dedicate a greater portion of their time to external business such as all bureaucratic tasks and wage-earning.

The separation of roles is not totally clear-cut, for men and women participate jointly in agricultural tasks. When husbands spend long periods abroad or are employed during the day in the non-agricultural sector of the economy, women take charge of most agricultural and bureaucratic tasks. Wives who are incapable of taking on these extra duties, because they are either weak or shy, are strongly criticized. An important consideration in choosing a wife is that she should be hard-working and active (*desinvolta*).

There is nevertheless a set of activities which are prohibited to members of each sex: men are forbidden to wash dishes or laundry, to sew, to sweep the floor; women are forbidden to climb trees and prune vines.

In this sexual division of labour males are more concerned with what the peasants call *produtos do ar* (literally, products of the air), that is, with things which grow well above ground level. (It must be remembered that vines, in this area, are grown either on pergolas or on trees.) Women are generally in charge of the *produtos da terra*, things which grow in or near the soil. Thus, the specific prohibition against women climbing trees may also be understood: they must not leave the ground (*terra*). Not only are women more rooted to the ground; they are also considered to be less mobile, for they are attached to a particular stretch of land, their *terra*. The task of keeping the household is left to women, and jobs which involve leaving the home are allocated to men. F. Lopes Gomes, discussing the nearby region of Barcelos, describes a rite which clearly underlines this point. When the newborn child has finished its first bath, people are careful to throw the water . . . in the fireplace if the child is a female, and out of doors if it is a male. Thus the little girl will be homely and 'a friend of the hearth' (*amiga do lar*), and the boy will not remain attached to the mother's skirts and to the earth (*terra*), but will travel the world as is proper (1965: 6).

In practice, although men and women often work together in the fields, they seldom carry out the same tasks. At harvest time, however, when larger groups of men and women work together picking grapes or cutting maize, an atmosphere of joyful excitement develops which is invariably accompanied by lewd joking. This usually takes the form of a battle of words between men and women, and always deals with the issue of the differences between the sexes. By means of joking, men and women attempt to re-create or to maintain the sexual division of labour which their communal participation in one single task has temporarily upset.

The following adage, which I often heard when participating in such communal tasks, points to the differences between the sexes: 'males look up, females look down.' This adage has three distinct meanings: it refers to the differences between male and female genitalia; it refers to the sexual division of labour; and, finally, it refers to a much wider utilization of the dimensional opposition above/below as analogically related to oppositions such as heaven/hell, life/death, mind or spirit/body, purity/corruption, socially beneficial/antisocial.

The story of Adam and Eve serves to demonstrate that women are morally and physically more susceptible to impurity. Statements such as the adage cited above validate the male claim to superiority, yet the position of women in this society cannot be considered underprivileged. The influence of women is indeed mostly limited to the sphere of the household. But, in opposition to what happens in urban circles, this does not reduce their power and relevance, since production is carried out at the level of the household.

II

In 1966, Cailler-Boisvert, writing about Soajo, argued that agriculture was entirely carried out by women due to male emigration (1966: 255). But, already as early as 1861, Furtado Coelho tells us that 'there is in this district the very ancient habit of handing over to the women most of the work in the fields. Here, women plough the land, hoe and spread the manure, while the men either are abroad or, those who remain behind, occupy themselves with other tasks' (1861: 10). This practice appears to be genuinely ancient: after having described their war dances, Silius Italicus tells us (in 344–53) of the soldiers from this region who joined Hannibal's army that

> Such is the relaxation and sport of men, and such their solemn rejoicings. All other labour is done by the women: the men think it unmanly to throw seed into the furrow and turn the soil by pressure of the plough; but the wife of the Gallician is never still and performs every task but that of stern war (1934: 139).

Similarly, Justin, the Roman historian says: 'The women do exercise themselves in household affairs, and in manuring of the ground; the men do live by their swords and by their plunder' (1672: 426).

But peasant women are not mere slaves, 'pack-horses' for their husbands as Camilo would have us believe (1885: 67). The fact that woman's role is mostly limited to the household and the market-place should not be taken to mean, as it does for the bourgeoisie, that women are deprived of economic power.

Emigration has been a feature of this area for many centuries (Serrão, 1974: 100–1). Whether the sexual division of labour is at the root of the marked tendency of minhoto males to emigrate or vice versa is a matter of dispute. It has been argued that the rise in male emigration since the 1890s has had the effect of giving more power to women in local life. In a simplistic sense, this is indeed true: if the husband is not at home, the wife's leadership is more crucial. It is in this sense that Cailler-Boisvert calls Soajo 'une communauté féminine rurale'. In effect, however, and in the long run, precisely the opposite occurs.

Economically speaking, the significance of women in *minhoto* peasant society is attached to the crucial role of agriculture and arable land. As the economic importance of emigration began to increase, particularly during the 1960s, agriculture became progressively less essential. The penetration of the capitalist sector into the rural areas had the same effect. The peasant population because increasingly dependent on cash income from wages. But, as a rule, it is men who emigrate and it is men who earn wages. It is also men who invest their earnings and develop small businesses (although in this case male domination is less complete).[1]

Even in the traditional allocation of agricultural activities, men were put in charge of the products destined for the market: cattle, vines, fruit trees, and pine woods. Overall their greater involvement in the capitalist sector of the economy means that, as a group, men benefit

---

[1] This pattern does not quite apply to areas such as coastal Minho, where local industries have developed and agriculture is more market-orientated.

from the progressive decrease in importance of the subsistence sector. As each household relies increasingly on money earned mostly by men, either through market-orientated production or through non-agricultural activities, the power of men in the home increases. Simultaneously, the penetration of the bourgeois worldview into the rural areas, via the media and the schooling system, has had the effect of introducing images of female dependence and passivity. The peasant women who adopt urban mannerisms in order to increase their short-term prestige, are in fact abdicating an age-old position of relative power and independence.

Numerous authors have referred to the 'matripotestality' or 'matriarchy' of Minho (e.g Willems, 1962: 70; Descamps, 1933: 191–2). While we may disagree with their formulations, evidence does suggest that, in rural Minho, the position of women is different from that in other regions of the country. This social position is also reflected in their attitudes and behaviour, especially in sexual matters. From an early age, women acquire a large amount of personal independence. Young women move about unchaperoned and their attitudes towards courtship are by no means passive. Pre-marital pregnancies are extremely frequent.

Once married, a woman is not immured in her home. She does agricultural work and often goes unaccompanied to the town and the markets. Male emigration means that women are left alone at home for long periods of time. Local residents claim that adultery during these periods of absence is fairly commonplace. The event is forgotten if the neighbours were unable to gather any definite information about the matter. Sometimes, however, the adulterous couple is not sufficiently careful, or the woman falls pregnant.

As a rule, neighbours are interested in spreading gossip about adultery. A woman's adulterous behaviour is seen to lower the prestige of the household, and this benefits the neighbours directly for, it must again be stressed, prestige is measured in relative rather than absolute terms. If the information is in fact more than a vague suspicion, the husband's mother might approach the wife, and give her a stern homily on the virtues of marital fidelity. If, however, there is sufficient evidence for the affair to cause public scandal, or if the woman bears a child, the situation for the husband becomes rather touchy. I was told that, if the woman is known not to have committed adultery again, the husband is likely to pardon her. I heard of two cases in which the offspring of adulterous relationships died extremely young and under somewhat suspicious circumstances. Often the husband, on his return, gives his wife a semi-public beating, and takes her with him abroad, thus putting an end to the whole event. However, if the wife persists in committing adultery, the situation is more serious. In this case the husband is branded a cuckold (*cornudo*), and his prestige is sharply diminished. Men thus branded seldom return to the parish, thus abandoning their wives.

As far as I could gather, the option of banning the wife from her own home has never been exercised. This would be unthinkable for peasants, for the home is the realm of the woman. Ultimately the highest sanction husbands can impose is to leave the home. The woman is then left in a difficult position, for she can neither get divorced and remarried nor bring her lover to live with her. The neighbours do not take kindly to such practices.

III

In Minho, when a peasant wants to refer to his wife, he often uses the expression *a patroa* (literally, the female boss). The use of this term varies interestingly between the genders. While the male form (*patrão*) tends to be employed mostly by outsiders in a slightly ironical tone, to refer to the male spouse, the female form is used mostly by members of the household, and in particular by the husband himself, to refer to his wife when speaking to outsiders. Again the undertone is ironical.

While there is a feeling that the male household head should have more power than the female, there is also a definite acknowledgement that the power of the woman at home is great and indeed often greater than that of her husband. This inconsistency in the definition of roles is profoundly experienced by the peasants. The use by the husband of the term *patroa* to refer to his wife expresses precisely this conflict. In the ironical twist of the expression a feeling of criticism and unease is implicit. By overtly admitting that his wife is his boss, the husband is covertly denying it.

This is not the case with the use of the male form of the term. I never once heard a peasant woman call her husband *patrão*; this would either be too clear an admission of servitude (if it were said seriously), or (if it were said ironically) it would imply that she presumed she was more powerful than the man. Such an implication would have a result contrary to what she had intended. Women are considered naturally greedy and lacking in self-control. If they suggest that they are equal to men, they simply prove the extent of their greed and their lack of control over their affects. Therefore, the male form of this expression is used only by outsiders who, when they call a man *patrão*, do so partially to imply that he is not really the 'boss'.

This expression has not been adopted by the bourgeoisie. It would be considered 'coarse' and 'improper' to imply both that a bourgeois husband is not fully dominant and therefore masculine, and that his wife is not fully feminine in her submission. As Lisón Tolosana has argued when talking of Galicia, the actual power of the male at home depends on the specific economic success and on the psychology of each particular man (1971b: 258–9). He suggests that different standards are used when talking to outsiders (who presume the existence of male domination). However, this duality of standards does not seem to be the best way of explaining the inconsistency in the allocation of power between the spouses. For the peasants of Minho, there is no doubt that women as a group are weak and impure. The fact that they hold so much power is just as problematical in the peasant worldview as when this fact is confronted by the attitudes of the bourgeoisie.

We are presented here with a contradiction in values and behavioural expectations. This should not disturb us, for cultures are not monolithic and contradictions may be expected to exist within each particular culture. As M. Douglas puts it, 'perhaps all social systems are built on contradiction, in some sense at war with themselves' (1966: 166). Indeed, numerous authors have argued for the existence of mechanisms by which each culture attempts to cope with such contradictions (e.g. Turner, 1957; Dumont, 1970). The manner in which the contradiction between male and female gender roles manifests itself in the Alto Minho in ritual and everyday practices will become clearer as this chapter progresses.

The relationship between the spouses as co-managers of the household, and many shared interests, often lead to the creation of strong feelings of partnership between them. Notwithstanding, husbands do not abdicate their right to punish their wives physically. (Local residents maintain that this practice is slowly dying out due to 'education'.) They emphasize the need not to *dar confiança* (give trust) to one's wife. This expression implies a distancing, an aloofness. Among other things, the wife must not be allowed to predict the husband's movements and choices; she must not be able to say, or even think 'I am sure that my husband will agree,' without having first asked his opinion.

Although a husband who always denies his wife the satisfaction of her small wishes is criticized, he is also not expected systematically to yield to his wife's desires. He must not 'spoil' (*estragar*) his wife. It is felt (and this idea is often expressed by women themselves) that if women saw all their wishes satisfied the world would be in chaos, for women always want more than they can have. This is one of the reasons why local residents object to the idea of women taking up positions of political power at national level.

Similarly, sexual relations between spouses are fraught with conflict. A man is strongly pressed to satisfy his wife physically. It is believed that women have strong sexual appetites and, should they fail to be satisfied, women will commit adultery. A wife too must answer her husband's sexual needs. This creates a situation in which both partners feel urged to perform adequately sexually. A local gynaecologist claimed that he found it exceedingly difficult to persuade couples to stop having sexual intercourse, for health reasons, even for short periods of time. His opinion is that both partners measure their success by the other's sexual gratification, and that thus a form of sexual competition takes place.

Great stress is laid on the husband's capacity to control his orgasm. A poor man in Paço who had fathered twelve children over a relatively short period was laughed at, for he was thought incapable of 'controlling himself'. *Coitus interruptus* is seen as the natural and correct way of performing birth control.

According to male informants, however, the reason for male control is that a man must 'laugh at' (literally, *rir-se de*) his wife while he is in a position to do so. Male residents complain that when a man is young, women 'laugh at' him, for he is incapable of controlling his orgasm. Similarly, when a man ages, he finds it difficult to perform sexually. Then again, women 'laugh at' him. In middle-age, however, a man learns to 'control himself' and then he can 'mount and dismount his wife as often as he wishes'. He can 'laugh at' her: sexually he has power over her.

Sexual conflict between men and women, and the threatening nature of female sexuality, are clearly manifest in yet another area, that is, in beliefs in witches. Witches in the Alto Minho are thought to be women and to attack only men. They appear only at night, and have a tendency to carry bluish lights on their bare buttocks. They generally beguile their victims by appearing as young girls dressed in white. Witches are not blamed for general cases of misfortune. If a man falls into their hands, however, severe damage, even death, may befall him. But usually, if their lures are ignored, witches are not dangerous. Personal accusations are made, but as a person who 'reveals' a witch is thought to be likely to suffer death, these are very infrequent, and I did not have the opportunity to detect any pattern in the women who were blamed. Broadly speaking, there are two types of stories told about witches; in my experience, one is more frequently recounted by men and the other by women.

The following is a witch story recounted by a man. It was considered to be particularly hilarious.

A certain man's wife had been looking tired and sleepy of late. Not finding any good reason for this, the husband became suspicious, particularly as he noticed that her backside was uncommonly cold in the morning. One night he decided to feign sleep so as to solve the riddle. After everyone had gone to bed and the wife thought that he was asleep, she called out his name softly. Since he did not answer, she pronounced a spell so that he should remain asleep until she returned, and left the room via the window. This disconcerted the man a great deal. He remained awake the whole night and was feigning sleep when she returned. She entered through the window and went straight to a big stone that was situated in a corner of the room, on which she sat. When she did this he could hear the noise: 'sheee'. [He understood immediately that she was a witch and that she was extinguishing the blue light which witches carry on their buttocks during their nightly wanderings. Heat in the genital and anal regions is commonly associated with sexual excitement.] The following night, the same thing occurred. But, after she had left, the husband got up and lit a big fire on top of the stone. He kept it alight the whole night till the stone was bright red. In the morning, as he heard his wife returning, he quickly brushed away the ashes and returned to bed. When she put her backside to the stone he heard the following noise: 'sheeeeeeeeeeeeeee!!!' followed by a great yell. Since then she never resumed her nocturnal outings.

The only means to cure a witch is to treat her the way husbands do their flirtatious or adulterous wives, that is to give her such a hiding as to draw blood. Short of that, nothing can deter a witch from her nightly rounds.

The stories told to me by women were of a rather different type. The following is a good example. One night, a relative of the mother of the woman who was telling the story

was going through the upland woods back to his house on the parish across the hills. At a certain stage he saw three beautiful young women dressed in white. They called to him and asked him whether he would like 'to walk or to ride'. [This is the witch's standard question; it is a sexual trap and one should ignore it and go on one's way.] He was a very strong young man and just the day before he had said that he was not afraid of witches, so he did not hesitate. He answered

that he would like to ride them all. Then they 'stole his senses' (roubaram-
-lhe os sentidos) and flew him away. Next morning, when the churchwarden of
a distant parish went to ring the bells for early mass, he found the young man
sitting numbly on top of the bell tower. The family took a good two weeks
to find his whereabouts. When he came back he could not speak. All that he
could say was, very softly: 'The witches . . .' He wasted away and died soon
after.

The victims of witches are always left in a dazed state. The sanction
for provoking witches is often slow death. It may also be, however,
temporary or permanent loss of sexual potency. Recently, a man from
Couto who was found one morning asleep inside a shallow water
deposit, claims that the witches flew him there from a distance. He had
to go to a white witch before regaining his potency (see chapter V,
sect. 16).

Both types of stories can be seen as comments on the potential threat
of female sexuality. In both cases, blame for sexually deviant behaviour
is placed on women. However, the stories diverge in their endings.
Whereas in the type usually told by men the witch receives a lesson
which cures her of all desire to continue practising as a witch, in the
type told mostly by women, the man receives a lesson on how he should
resist temptation.

Through recounting witch stories, men and women perform a battle
of the sexes which is acted out even more clearly during big communal
tasks at harvest time, when the sexual division of labour is temporarily
upset. Then the jokes and the witch stories, are not innocent, for in
spite of the apparent good nature of their humour, they hide a very real
hostility between the sexes (cf. Silverman, 1975: 43).

When a man sees witches but does not want anything to do with
them, he shouts out to them that they are 'whores' (*putas*), which is supposed to infuriate them. The use of this word in this context is interesting. Although strictly speaking it refers to prostitutes, the word *puta* is
used in everyday speech as a term of abuse in a variety of circumstances.
In adjectival form, for instance, it is applied to parishes or hamlets
where illegitimacy (but not necessarily prostitution, for the locals do not
confuse the two) is particularly common, as in 'Couto is a whorish
parish' (*freguesia putanheira*). Although the word describes women who
allow their sexuality to become threatening to society, its everyday
usage is wider, referring to the particular antisocial nature of women in
general. When a daughter commits a mistake due to carelessness, for
example, her mother may well call her *puta*.

Marriage, and an attachment to the household and the land, are the means by which women's sexuality is redeemed. Nevertheless, in a very real sense, the jeopardy to the moral order represented by female sexuality is never fully eradicated: deep down inside all women are *putas*.

The potential independence of female sexuality represents a threat to paternity and, therefore, to men's basic source of authority in this society, as heads of household. Furthermore, it must be noted that these opinions concerning the nature of women do not represent an exclusively male view of the male–female conflict. Women's unredeemed sexuality does not threaten only the position of males, it jeopardizes the very elementary social unit. Therefore, it affects both males and females in their identification with the society's central institutions.

9. Sex and pollution

In a society where women are favoured heirs, where uxorilocality and uxorivicinality are preferred, where women participate fully in the duties of headship of the elementary social unit, where they are in control of that aspect of production which is cognitively most stressed (subsistence agriculture), and where male emigration is a long-standing tradition, man's insertion into the social tissue is necessarily problematic. As brothers and sons, men tend to be gently pushed aside, and as husbands their position of authority has to be achieved. The conflict between man's right to rule and woman's effective power is, therefore, necessarily intensely felt.

The material presented in the following chapters appears to support M. Douglas's thesis that sexual pollution tends to coexist with an ambiguous definition of gender roles (1966: 169). Indeed, as M. Bloch and J. Parry have argued, 'fertility is separated and made superior to the biological processes of sex and birth by analogy with the taken-for-granted difference between the sexes' (1982: 24). The reproduction of the household and the effective institution of male authority demand a shift of fertility from sex and women, to marriage, household, and men—the postulation of a form of pure reproduction in which both genders participate equally but differentially and which is typified by the ritual of bread-making. But, following Bloch's insights relative to funerary rituals, it may be argued that the institution of this image of social fertility cannot be carried out positively as its practical effectiveness is constantly denied by the everyday reality of biological fertility. Thus, it depends on setting up a 'phantasmagoric' contrary, in relation to which it can then be defined. Once again, therefore, 'the creation of a symbolic order is dependent on negation' (Bloch 1982: 218) and the creative role is women's, for they operate as pivots between social fertility and biological (and now, antisocial) fertility. Women's dual nature (as biological and as social beings) is thus more conflictuous and more strongly felt than man's dual nature.

I

In church, when the members of the parish unite in an act of sublime contact with the divinity, men are placed nearer the altar, while women stand in the lower, western half of the nave. The only time when women go above this line is to receive the Host. In this way, men are prevented from seeing women in church. As their eyes do not fall upon the temptress, they are able to exercise full restraint.

The association between sex, sin, and death is, and has always been, a central feature of Christian thought. Bodily decomposition and moral or spiritual corruption are closely identified. The dogma of the assumption of Our Lady depended for its authority on a symbolic equivalence between sex and death. In the bull which established the dogma, Pope Pius XII quotes John Damascene: 'There was need that the body of her who in childbirth preserved her virginity intact, be preserved incorrupt after death' (quoted in Warner, 1978: 94).

Sex is polluting and spiritually dangerous for both men and women, but not equally so. It is considered to be particularly polluting for women and, spiritually, women are measured in terms of their resistence to sexual temptation in a way in which men are not. Sexual pollution, then, is asymmetrical.

The unavoidably negative nature of sex is illuminated, for example, in the following folk-tale:

The Girl who Wanted a Husband with White Testicles[2]

There was once a girl who did not like men with dark testicles. She wanted them white. Thereupon, she asked her betrothed whether he had white (or light, *brancos*) testicles. Afraid of being discovered, he was forced to admit that his were dark. She therefore refused to marry him. This scene repeated itself with a few other suitors until a certain man decided to deceive her. One day, he waited

---

[2] The reader should be aware that lightness of skin is valued as a sign of cleanliness and urbanity. The value attached to the proverbial darkness of testicles is closely related to this conception.

till she was going to the river and, as she was arriving, he started soaping his testicles, creating a great deal of lather. The girl approached him and asked him about the colour of his testicles, whereupon he answered that, to his great misfortune, they were white, and that he had already missed a few marriages because of this. She immediately asked him to marry her.

They got married and, after the wedding feast, they went to bed (*na noite da boda foram para o treino*). When they were satisfied, he fell asleep, but she remained awake. She switched on the light, lifted up the bedclothes, and saw his dark testicles [the expression used here is *amulatados*, literally, like a mulatto]. She got very upset and decided to throw herself out of the window so as to commit suicide. As she was about to do this, however, she banged her head on the window-sill and fell backwards, fainting and bruising her forehead.

The husband awoke from the noise and, after she came to, asked her what the matter was. When she told him, he answered: 'Don't you have a bruise on your forehead? How then do you expect my testicles to look after we have made love?'

The moral of the story is that, if the couple were to make love at all, the testicles would have to be dark, even if there had been men born with white testicles. The final analogy between the bruise and the testicles is significant: the colour of the testicles, like the bruise, is a blemish. By demanding a husband with white testicles, the girl was attempting to overcome what the locals perceive as an unavoidable law of nature: that sex is morally negative, and that it is dirty.

Local residents often express the view that the sexual activity of men is good for their health, for it purges them of semen, which is 'like a poison' (*como um veneno*). Concomitantly, however, it is also commonly accepted that too much sexual activity in men speeds up the process of ageing and impotence. This applies both to copulation and to masturbation. These two views, however, appear to be contradictory. How can sex be healthy if it speeds up the process of ageing?

Such apparent contradictions cause no great discomfort to the inhabitants of Paço and Couto. As a rule, when confronted with them, they are ready to admit that perhaps they are mistaken. The important thing to realize here is that, although superficially these two conceptions may seem to be in conflict, at a deeper level there is no contradiction, for all three instances are consistent in the values they express: if testicles are analogically a bruise or blemish, and if the semen is analogically a poison, then sexual activity itself can well be seen to speed up the ageing process. The final conclusion is that sex is polluting (blemish), it is dangerous (poison), and it is attached to the passage of linear, irreversible time (ageing).

II

In the version of the Adam and Eve myth referred to at the beginning of this section, the informant commented that because women were made from a man's rib they were incomplete. Eve, unlike Adam, was not made 'in God's own image'. As such, Eve did not share directly in man's semblance of the divinity. If the distance between God and Satan is seen as a continuum (a notion which the belief in saints and angels, and in minor devils and witches, seems to justify), it can be argued that women as a group are further away from God than are men, and thus nearer to Satan. This is definitely somewhere in the peasants' minds when they argue (only half-jokingly) that women go to church more often than men because they have more sins to 'pay' for.

The sin of Eve is thought to be relived in all women. Eve was incapable of controlling her desires in spite of her knowledge that punishment would be imminent. Women's incapacity to control their affects is particularly evident in their greed. This, in turn, expresses itself mainly in three areas: gluttony, 'envy', and lust.

A gluttonous person is called, in local parlance, a *lambão* (from *lamber*, to lick). In everyday language this word is extended to apply to instances of unreasonable greed other than mere gluttony. When applied to oneself, or used endearingly, this word becomes blander. When used as a term of abuse, however, it is very powerful. A person who is accused of being a *lambão* runs a risk, for the neighbours are not eager to enter into any form of reciprocity with such a person. Neighbours fear that people who are greedy cannot manage their affairs properly and will eventually find it impossible to repay a loan.

Although individual males may be accused of being *lambões*, this expression is most commonly applied to women (*lambôna*). Gluttony itself is almost specifically a characteristic of women. Men, for instance, are held to prefer eating savoury food. This is felt to be less gluttonous than the preference for sweet things, which is usually assigned to women. Typically, at a wine-harvesting party I attended, the lewd joking throughout the day centred around one particular joke: 'Girls prefer sweet things, such as quince jam, grapes, sweets, rice, chicken, etc.' This joke rests on a pun on quince jam (*marmelada*) which also means 'foreplay' in colloquial speech (female breasts often being referred to by the word 'quince'). The twist provided by the final two savoury items (rice and chicken) serves to indicate the existence of a pun, and, at the same time, it doubles the absurdity. It is worth noting that this doubling can only occur because of an unstated binary opposition between sweet and savoury.

Unreasonable gluttony or hunger is often expressed by analogies with animals. For example, 'I ate even more than an animal would' (*comi que nem um animal*); or 'I have a dog's hunger' (*tenho uma fome de cão*). Control of one's affects is the most important characteristic of righteous social life. It is this control that gives rise to trustworthiness and social order. The joke about quince jam makes an analogy between gluttony and concupiscence, thus highlighting their similarity as manifestations of unreasonable greed. This analogy is frequently expressed in the use of the verb 'to eat' (*comer*) to refer to sexual intercourse.

Greed is also related to physical corruption. When Adam ate of the apple, it got stuck in his throat; Eve's bite, however, went all the way down. For rural *minhotos* this is a validation of their belief that, 'while men are clean inside, women are dirty.' They argue that, while men do not have a *ventre*, women do. It is inside this *ventre* that are found all the 'rotten' (*podre*) substances which surround the baby before it is born and which come out during menstruation and childbirth, which are also results of the Fall.

During menstruation, women are fussy, irritable, and greedy. Similarly, during pregnancy, they are prone to experience uncontrollable and unreasonable food cravings. It is believed to be very dangerous not to satisfy these cravings, because, should they remain unsatisfied, the child would, in the future, unwillingly cast the evil eye upon others. An analogical relation is therefore established between gluttony and envy (evil eye), and between these two and physical corruption.

In Paço and Couto, women often refer to menstruation by the expression 'the sadness of women' (*a tristeza das mulheres*) for it reminds them of their impure condition, and of the danger which this impurity represents to the group. In the Alto Minho, the fear of menstruating women and their proclivity for casting the evil eye is frequently encountered. Menstrual blood itself is greatly feared for its destructive power. For example, a few years ago, in Paço, a woman leaned on an olive tree and a few drops of menstrual blood are said to have fallen on a branch. When this branch dried out shortly afterwards, the blame was laid on the menstrual blood. When women go to market, they are not permitted, as men are, to jump or step over goods which are displayed on the ground. This is because the vendors fear that the women may be menstruating, in which case the tiniest drop may fall on their goods. These, then, would not be sold, because of the awesome magical powers of menstrual blood, which would repel the customers. When cattle drink from a pond or reservoir where the water, perhaps, contains menstrual blood, they are thought to contract a disease which first manifests itself by causing white patches on their hide.

There are many more examples of this fear of menstrual blood. My impression is that new associations—'beliefs'—appear and old ones are forgotten rather frequently. These are all surface-level conceptions whose deep-level meaning remains stable: menstruation is associated with impurity and greed, antisocial tendencies which, if allowed to develop, would give rise to chaos in society.

Furthermore, menstruation is valued ambiguously. Regularity of menstrual periods is greatly desired, for it is taken to be a sign of a fertile woman. A woman whose periods have become irregular or have completely ceased in the prime of her life, is said to be *estragada*. In this context, the word would be translated by the English phrase 'broken down': the woman is like a machine which no longer fulfils its predetermined function.

It is believed to be harmful for women to remain for long periods of time with their feet in cold water, or to sit on cold, damp stones, for they run the risk of having their 'blood stop', and thus of becoming *estragadas*. Cold and humidity are antagonistic to the heat which, together with bodily vigour and health, is associated with regular menstruation. On the one hand, these qualities are all signs of well-being and fertility, and as such they are cherished; on the other hand, they, like bodily needs, are also associated with the animal side of humanity, and as such, with its fallen condition.[3]

III

The dangerous ambiguity perceived by the locals in that area bordering humanity and animality is encountered in the concept of 'monsters' (*monstros*). Minhotos believe that women can give birth to creatures which are half-human, half-animal. By means of this concept, they group together a large number of aberrations in the human breeding process which medical science would explain as discrete phenomena (e.g. miscarriages, phantom pregnancies, deformed babies) and others, the existence of which medical doctors may deny. Different explanations are given for specific cases. What makes a particular person choose one

---

[3] A further example of this identification of bodily heat with antisocial tendencies can be taken from the first witch story reported above. There, the returning of the witch to her 'social' self was marked by the cooling of her buttocks.

type of explanation over another is not fully clear to me. Once more, however, we are dealing with apparently different surface-level explanations which, at a deeper level, are essentially equivalent.

The explanations I have encountered fall roughly into three broad categories. First, women are said to conceive monsters as a result of the ingestion of water which has been polluted by the washing of dirty underclothes, that is, water polluted with bodily rejects (impure substances which have come to represent man in his fallen condition,—the animal side of man). Second, monsters may be the result of copulation in impure circumstances, such as during menstruation or during the forty days which follow childbirth—both of these are instances of man behaving like an animal by not refraining from impure contact. Third, monsters may be the results of bestiality, either actual or metaphorical. If, during copulation, the woman looks intently at an animal, the child conceived is thought to look like that animal and will be called a 'monster'. Cases of male bestiality were reported to me, but it seems that actual female bestiality is too revolting a subject to be contemplated.

It is believed that monsters should be killed immediately after birth, for otherwise, when they grow up, they are certain to kill their mothers. This is validated by the belief that monsters are neither human nor animal. I propose that an analogy is being made which runs along the following lines: animals and humans alike respect the most basic 'natural' law, which is to love one's mother (here we must not forget the strongly matrifocal tendency of the local family structure); as monsters are neither animal nor human, they must act in an antisocial fashion. Monsters, therefore, kill their mothers.

Because sex is the area in which man most closely resembles beasts, a breach in the rules of sexual conduct is often castigated by the locals by means of abuse using animal names. The very word *animal* is a form of abuse meaning someone (usually a male) who behaves in an uncontrolled and coarse fashion.

Animal sexuality itself, with all its connotations of chaos and pollution, particularly when it takes place within the confines of the household, is strongly discouraged. 'Self-respecting' people (*gente de respeito*) in Paço and Couto consider it *coisa fraca* (literally, weak thing, i.e., not prestigious) and 'scandalous' to keep stallions, male pigs, rams, and goats in their households. During his Easter visit, the priest does not enter such households. At that moment, when all households are linked in a chain of order and purity, a household where sexuality runs riot is not allowed to become a weak link in the chain. Such a household cannot fulfil its main symbolic function: reproduction within purity.

It is not surprising, therefore, that only poor people with low prestige have recourse to this means of earning money. Indeed, in the case of pigs, rams, and billy-goats, I found that in both parishes these were mainly owned by landless people, in more than one instance unmarried mothers.

IV

The uncomfortable relation to the natural world is not limited to that between humans and animals, as the local use of the term *vício* demonstrates. Cutileiro, in his ethnography of a southern Portuguese rural community, describes *vício* as 'the predisposition responsible for the potential social dangers attached to (the woman's) active social life' (1971: 99).

This does not exhaust the possible implications of the term. The following is an extract from field notes I took during a conversation with a local woman who was explaining the meaning of this word to me.

Cutting wood for building or carpentry must be done in January because the wood lasts longer. It does not get borers. It is without *vício*. When the tree gives off shoots (*dá rebentos*) the wood is soft.

When the tree is budding (*arrebentar*), one says it has *vício*. Before January you can twist a thin branch. In March, however, it will break (*arrebentar*). As the leaves fall in autumn the trees get weaker: they no longer have *vício*. It is like people. When they are young and while they have children, women are strong; when they are past menopause, they lose strength.

This analogy between the life cycle of women and the yearly cycle of trees is extremely commonplace. The question becomes more complex, however, when we start to explore the meaning of the term *vício*. This, surprisingly, is also used to refer to antisocial and self-destructive features of things or people, such as addictions, general flaws, and bad habits, as well as what the Church calls *pecados veniais* (venial sins). Taylor's Portuguese-English Dictionary (1958) provides the following meanings: '*Vício* (masc.), vice, failing, weakness, besetting sin; bad habit; addiction; depravity; immorality; rut, oestrus.' The word's association with fertility is therefore surprising. Yet the repeated use by the above informant of words derived from the root *rebento* (meaning 'to give off shoots', 'to burst', and 'to break up') clearly stresses this relation.

The use of the word *vício* in local parlance is the result of the merging (or non-differentiation) of two words which are both derived from the same Latin root: *vício*, and *viço*. The Latin root *vitium* means: 'fault, defect, blemish, imperfection, vice; moral fault, failing, error, offence, crime; a defect in the auspices or auguries' (Lewis and Short, 1962: s.v.). The merging of these two words, which is not common among the bourgeoisie, can nevertheless be traced in more particular usages still referred to by dictionaries. Morais, for example, after enumerating a wide range of meanings for *vício* which are more or less covered by Taylor's translation quoted above, gives the following meaning for the expression *ter vício* (literally, to have *vício*): 'for a plant to produce a great quantity of shoots which damage its flowering, diverting uselessly the vegetative force of the resin'. *Viço*, in turn, has two distinct entries. The first is 'the vegetative force of a plant; vigour of vegetation', and a few other derivatives. The second is 'the same as *vício*'. Finally, the 1865 edition of Viterbo's *Elucidário* includes the following entry 'Viços-Vícios'.

It is apparent, then, that the merging of the meaning of the two words is (or has sometimes been) common. In some instances it was effected under the blanket term *viço*, while in the Alto Minho today (and in the Alentejo), the term *vício* is used. The complexity of meanings attached to these terms becomes even clearer when we realize that in popular speech both *vício* and *viço* can mean the heat of animals (*cio*), and that one of the standard meanings of *vício*, according to Morais, is 'sensuality, lasciviousness, lubricity'.

Once again, therefore, we find that bodily vigour is associated with fertility, sex, and sensuality and that these qualities are placed in a morally perjorative light, for they are identified with antisocial and self-destructive qualities and with animal sexuality. When physical strength is at its peak, moral strength is at its nadir.

V

It is not only women who are considered morally inferior. Peasants as a group believe themselves to be inferior to the bourgeoisie, for they see their life-style as 'dirtier', and themselves as incapable of restraint.

In spite of what may be considered a rather stern judgement of sex, the peasants of the Alto Minho cannot possibly be considered puritans. Their attitudes towards sexual activity are rather lax when judged in the context of Portugal as a whole. This is manifest not only in their actions but also in their speech. The use of foul language is extremely common among the peasantry. It is used either as an expression of familiarity and relaxation or anger and antagonism. By punctuating their phrases with foul language the peasants instil their speech with an emotional content. Most foul language is restricted to words referring to sex and bodily rejects, and these are equally used by all.

Yet the peasants' attitude to foul language is not value-free. It is said of a person who speaks in this way that he *fala mal* (speaks badly) or that he is *malcriado* (badly brought up). People who use this type of language themselves agree that it is improper. Nevertheless, peasants in general judge it to be extremely difficult to avoid doing so. For them, this would be a sign of distinction and status. When the local residents complain that 'we cannot even speak Portuguese properly,' this is one of the aspects that they have in mind. The capacity to avoid 'speaking badly' is used as an index of local stratification.

The following tale throws some light on these matters:

O Amigo Malcriado (The Badly Brought Up Friend)

There were two young men who were very close friends. One day, one of them decided to get married. But he was very worried because he had to invite refined people (*gente fina*) to the reception and his best friend 'spoke so badly' that inviting him would be very embarrassing. He decided not to tell his friend of the marriage until after the reception.

The friend heard of this and was very hurt. When they next met, he complained bitterly and the groom had to explain that he was very worried about the friend's way of speaking. The friend, however, protested loudly, saying that he was no animal and that he could behave properly whenever this was necessary. So he was invited after all.

On the day of the wedding, many 'refined' ladies turned up wearing gloves. After the service, when they were leaving the church, the ladies took off their gloves to shake hands with the other guests. But, when the friend of the groom saw the hands of a particular lady, he could not take his eyes off them. He stared so intently and for so long that the lady had to ask him why he was looking at her hands in that way. He answered that he had never seen such white hands. To this she retorted that, since she had been eight years old, she had always worn gloves. But he dismissed this explanation: 'Yes, yes,' he said, 'but the fact remains that I have been wearing underpants since I was five and my *culhões* [very rude word for testicles] are still dark!'

As in the tale of *The Girl who Wanted a Husband with White Testicles*, the punch line of this story rests on the particular nature of the sexual organs, which, even if covered, always remain dark. As with the earlier tale, testicles cannot be both sexual and clean (for that is the implication which is attached to white or light skin). The joke relies on an opposition between the lady, who is 'refined' (not a peasant), and the man, who is rude and 'speaks badly' (a peasant or a member of the lower urban classes). Whiteness of hands is associated with the lady and darkness of testicles is associated with the rude friend: the lady is to the lower-class man as her hands are to his testicles. His foul language means that he is impure. This connection between impurity and foul language is frequently expressed. For example, when a person speaks foul language, he or she is said to have a 'dirty mouth' (*boca suja*).

Sydel Silverman, in her study of the inhabitants of an Italian hill town, tells us that 'their premise appears to be that it is in the towns (or cities, or villages like towns), or living in the manner of the town, that man is most human' (1975: 3). Oddly enough, this comment, which applies to the bourgeois worldview of the Alto Minho, applies equally to the peasant worldview. Peasants conceive of themselves as living somewhere between the ideal 'human' environment (a town) and nature. That is why they speak of their lush and exceptionally beautiful countryside as a *deserto* (desert), for the human presence there is subordinated to the presence of nature. Locals stress repeatedly that their life is 'dirty' and that their work is 'slavery': theirs is an impure and arduous life. They dislike silence and the only places they unreservedly classify as beautiful are big cities. Although they complain that they 'cannot speak properly', they greatly appreciate rhetoric, and they will travel far, simply to listen to a famous preacher—not for his message, but quite consciously because he *fala muito bem* (speaks very well).

Individual peasants are thought to be more or less *atrasados* (retarded, only half-socialized), that is, the contrary of *educados* (educated). The extreme examples of this feature are the people whom locals call *bichos do mato* (literally, animals of the bush or jungle). These people are always characterized by at least a few of the following features: faulty speech; speech punctuated by long periods of silence; the use of extremely foul language; being very suspicious, inhospitable, and unsociable; working extremely hard; living largely in isolated conditions; a lack of control over bodily rejects (carelessness in their disposal); being at times very violent due to a lack of emotional self-restraint; and finally adhering deeply to that which the bourgeoisie calls 'superstition'. Not all peasants are said to be *bichos do mato* but they are also not *senhores* (people of high status). Their incapacity to control their foul language is taken by themselves, as well as by the bourgeoisie, to be a sign of this.

On the whole, the provincial bourgeoisie reacts extremely strongly to foul language. It is part of their image as *educados* to avoid speaking in this way. Members of the urban élite express disapproval of foul language in highly emotional terms. The 'liberalization' of values which has taken place in the cities since the 1960s, however, means that the practice of 'speaking badly' is assuming a certain prestige among the youth of small towns, who always attempt to imitate city trends. This presents the older generation with a conflict.

Among the bourgeoisie, the concern with sexual restraint and control over bodily processes is not confined to the use of language. Stronger standards of marital fidelity are enforced, particularly on women, and a serious concern for the virginity of unmarried girls is manifest. While peasants do not hold to these standards, they nevertheless judge them positively. Peasants use sexual restraint and control over bodily processes as indices of social stratification and, as they argue that those whom they call *bichos do mato* are too unrestrained, so they argue that those whom they call 'nobles' are too restrained. 'Nobles' are members of a rural petty aristocracy which is rapidly disappearing because, during the past twenty years, most of their lands have been sold to returned emigrants. They are mostly engaged in the liberal professions in the cities and return to the land only at harvest time. The residents of Paço and Couto expressed to me the belief that most 'noble' couples sleep in separate rooms and that it is frequent for the wife to allow her husband to visit her only on a specified number of nights per week or per month. Of this my informants were particularly critical because, they argued, too much restraint eventually leads to unrestraint, which is why 'noble' men are believed to sleep with servants.

The apparent paradox of the peasant view of themselves as incapable of restraint and their positive evaluation of bourgeois, 'civilized' ways, should cause no surprise (cf. Elias, 1978). A similar process has been studied by James Peacock in Java in relation to the confrontation between the unrefined *kasas* ways of the Surabaja proletariat and the *alus* ways of the élite (1971: 155–67). From an individual perspective, the attitude of the *minhoto* peasant is somewhat akin to that of the layman who values the monastic way of life as superior to his own but does not feel capable of following it.

As Elias has pointed out (1978: 116–17), the spreading of new manners is closely related to a society's structure. In the long run, it might be argued that the distinction between peasant and bourgeois ways corresponds to a process of unidirectional historical development; look-ing at it closely, however, we may conclude that the acceptance by the peasantry of the relative superiority of bourgeois manners reflects an interiorization of its position of cultural inferiority within a broad cultural tradition. Within this tradition, each of the worldviews is influenced by the other, nevertheless preserving its relative autonomy, which is obtained by reference to a specific basic cultural prototype. Yet the relative weight of each of these worldviews within the wider culture varies and is an essential fact in maintaining the unitary aspect of the broad cultural tradition. If, on the one hand, there is a spreading of 'civilized' manners from the urban strata to the peasantry—such as the custom of eating from individual dishes, which the inhabitants of Paço and Couto adopted only three to four decades ago—on the other hand, the peasantry is maintained in a similar relative position. (The same may not be said of the relations between the aristocracy and the bourgeoisie.)

VI

If fertility, wealth, and physical well-being are essential for the survival of the *casa*, so is an orderly social life, and this requires a control of fertility, acquisitiveness, and man's bodily desires. Should these run rampant, the ideal of the subsistence prototype would be unattainable. For the *minhoto*, human society is situated between heaven and hell, between God and the enemy (*O Inimigo*, the Devil), between dedication to the soul and enslavement by the body. This battle is waged inside each human being individually, as well as in each social group. Man's natural tendency is to yield to the base forces in him. Restraint, there-fore (and in particular sexual restraint), heralds the victory of the soul: man's option for an orderly social life, rather than chaos, for heaven rather than hell.

Each individual has his or her own place in the scale that extends from ultimate surrender to the spirit (heaven above) to ultimate sur-render to matter (hell below). But human society is composed of groups of individuals. These groups, too, may be classified as being higher up or lower down along this scale. Both women as a group, and peasants as a whole, are seen as unrestrained and as slaves to matter. This is not to say that all women are damned, but rather that they have to struggle harder.

10. Pregnancy, childbirth, and baptism

And the blots of Nature's hand
Shall not in their issue stand;
Never mole, hare-lip, nor scar
Nor mark prodigious, such as are
Despised in nativity,
Shall upon their children be.

W. Shakespeare, *A Midsummer Night's Dream*

In important respects the set of prohibitions, rites and beliefs which surrounds pregnancy, childbirth, and baptism corresponds to an attempt to bring under control the dangers perceived in the process of human reproduction and to transform the still animal-like child into a full member of society.

The residents of Paço and Couto refer to these prescriptions and prohibitions by the term *adágio* (adage) and their attitudes towards them are fraught with ambiguity. When asked whether they believe in these *adágios*, rural dwellers tend to answer equivocally, for they are all too well aware of bourgeois prejudice, which classifies them as 'superstitions' and considers those who believe in them to be 'backward' (*atrasados*). The *adágios*, however, still make sense to the *minhoto* peasant and even those who claim not to believe in them feel that they should be 'respected'. Their number and variety is so great that I can present only a few examples here. I have, nevertheless, attempted to cover most types that came to my attention.

I

Although most of the prohibitions attached to the period of pregnancy are phrased in a positive fashion (i.e., if you do *x*, *y* will follow), their real meaning is only understood when they are looked at as *ex post facto* explanations for events which the locals feel require an explanation. On the whole, their internal logic is that of sympathetic magic, as they are based on the establishment of fairly simple analogical connections between two events or objects to which a causal value is then ascribed. Thus, their sociological significance lies less in the particular analogical connection on which they are based than on the aspects of social behaviour which they choose to highlight. In this way, the following set of *adágios* can be seen to reflect a concern with the mother–child symbiosis.

A significant number of these prohibitions relate to the oral gratification of the mother, whether positively or negatively, directly or indirectly. The first to be considered states that *the pregnant mother must not eat octopus or lamprey, for otherwise the child will be born with weak bones or no bones at all.* Their bonelessness makes octopuses and lampreys classificatorily anomalous. They are also considered to be relishes. Pregnant mothers are often accused of being particularly greedy (*lambonas*); this prohibition is a moral indictment against the mother's tendency to oral self-indulgence, and the importance for the formation of the child of the need to control this moral failing.

The next prohibition to be considered carries this connection one step further: *the strong food cravings felt by pregnant women should be satisfied, otherwise the child will unwittingly cast the evil eye* (cf. Lévi-Strauss, 1966: 79).

If asked, the locals reply that what causes the evil eye is the *invejedade* ('enviousness') of the neighbours. It may, therefore, seem strange that one of the most important reasons why particular people are accused of casting the evil eye is apparently unrelated to 'envy'. The unstated connection between these two convictions becomes clear when we consider that the pregnant mother's strong cravings for certain foods are thought to result from her incapacity to control her desires, which is associated with her condition. If she is denied the satisfaction of her cravings, she is left in a state of frustration which is akin to that of 'envious' neighbours. An analogical connection is being established between 'envy' and 'greed', both of which are equally antisocial manifestations of lack of restraint.

A similar connection may be seen in the prohibition which states that *if the pregnant mother turns her head away, or glances backwards, during the elevation of the Host, the child will unwittingly cast the evil eye.*

The turning back of the head during the elevation of the Host is a symbolic rejection of a very special kind of food. During Mass, God is literally 'consumed' by the members of the congregation. The Host (itself a form of bread) is the holiest of foods; its consumption purifies and brings blessings to the neighbours who are united in their church. To reject the Host is to refuse to participate in the ultimate 'social' act, the act that unites all the neighbours with the divinity. In turning away from the Host, a pregnant woman is considered to be opening the way to those antisocial tendencies which, later on, will manifest themselves in the child.

Finally, *the pregnant mother must not kiss (and to a lesser extent, touch)*
a corpse, or the child will be mute. Once again, this prohibition follows
the logic of sympathetic magic: the corpse is, as it were, mute. As
Thomas puts it 'le silence fait corps avec la mort, naturellement
puisque le cadavre est muet, et culturellement puisqu'il est "outre-
signifiance"' (1980: 59). The prohibition also stresses the need for the
mother, who is full of life, to restrain herself from coming into contact
with the substance of death.

A further set of prohibitions has great currency in Paço and Couto: *if*
the pregnant mother touches flowers, strong smelling smoked meats, mice,
moles, or the spleens of pigs, the child will be born with a birthmark. To
prevent this blemish from appearing on a part of the body where it
would deface the child, the mother must touch the object and immediately put her hand to her buttocks or her thighs. In this way the
child's birthmark will be deflected to that area.

The particular analogical connections between birthmarks and the
objects cited do not really concern us here. These connections are sometimes buried deep in the history of the language—for instance, *baço*
(spleen) derives from the Latin root *badiu*, meaning 'reddish' (Corominas, 1980). In most cases, they are merely based on simple
similarities between birthmarks and the objects cited—their reddish colour, the fact that they stand out, their hairiness.

The peculiar interest of this set of prohibitions lies rather in the fact
that a need is felt to explain birthmarks at all. The places chosen by the
mother for the birthmark (the thighs and buttocks) are significant, for
the similarity of dark and hairy birthmarks with dark and hairy genitals
should not escape the reader. It is the mother's incapacity to control
her behaviour during the impure period of gestation that explains the
appearance of these blemishes which, like genitals, are better not
seen.

II

The prohibitions so far considered concern solely the mother–child
relationship. However, the importance of the concept of *casa* (household) in the local worldview is such that we must not be surprised to
find another set of pre-natal prohibitions which, this time, apply to
all members of the household: 'those who eat together'. Concomitantly,
the sanctions which are presumed to result from disregarding these prohibitions no longer apply only to the child, but to most of the products
of the household.

If these prohibitions are not respected, the local inhabitants believe that *the offspring of any pregnant animal or person belonging to the household will be born with some physical deformity.* Usually, the deformity is related to the nature of the infringement. Some informants extend this also to the cutting of wood (which will get woodworm if cut on certain days), and the picking of cabbages (which will similarly be attacked by worms).

On certain days of the year, *it is forbidden to prick, saw, cut, tie, or wring* anything. These are all violent acts which imply a change in the boundaries and the shape of the object in question. Furthermore, most of these acts involve sharp metal instruments.

The prohibitions considered earlier assumed that the behaviour of the mother would be reflected in her child, who was understood to be passing through the vulnerable stage of formation. In this new set of prohibitions, actions of members of the household which change the boundaries of objects are seen to be reflected in the products of the household which happen to be in the same vulnerable state of metamorphosis, of morphological change. In Paço, a certain man who had been tying vines the whole day got up in the middle of the night and undid the whole of his day's work when his wife told him that she suspected she was pregnant. He was afraid that the child would be born with his arms or legs 'tied up'.

The analogical connection being made here is the precise opposite to that which underlies the belief that a werewolf (the seventh of a line of seven children of the same sex) can only be freed from his 'fate' (*fado*) by being wounded with a sharp metal instrument so that he bleeds. The werewolf is in a constant state of metamorphosis; every night he changes into an animal and is forced to run around in a frenzy. By wounding him with a metal object, one is arresting this process of metamorphosis. On the contrary, in the case of the child and of the offspring of household animals, the process of metamorphosis has to be carried out to its desirable completion.

This throws some light on the use of sharp metal objects in many other contexts. Metals, and particularly iron and steel, are the most stable substances available locally, and, at the same time, they are the most damaging. As such, they are frequently employed to mark either a definite break or a strong juncture. Metal objects are used to protect the pre-baptismal baby from witches, thus making a barrier between the child and its corrupt origins. The contrary logic can be seen in the fact that, in the 1930s, blacksmiths were still considered to be surgeons particularly able to cure wounds (Pires de Lima, 1938: 180).

In varying degrees, all the types of pre-natal prohibitions analysed above are explanations of misfortune. In general terms, in the first set, the perceived misfortunes were explained by means of the moral vulnerability which is seen to characterize the mother during the period of gestation, and were associated with the impurity of birthmarks and the evil eye. In the second set, where the prohibitions affect the whole household, the misfortunes were blamed on the vulnerability of the gestation period itself, when it is easy to misdirect the process of morphological change. Reproduction, therefore, not only of people and animals but also of households in general, is characterized symbolically by both moral and physical weakness and is particularly exposed to anti-social tendencies.

But the difference between the two types remains significant. In the second type, we witness the shift of reproduction from the impure female fertility to the fully 'social' fertility of the household. It is significant that this shift should be accompanied by a change in the kind of vulnerability implicit in the explanations. In the first type, this is of a moral kind and is attached to pollution; in the second type, it is merely morphological.

III

Misfortune attached to childbirth, however, is not limited to physical deformities. Mothers may have miscarriages, still births, or their children may die at a very early age. When this takes place sporadically, or due to reasonably clear external causes, the local inhabitants may limit themselves to consulting a medical doctor. However, should the same woman suffer the same misfortune repeatedly, and particularly if doctors do not succeed in finding a cause or cure, people feel that a wider approach to the problem is necessary. The mother is likely to promise a votive offering to a saint or to the Virgin Mary in the hope that she may be successful. The *minhotos*, however, are aware of a specific remedy for this problem, and I believe that *in extremis* few would not have recourse to it. This is the so-called midnight baptism.

There is a fifteenth-century bridge over the river Lima near the town of Ponte da Barca which, because it connects two boroughs and runs in a north to south direction, fulfils the necessary conditions for the success of this ceremony.

E. Cruz, who himself participated in one of these ceremonies, describes it thus:

Of an evening, during the last month of pregnancy, just before midnight, the woman comes to take her post on the semicircular landing in the middle of the bridge, where the coat of arms marks the division between the boroughs of Ponte da Barca and Arcos de Valdevez. There, she waits for the first person to pass who then becomes the 'godfather'. This person is asked to perform a 'baptism' with river water which has been collected from the same spot by means of an earthenware jug attached to a rope. . . . What is essential is that the godfather should pass by accidentally and not on purpose and that, after midnight, no other *living breath* (*fôlego vivo*), be it a cat or a dog, should have crossed the bridge before him. The first *living breath* to cross the bridge must make the baptism and, as an irrational creature *has no soul*, the ceremony obviously can only be performed by humans.[4] The ceremony of the baptism is simple. Having dipped in the water a branch of an olive tree, one has to spray the belly of the woman, repeating the formula: 'I baptize you in the name of the Father, the Son, and the Holy Ghost.' It is important not to say 'Amen.' . . . That is reserved for the priest, in the other baptism, after the child is born. One also does not give the child a name, since one cannot know its sex. (*Notícias da Barca*, 8/1980: 16).

Afterwards the parents serve a meal to the godfather who is to eat as much as he wishes. If possible, the same godfather should be used for the church baptism.

But what is the significance of the river? The river Lima was called by the classical authors *Lethes, Oblivio*, or *Flumen Oblivionis*. These names referred to a tradition, of which borough residents are still aware, which reported that those who crossed this river would forget their place of origin. A similar tradition is found today in relation to the fountain of *Fontaínhas* in the town of Ponte da Barca, near the river. Strangers who drink of its water are supposed to become so attached to the borough that they will never again want to return home. There appears to be a consistency in all the beliefs and customs related to rivers in Minho. In customs such as these, an analogy is being drawn between the water which runs and washes things away and people's memory. Furthermore, rivers are boundaries on the face of the landscape, and popular songs are full of references to the difficulties attached to crossing them. Rivers, therefore, are like seams: they divide the land into separate spaces.

---

[4] This may also be due to fear that the Devil in animal form should be attempting to take control of the future child's soul.

The various rites which make up the ceremony of the midnight baptism present a set of similarities. The ceremony is performed at midnight; over a river (an important dividing line); at a mid-point between the two banks; the water has to be drawn up from the centre of the bridge; and the place chosen is the precise borderline between two boroughs. Thus, the people choose the time and place which best represents liminality. The demand for an officiant who does not know in advance that he is going to be chosen may be interpreted similarly. If the officiant had been forewarned, this would represent a continuity.

But it must not be forgotten that this ceremony is a baptism and that baptisms are rites of purification. The pregnant mother is thought to be undergoing an impure and dangerous state. By baptizing the child while it is still in the womb, the people are bringing forward the moment at which the child receives a soul and is thereby protected by the grace of God.

Not only is baptism a ritual of purification; it is also a rite of incorporation (Van Gennep, 1960: 62). After baptism, the child is a member of society in its spiritual sense, and it therefore enters the realm of order and purity, leaving behind it that of chaos and corruption. By combining symbols of liminality with the symbolism of purification and incorporation, the midnight baptism can be seen as an attempt to bring control into the pregnant woman's dangerous state of liminality.

E. Cruz's account is equally interesting from the point of view of the relations between the bourgeoisie and the peasantry. He tells us that:

it is not only the rude creatures of the people (*creaturas rudes do povo*) who have had recourse to the midnight baptism. Even among people with some education (*gente de cultura média*), in my region, the belief in its efficacy is widespread . . . It is the truth of the facts that has ensured the strength of the belief. I could cite names of people who have distinguished themselves in this region and whose life, I have heard, is attributed to the miraculous effect of such baptisms. (loc. cit.)

The recourse to what they themselves call 'fantastical superstitions' by members of the bourgeoisie is certainly not limited to this ceremony. The inhabitants of small provincial towns are people who, despite being the most outspoken opponents of the peasant worldview, have lived too long in close contact with it for the symbolic significance of the rites, practices, and beliefs described here not to affect them. Ethnographic and folkloric writers often refer to this fact with some surprise, for, considering the militant attitudes of the provincial bourgeoisie, its performance of these ceremonies appears to the actors themselves as a blameworthy form of hypocrisy and weakness.

But is is not only members of the bourgeoisie who are presented with personal conflict resulting from the clash of the two worldviews. The peasants themselves, when confronted with bourgeois prejudice, are tempted to deny the value and even the existence of practices which the urban élite rejects. Peasants 'are afraid of the ridicule, of the nickname of yokel (*parôlo*) and only in hiding, when even their shadow cannot spy on them' will they practice these ceremonies (Lopes Gomes, 1965: 4). Some of the customs discussed above, therefore, belong to the group of ceremonies which, although sometimes enacted by members of the bourgeoisie and often by the peasants, tend to be hidden from the casual observer and are practiced mostly in secret.

IV

The actual techniques of childbirth have changed considerably over the past thirty years. Nowadays, according to the estimate of local doctors, approximately 31.4 per cent of all births in the borough take place in the maternity hospital in the town. Previously, medical assistance at childbirth was difficult to obtain. The members of wealthy households took time off to look after the mother and child. Poorer households, however, could not afford any such luxuries. And, of course, landless unmarried mothers were the most unprotected of all. Their children were often born in the fields, for they worked till the last moment, not being able to dispense with their meagre earnings. Informants often express surprise at the fact that these children survived at all, as they were almost uncared for.

After the birth, the placenta must be expelled and it is said of a mother who had not yet done so that 'she is neither pregnant nor has she delivered'. This liminality is considered to be dangerous and the mother is not allowed to leave the house in this state. Moreover, no part of the placenta should be taken out in the house before all of it has been expelled. As a matter of fact, in the past, the placenta was buried inside the house; either in the byre (if it occupied the ground floor of the house) or underneath the pile of wood which is kept in the corner of the kitchen to burn in the hearth. These spots are supposed to consist of 'fat earth' (*terra gorda*), i.e. fertile earth. A nail is hammered into the spot where the placenta has fallen. It is believed that if this is not done and a drop of wine should fall upon this spot, the mother's blood would lose colour and she would go mad.

As with bodily rejects, the dropping of the placenta is seen as a breach of the normal boundaries between the human body and the external world. The spot where the placenta has fallen remains associated with the woman. We know that wine is often used as a symbol of life force. The spilling of wine, therefore, is metaphorically related to the wasting of the woman's life force. We are already familiar with the role of sharp metal objects as means of effecting a symbolic break between two areas, spheres, or states. By hammering a nail into this spot, the local inhabitants are symbolically marking a break between the mother and the earth.

The *minhoto* proverb which states that 'a woman who has just given birth is neither replete nor clean' (*mulher parida, nem farta nem limpa*) establishes a connection between impurity and greed (gluttony), and between these and the process of childbirth. Furthermore, as we have seen, childbirth is a moment of danger to the mother. By waiting until the process is fully completed inside the household, and by burying the placenta in the home, the peasants are once more employing the symbolism of the household as the safe and 'social' environment *par excellence*, as well as preventing female fertility from manifesting itself outside the context of the household.

The period of liminality connected to childbirth is not fully complete until approximately forty days have passed after the birth. Till then the mother is not thought to be fully healed, and she is still considered impure. Thus, in the old days, she was forbidden from going to church during this period. After the forty days, she had to go through the ritual of churching so as to be readmitted into the church, as if her period of liminality had temporarily or partially placed her outside the bounds of Christianity. (This ritual has now been abolished by the church.)

During the 'quarantine' the mother is not only unclean, she is also not *farta* (to be full, replete, satisfied). It is believed that, if a mother is not fed properly after giving birth, she may become very weak and even wither away and die. She should therefore eat one chicken, one gourdful of wine, and one loaf of bread each day. (This is an ideal to which only the very wealthy households manage to adhere.) This is considered a very 'pure', healthy, and somewhat extravagant diet. A woman who is not satisfied by this is truly very greedy.

The mother's state of impurity is reflected in greed. But while the mother's pre-natal cravings are irregular, unpredictable, and usually attached to unwholesome foodstuff, her post-natal greed is regular and normally assuaged by wholesome food. These differences may be interpreted as manifestations of the belief that the actual moment of childbirth (when the previously single mother becomes a duality of mother and child) is the most dangerous and impure. As she moves towards it, the mother is distancing herself from the norms of social control and righteousness; as she moves away from it she is being reintegrated into society in its spiritual sense.

Not all children survive birth; indeed some are even born before they are fully formed. The word *aborto* is normally used to refer to still-births, miscarriages, and induced abortions. A midwife told me that she always baptized these births, just in case they still had some life in them. This practice was taught to her by a priest, and I do not know how widespread it is among the peasantry. This woman used to collect the *aborto* in a chamber-pot and baptize it using the formula 'If you are still alive, I baptize you in the name of the Father, of the Son, and of the Holy Ghost, Amen' (*Se ainda estás vivinho* . . .). The use of the chamber-pot, which was her own choice, seems to me to be a significant indication of the fact that she categorized miscarriages as impure substances.

When seriously deformed children are born at home, they are baptized and then allowed to die. They are given a rather summary burial, which accords with Hertz's observation that, throughout the world, such burials tend to be 'infra-social events' (1960: 84). In the past, these *abortos* and *monstros* were buried inside the house, in the same spot as the placenta. According to Hertz, this type of burial represents a return to the 'world of spirits'. In his analysis of a similar practice among the Venda, Schutte argues that it consists of a 'ritual reversal of birth' (1980: 262) which I feel to be a more appropriate explanation. The identification of the child with the mother and the analogy between the mother and the household encountered above in the prohibitions on work, must be borne in mind. The child who dies so young, or who has hardly been born, returns whence it came. This child is a product of the household and is thus buried within it, as it has not yet assumed an independent personality.

Of late, the practice of burial inside the house has been less frequently adhered to and often the father secretly buries the child in the cemetery at night. This reflects changing attitudes to the conception of the household. The child is no longer seen mainly as the product of the household, for the pivotal role of the household, strong as it remains, has diminished. This obviates the necessity for the burial taking place within the house.

Immediately after birth, the child is thoroughly washed. This bath is not an innovation imposed by scientific concepts of hygiene, but rather an old practice of great significance within the peasant worldview. It is said that if the child is not well washed it will be 'suspicious' (*desconfiado*) in later life which, as we have seen, is one of the characteristics of semi-socialized people—*bichos do mato*. Like baptism, this bath is a rite of purification and separation.

This first event in a person's life is seen as determining the rest of it. For this reason, valuable objects are put into the bath so that the child may grow to be rich. Similarly, the water is very frequently disposed of by throwing it from on high into a hole in the ground 'in such a way that it runs' (*de maneira que corra*). The purpose of this is to ensure that the child will not grow up to be a frightened person (*temporato*).

In Paço and Couto mothers are said to develop a dark film on the skin of their faces during pregnancy (*pano*). This is seen to be related to the impurity of their condition and the only way to get rid of it is by washing the face with the water of the child's first bath. As it cleansed the child's impurity, so this water cleanses that of the mother.

The practice of burning the child's umbilical cord in the hearth immediately after it has been severed is strongly enforced. It is thought that if mice catch it, the child will become prone to stealing. If this does occur (and particularly in cases of kleptomania) the mother must catch a live mouse and boil it in a soup until it almost dissolves. This soup is then given to the victim who must be unaware of its composition. It is claimed that, after this meal, the person no longer feels the urge to steal—a form of greed—and that simultaneously he feels he is extremely *farto* (replete), which means that his greed will have been satisfied. The mouse's theft prevented the full separation of the child from the mother; the child's 'socialization' was, therefore, not effected as its desires remained unrestrained. By inverting the original situation in which the mouse ate a part of the person (the umbilical cord), the remedy helps the victim to be liberated from the greed inherited from the mother's womb.

Until the child is one year old or, according to other informants, until it has begun to speak, its hair must not be cut, and its nails may only be chewed off by the mother. If this prohibition is disregarded, it is thought that the child may become mute. It is evident that, even after birth, the child is perceived as morphologically unstable. Hair and nails are parts of the body which grow until death (and in some cases continue to do so after death). By cutting them with a sharp metal object, the mother would analogically be preventing the child from developing that quality which it acquires last, the capacity to speak.

As we have seen, the mother–child symbiosis of the pregnancy period is not abruptly resolved at birth. This is made clear both in the treatment of the dark film which develops on the mother's face and by the fact that the mother is the person who must chew the child's nails. It also becomes evident in the prohibition against drinking or eating while breast-feeding. Should this be done accidentally, the child runs the risk of later suffering from gout. To prevent this from happening, mothers used to attend Mass on the feast day of St. Gregory and suckle their children facing the altar at the elevation of the Host. (The present priest abolished this practice as he felt it was 'improper'.)

The symbolic relation between mother and child means that, by eating at the same time as the child, the mother is passing on to her offspring her gluttony or, in other words, her incapacity to control her desires. This interpretation is supported by the nature of the sanction which results from the breach of this prohibition: gout. This complaint is associated by the locals with overeating. The rite on St Gregory's day sheds some light on the significance of the elevation of the Host during the Mass. As was the case with some of the pre-natal prohibitions examined above, if the mother turns away at this moment, she is rejecting the purest of all foodstuffs; on the contrary, in symbolically eating the Host, she transmits to the child the purity it symbolizes.

V

The period between birth and baptism was, in the past, considered to be particularly dangerous. The residents of Paço and Couto say that until the 1950s people used to be scared that, if the child left home during this period, the Devil might get hold of it, and the child might die. It was common to cover the child with a pair of trousers belonging to the father, or to place a pair of scissors or an ox yoke upon the cradle. This was thought to be a protection against the witches who, coming up against these instruments, would be unable to reach the child. The father's trousers, like his hat in the bread-making ritual, effect the shift from the impure and dangerous female fertility to the safety of (male *and* female) household fertility. As for the scissors (sharp metal object) and the ox yoke, we have already encountered them in pre-natal prohibitions which apply to the whole of the household. There, they perform the role of instruments of morphological change which affect the boundaries of, and deform the products of, the household. Here, they create a barrier between the child and the antisocial world from which it has only recently departed, and to which it still partially belongs, as it has not yet been integrated into Christian society. Like the trousers, the ox yoke represents domination over animal force (in the case of the yoke, as represented in oxen; in the case of the trousers, as represented in female sexuality).

Until the middle of the 1890s, children in Paço and Couto were baptized during the first eleven days of their life. Later, there were exceptions to this rule, but the practice was still adhered to by an overwhelming majority of people until the 1950s, when the time-span between the two events began to widen. According to the locals, there are two principal reasons for this. Firstly, the new priest, who arrived in the mid-1950s, thinks that it is 'superstitious' to baptize children hurriedly, and therefore refuses to change his routine in order to do so. Over the past five years, in fact, he has instituted the practice of group baptisms, which take place twice a year, in August and during the Christmas season (the periods during which the emigrants take their vacations). Secondly, the local inhabitants acknowledge that infant mortality has decreased radically and that they feel safe that children will not die before baptism.

Nevertheless, the fate of those who die before baptism is still greatly pitied by parents, relatives, and neighbours alike. It is believed that these children 'remain in the dark' (*ficam às escuras*); they go neither to Hell nor to Heaven. It is thought to be unfair that such 'pure little creatures' (*creaturas tão purinhas*) should miss the benefits of Heaven. Furthermore, baptism is thought to be prophylactic and therapeutic. Even the priest admits that weak and ailing children should be baptized as early as possible since this may prevent early death.

Prior to baptism, the child is thought to have no soul and the locals express anger at the idea that some people never baptize their children, for they believe that such children 'remain like animals' (*ficam como animais*). By this they do not necessarily mean that such children behave like animals, but rather that spiritually they are akin to animals. Baptism is the door to human society proper. In the past, to further the distance between the child's impure origins and its membership in society, its parents were not allowed to attend the baptism. Even today it is common for the mother not to attend the ceremony, in spite of the priest's injunctions to the contrary.

As opposed to weddings, to which many guests are invited, or to funerals, which most people who have relations with the household of the deceased feel obliged to attend, baptisms are usually attended by a small but usually uninvited group of relatives and close neighbours.

On the morning of the event, the church bells announce to all the neighbours that a baptism is going to take place by ringing as for a *festa* (*toque de festa*). Previously, only the baptism of an illegitimate child was not celebrated in this way. Now, the priests insist that bells should ring for one and all.

In the past, baptism was a complex ceremony, the symbolism of which was vividly experienced by the faithful. Today, the priest has abolished this, and substituted for it a simple ceremony which is almost destitute of meaning for them.

At the baptism, the child receives its name. Before it became common for parents to attend the baptism, the name of the child was chosen by the godparents who were expected to consult the parents before reaching a final decision. Nowadays, the emphasis on the choice of the name is on the parents, who nevertheless do feel obliged to consult the godparents. As it happens, it is frequent for the child to receive the name of its grandparents, whether or not they are still alive. This practice is consistent with the fact that it is very common for grandparents to be godparents.

The role of the godparents is 'to do what the parents cannot do' (*fazer o que os pais não podem*). From a spiritual point of view this means that the parents cannot lead the infant to the baptismal font. From a material point of view, it means that godparents see to it that the parents bring up the child properly, and godparents may be called on to look after the child if it is orphaned.

In Paço and Couto at present, the godfather provides the *baeta* (baize; originally a warm, coloured type of flannel in which the child was wrapped). The godmother's gift is the baptismal dress. (It is interesting to note that traditionally the male gift had to be bought, while the female gift was made at home.) Both godparents are responsible for the expenses of the ceremony and, furthermore, it has become common for them to give the child a piece of jewellery.

Nowadays, the duties of the godparents are usually limited mostly to the ceremony. The choice of godparents lies with the parents. Although in theory it should not be a problem to find godparents, for it is believed to be a sin to refuse if asked to be one, in practice the choice is often difficult. Many people who are approached by the parents do not refuse outright to become godparents, but suggest that someone else would be more suitable. This is tantamount to a refusal. This difficulty, which is a recurrent theme in folk-tales, is augmented by the fact that parents want to choose godparents who have greater prestige than themselves.

In practice, and particularly in the case of elder children, the problem is usually resolved by resorting to the grandparents, who are both eager to help the parents and, because of the age gap, sufficiently prestigious. When no other godparents are available, the elder siblings of the child may be chosen to perform this task. Finally, people may choose saints as godparents for the child. This option may be taken during emergency baptisms, when no other godparents are available, or as a result of a promise made by the parents. Many of the children in Paço and Couto who were given saints as godparents were illegitimate children whose mothers had not been successful in finding anyone willing to take responsibility for their future. This may also partly account for the fact that illegitimate children were, as a rule, baptized later than legitimate children.

In Minho, the role of *compadrio* (the relationship between parents and godparents) is not as important as it is in the south of Portugal, where it assumes a much greater role in social life as a whole. Cutileiro's description (1977) of the institution, in his chapter on spiritual kinship, nevertheless remains largely applicable to this area, and I shall therefore not repeat it here.

In spite of all the implications of reciprocity, the *compadrio* is in fact an asymmetrical relationship. In asking people to become godparents, parents are indebting themselves to them. This imbalance is acknowledged as a patron-client relationship when a share-cropper or a day-labourer asks his landlord or master to be the godfather, or when a townsman accepts the role of godfather of a peasant. When the relationship is created between neighbours, however, it assumes a different perspective, for it favours the maintenance or the creation of a type of relationship of 'friendship' between wealthier and poorer households which phrases itself in terms of reciprocity between equals, while in fact hiding a form of economic dependence.

VI

Rapariga, tu és tola!
Eu não sou o teu amante,
Ou tu nasceste sem lua,
Ou no quarto minguante.

Minhoto song[5]

[5] 'Girl, are you crazy! / I am not your lover, / Either you were born without moon, / Or when the moon was waning.'

Minhoto peasants, like so many other peoples throughout the world, believe that the sun and the moon have power to influence events on earth. This is not to say that they anthropomorphize heavenly bodies, but rather that their power is much like that of fire—a force which can do good or evil depending on the way in which it is utilized. The term used to refer to this power is *força*, which can mean force, strength, power, might, or vigour.

The sun and the moon, however, are very different from each other and their *forças* are therefore, in many ways, opposed. A *minhoto* adage says that 'as the moon rules the night, the sun rules the day.' The two powers must be kept apart. Eclipses of the sun are feared because they confuse the categories of day and night. As a resident of Couto once observed, 'it is like a battle, the moon wants to win over the sun.' But the sun is, and should remain, the stronger of the two. If the moon were to win the 'battle', that would denote the end of the world: complete chaos.

The *minhotos* evince a particular concern with the power of the moon. They believe that this power is of a specific kind and concerns specific things—a belief which is by no means unique to the Alto Minho. The concepts which I discuss in this section concern mainly the phases of the moon and their relation to human, animal, and vegetable growth and reproduction.

As in the case of the *adágios* described above, belief in the power of the moon is opposed by the bourgeoisie. Peasant statements about it, therefore, are often ambiguous. The residents of the 'lower halves' (*meias de baixo*) of both parishes are, as a rule, not very eager to admit to this belief. The residents of the 'upper halves' are highly critical of this attitude, which they see as a false attempt to claim bourgeois status. They point out that, although the residents of the 'lower halves' deny belief in such things, 'they still perform their agricultural tasks at the same time as everyone else' (a timetable based on the phases of the moon).

Local residents call the waxing moon 'new moon' (*lua nova*). This is contrary to bourgeois practice, which uses this term to refer to the period when the moon is invisible. The peasant terminology implies an interpretation of the phases of the moon which stresses the fact that, for a certain period of time, there is no moon at all: we are 'between moons' (*entrelunho* or *antrelunho*). The moon at the beginning of its cycle is growing in 'strength' or 'power' (*força*). Thus, the full moon is called alternatively *lua cheia* (literally, full moon) and *a força da lua* (literally, the strength or power of the moon). Similarly, the locals often speak of something having been done 'when the moon was strong' (*no forte da lua*) or 'when the moon was weak' (*na fraqueza da lua*). The 'strong' period extends from the moon's first quarter to the day after full moon: in other words, the waxing of the moon, when it is in its full potency as opposed to the 'weakness' of its first appearance in the sky. Once it starts to diminish, the moon manifests an increasing 'weakness': this is the waning of the moon. Finally, when it disappears, there is thought to be no moon.

The strength of the whole natural world is thought to increase and decrease according to the phases of the moon. For example, *minhotos* believe that sea air is very healthy. When they go to the seaside for therapeutic reasons, they always choose to do so during the 'strength of the moon' because then the tides are at their fiercest and the wind is said to be stronger and to 'penetrate the flesh and bones' more readily. This is supposed to be very healthy 'for the bones'.

With regard to plants, the general rule is that most species should be sown, planted or grafted during the *forte da lua* (the waxing moon), so as to ensure better growth. There are, however, many specifications for plants which do not follow this rule. Timber, for example, should be cut during the waning moon, for during the waxing moon the tree has too much sap and will therefore not dry, but also develop borers. This is the same explanation, the reader will recall, given for not cutting trees with *vício* (when the sap is rising) and for not chopping and gathering wood on certain days. As in so many other instances, the processes of growth and gestation are believed to be accompanied by vulnerability and weakness.

These prescriptions and prohibitions deal with the basic presupposition that the cycle of the moon is accompanied by a process of increasing strength which is then followed by a decrease. The moon's 'death' also heralds its rebirth, just like the death and Resurrection of Christ, which is relived every year on the first Sunday after the full moon which follows the vernal equinox (Easter).

Local residents believe that the conception of both humans and animals should take place at night. As they put it, 'one always waits till night-time for those things.' Sows, she-goats and cows are always left overnight for fecundation. This is done not only because copulation is an 'improper' thing that ought not to be witnessed, but also because, as they point out, it is the moon which 'rules' over these matters. Children and animals which are conceived or born during the full moon or during the waxing moon will be both stronger and more intelligent. When a woman has an easy labour, people say that conception 'took place during the strength of the moon'. This is a proverbial phrase: they are not concerned to establish when it actually did take place.

On the other hand, children who are born or conceived during the waning moon or the period without moon are said to be *sempre ríticos* (rickety). This weakness does not apply only to their bodies but also to their minds. There are a number of dialectal words expressing this idea. The locals refer to someone who is idiotic or scatter-brained as *luato* or *antrelunhado*. The song quoted as an epigraph to this section expresses this belief in the weakness (mental, physical, and even moral) of children born during these periods—the girl was behaving amorously towards a man who was not her lover; there was something immoral about her indiscriminate behaviour. Thus, the singer concludes, either she 'was born without moon, or when the moon was waning'. The period without moon (*antrelunho*) is particularly mistrusted, and it is believed that this is the time when witches emerge.

While witches come out during the death of the moon, Christ's redeeming death took place during the full moon. The moon is a symbol of death, rebirth, and of life continuing through alternation. In this, it is similar to females, whose fertility follows the moon's cycle. It is no wonder that the Virgin Mary, when depicted as Our Lady of the Conception—Portugal's patron saint—is associated with the crescent moon.

In the light of this, the following *adágio*, which puzzled me for a long time, becomes comprehensible: *If the moon is in its strength during Christmas Eve, there will be a good harvest of wine during the year to come.* We have already encountered a set of beliefs concerning the prediction during the Christmas season of the weather of the year to follow. Just as a child's life is affected by the gold put into its first bath, so the year can be influenced at the moment of Christ's yearly rebirth.

When the moon is in its 'strength' at the moment of someone's birth, this person will become strong and healthy, full of life force. But how is this connected with wine? Why should the full moon on Christmas Eve herald a good wine harvest? Onians, in *The Origins of European Thought* (1954), argues that wine was regarded by the Romans and Greeks as 'liquid life'. This symbolic connection remains extant today: people drink 'to health' (*à saúde*); wine is the basis of hospitality; and peasants continuously prescribe wine to each other as a means of enhancing health. For them, wine produced locally is particularly therapeutic and prophylactic, for it is full of life force. This is particularly true of red wine.

Although local white wine is more marketable and of superior quality to the red, peasants prefer to produce red wine. Their explanation for this is that they produce wine mainly for home consumption (which in many cases is not true). The only times white wine is consumed locally are at breakfast and during the Mass. Although peasants are aware that the alcoholic content of the white wine is the same as that of the red, they still maintain that it is less 'strong' or 'heavy'. It is therefore felt to be more appropriate for Mass than red wine which is too hearty, too full of a life force which may run rampant.

Although Onians appears to disagree with authors who have established a connection between wine and blood in classical times (1954: 278, note 3), it must be stressed that this connection is firmly established in present-day Minho. Not only are peasants brought up to see the blood of Christ in the form of wine, but wine is also connected with blood in normal, everyday language. When the peasants trample their grapes, they proudly display to visiting neighbours their legs covered in dark red pulp, always stressing how 'it even looks like blood.' While the wine is fermenting, they stir it with a long stick so as to 'give it colour' (*para dar côr*). If the wine still turns out too light, this is considered unfortunate. This concern also explains their preference for drinking out of opaque white mugs, and the gesture which is always made by the men of twisting their wrists in such a way as to let the wine swill around the mug and show off its dark reddish tint against the sides.

Christmas being an epitome of the whole year, if the moon is in its full 'strength' that night, the year ahead will be characterized by much life force which, in turn, is best represented by the good wine harvest.

VII

Whatever may take place in other regions of the world (Lévi-Strauss, 1973: 251–61), in Portugal the attribution of the female gender to the moon and of the male to the sun is certainly significant. Like women, the moon is in charge of 'all things growing'. The moon is said to be weaker than the sun; furthermore, the sun's strength is seen as constant whereas that of the moon is changeable. This corresponds precisely to peasant views of the relative moral and physical strengths of the genders, and to their ideas of female fickleness and recidivist impurity.

Furthermore, we should not be surprised to find that the difference between bourgeois and peasant manners should be phrased in a similar idiom. All of these oppositions are based on the same underlying premises. Any attempt to specify these premises must necessarily remain at a very general level and thus can at best be only partially satisfactory.

The soul and the body, men and women, the sun and the moon, and urban and rural peoples, represent contrasting but complementary principles whose differentiation is predominantly characterized by a perceived opposition between restraint and fertility respectively. The very existence of the prohibitions and prescriptions described above is itself a proof of the culture's sense of the problems inherent in the necessary complementarity of these principles. A concern for satisfaction of bodily desires alone would only give rise to *vícios*; an attachment to the land alone would transform anyone into a *bicho do mato* (wild beast). These have to be tempered by restraint and order, by sacraments, the household, social norms. Fertility is desired, but it must be shifted from the disorder of female fertility to the order of household fertility. Peasant society is not merely concerned with the procurement of a bountiful life, but rather, of a bountiful *and* orderly, 'social' life.

IV

Household and community

At the levels of the hamlet and the parish, the very strength of the *minhoto*'s attachment to the *casa* leads to a divisive tendency and to social conflict. In a situation of conflicting interests, the peasant may be quite ruthless in attempting to advance his own household. Parish society is fairly restricted in numbers; competition, therefore, both for economic and for prestige goals, can be very intense. One household's success is far too often another household's failure.

The existence of this divisive proclivity is acknowledged but regretted, for it is seen as a serious failure to achieve the accepted ideals of parish and hamlet life. Parish residents, therefore, have recourse to a set of institutions, prescriptions, and prohibitions, the purpose of which is to bring under control this divisive proclivity and to create and reinforce the experience of community which is so cherished and important a part of the peasant worldview.

The meaning of the term community must be clarified. Like many other concepts in sociological thinking, this is a polythetic concept (cf. Needham, 1975). Broadly speaking, community can be used to refer both to 'a complex of social relationships' and to 'a complex of ideas and sentiments'. A typical example of the use of the term which confuses both meanings is Robert Redfield's classic essay '*The Little Community*' (1973). I have found it necessary to distinguish between the two notions, but I am aware of not having done so fully, for there is a certain logic to this ambiguity. As Calhoun puts it 'the experiential dimension [of community] is not independent of the structural; the sense of belonging to a community is directly founded on the social relationships through which one does belong to a community' (1980: 109). It may be, therefore, that the experiential aspects are not entirely separable from the structural. One conclusion, however, may be drawn from the awareness of this ambiguity: what transforms a group of people into a community is the strength of each person's investment in a set of communally defined interests. This strength may vary, and as such there may be more or less community. To quote Calhoun again 'community must be seen as a variable' (1980: 109).[1]

But community is not only variable in the sense that it may be stronger or weaker; there may also be communities within communities, and communities being created at the expense of other communities. It is, therefore, necessary to specify at which levels one can identify community in the Alto Minho, how it manifests itself at each level, and whether, in its various manifestations it has undergone change in recent decades.

11. The experience of community

I

The association of social groups with tracts of land from which they derive their identity is an essential aspect of *minhoto* life. Members of the same borough, in opposition to outsiders, or alternatively neighbours of the same parish in opposition to strangers, are called *conterrâneos*, once again stressing this association with the land (*terra*). This relation is one of property, which is yet radically different from a notion of private ownership of the land. The *minhotos* think of their society in terms of a set of hierarchically related socio-geographic units: households join up to make hamlets, which are grouped into parishes, which, together, form boroughs; these are united in districts, a number of which comprise a province, Minho. From the perspective of our interest in rural community, these groups have different characteristics.

Hamlets consist of a set of households which may be scattered around the fields, although there is usually a central core of houses. This core tends to be demarcated by a small square, a fountain, a shrine to the souls in purgatory, a chapel, or similar areas of communal use. Its residents develop close personal links and remain almost permanently informed of one another's lives and significant social actions.

Parishes, too, share the features of community: their members are relatively familiar with one another, and they have both diffuse and specific obligations to perform which are communally defined. Nevertheless, the relations between members are weaker than those within the hamlet, for face-to-face contact is less frequent and tends to take place only around the core of the parish: the cemetery and the nearby church.

[1] Cf. F. G. Bailey's concept of the 'moral community' for a different but related formulation of the same problem (1971: 302-3).

Similarly, the dependability between members, which is most marked at hamlet level, has less opportunity to manifest itself at parish level. It tends to do so during large ceremonial occasions such as Easter, St Sebastian's Eve, St John's Eve, and All Souls' Day; and to a lesser extent around ceremonial occasions of personal significance, most noticeably at funerals (Feijó, Martins, and Pina-Cabral, 1983; Du Boulay, 1974: 44).

The parish assumes its greatest relevance as the frontier between the folkways and the stateways, to use an expression of Robert Redfield's (1973: 130). The Church Committee, the priest, the Parish Council, the *mordomos* (organizers) of the *festas*, are all representatives of a group of people related by communally defined interests and by a familiarity based on face-to-face contact. They act as intermediaries between this world of folkways and the external world of stateways with its impersonal definition of means and ends.

Community cannot be claimed to exist at borough level, for there is no specific relationship between all the households which make up the borough, or their members. Yet there is still something of community, for the residents of the town which is the centre of the borough tend to express their identity at borough level, even though they only have relations of community proper at the level of the town's parish. It is almost as if the town represented the borough—a notion which is supported by the fact that town and borough always have the same name in the Alto Minho, and by the fact that the town's *festas* are attended by people from all parishes of the borough (cf. Silverman, 1975).

The hamlet—or, in the case of the town, the neighbourhood—is then the floor of community on which the other levels are raised. It is at the level of the hamlet that the individual learns the experience of community and that he integrates the values which give body to it in *minhoto* rural society.

The experience of community is doubly specific. On the one hand, it is dependent on the images by which people measure their communal life and cannot be transposed to another cultural universe: it acquires a substance only through each culture's basic cultural prototype. On the other hand, its individual members are not substitutable. Unlike a university faculty, for example, a community is formed by its individual members, not by role-performers, and, in order for a new member to integrate himself, he has to acquire a past in the community; he cannot simply slip into a prefashioned role. In the Alto Minho, this is true whether we consider households or persons as the elements of community.

II

After the baptism, the child begins its process of integration into human society. The first social group of which it becomes aware is the household. This is its major source of identity, and to it the child owes its greatest allegiance. Progressively, however, it explores the world and begins to participate in social relations which are wider than the sphere of the household. The child first becomes aware of inter-household relations in the context of the peer group. It is here that the child learns of both the particular images which give substance to the group's experience of community and the individuals which compose the community.

Usually confined to the boundaries of the hamlet, the peer group is an important source of identity. By the time they are eight or nine years old, the children of a hamlet are already organized into play groups. These tend to correspond to age-groups which include people born within a period of three to four years. Throughout life these people will always address one another by the familiar second person singular. This form of address is used only between peers, spouses, siblings, and by parents to children. Peer groups are informal groupings, but they are very close-knit and lasting and they have a definite role to play in hamlet life. Their existence is an accepted and cherished fact of traditional social patterns. These groupings have a greater impact upon local society during the period which immediately precedes marriage.

Peer group allegiance counterbalances household allegiance and many of the roles which are performed by the peer group at the level of the hamlet exploit this feature. It is the *nôvos* (the young ones) who organize such activities as dance and theatre groups. They also play an important role in helping to plan most *festas*. Similarly, it is the self-acknowledged role of the peer groups to minimize and resolve strife between households at hamlet level. Time and again, cases in which the 'friendship' of the children of two households had been central in the process of re-establishing relations after a conflict were reported to me. The peer group also has an important role in imposing group coercion and sanctions upon individuals or households who fail to live up to communally accepted standards. Sexual relations, or activities which are not accepted by the group, are punished mainly by means of *chacotas* or *tocatas* (rough music) and by general harassment which may at times be very brutal and compelling. Stingy people find their property is stolen; unfriendly people are disturbed during the night; excessively zealous and religious people are made fun of; and strangers who refuse to participate in local life are continuously provoked.

Peer groups are not only a source of communal action and entertainment; they also function as courtship groups. Courting a girl outside one's natal hamlet or parish was a difficult matter before the present progressive disintegration of peer groups began. The stranger was carefully assessed. If he presented an acceptable image, he had to pay a small entrance fee which usually meant that he had to offer a round of drinks to the local 'boys'. If he behaved in an undesirable fashion, or if he attempted to steal the girl-friend of a local youth, he would be very roughly treated (cf. Pitt-Rivers, 1971: 9). The locals do not object so much to outsiders marrying into their hamlets: what they really do object to is the prospect of a future neighbour of whom they do not approve.

When they get married, young people abandon their group activities, as they are now considered to be too busy looking after the interests of their household and family. On marrying, people are seen to become more selfish and more impure. In the past, the church bells were not rung for this ceremony. When the priest pronounced the banns in church, the bride and groom were never present, as they were said to be 'ashamed'. Their peers would nevertheless tease them about having 'fallen from the altar', like a saint who had lost his sanctity.

As people 'made bread with the sweat of their brow', the toil and struggle which are necessary for survival are seen to cause them to be mean and impure of heart. Only the young, who are still free from 'responsibilities', are thought capable of genuinely pure and disinterested action. They can overcome the divisive tendencies which arise from the strong allegiance of adults to their households and thus they represent the cohesive forces of the wider group.

The early experience of community through communal action is not completely erased by marriage, or upon the onset of adulthood. As they grow older, children create more specific 'friendships'. These survive the changes brought about by marriage, and usually lead to the creation of the links of 'friendship' between households which form such an important part of hamlet life. Furthermore, a sense of belonging remains, which means that the individual's consideration of alternative courses of action is strongly influenced by the set of communal relations to which he belongs (Calhoun, 1980: 119). It is in the context of the peer groups that children learn how to operate in groups of equals (cf. Schlumböhm, 1980). This process of socialization is a *sine qua non* of the experience of the ideology of egalitarianism which is a central corollary of the subsistence prototype.

The experience of identity which each individual member has shared with all other members of his age-group is never fully erased or denied by the differences in wealth and prestige which only become fully evident at the onset of adulthood. As the members of a community are not substitutable, each experience of community is specific to each set of individuals. This means that the concern with equality encountered in the Alto Minho corresponds to a real experience of identity between specific individuals.

By this argument I do not mean to deny that equality can be, and at times is, manipulated. Such manipulation is in fact unavoidable, for there are two levels at which one may reckon community. The fact that the two central notions of *casa* and vizinho each have two different meanings suggests that one may consider the elements of community to be individuals—a reckoning which is most appropriate to the level of the hamlet—or one may consider that the elements of community are households, this being most apposite at the level of the parish. The latter reckoning excludes landless peasant families from community, which the former does not. (See pp. 3–4 above). But even if one sees community as being formed by landed households alone, there are still great differences in wealth and reputation to be accounted for.

Two largely independent conclusions may be drawn from this argument. First, it becomes clear that the feeling of equality manifested by hamlet residents is based on peer group socialization and is actually independent of actual differences in wealth and reputation. Second, the notion of a hierarchy of communities is further developed by the realization that these levels are interdependent and that it is at the level of the hamlet, and in the relations between individual persons, that this experience of community reproduces itself at all levels.

III

At the level of the parish, the action of the hamlet peer groups does not always express social cohesion. Until the 1960s, peer groups often enacted the conflict between the upper and the lower halves of these parishes. Fights between hamlet peer groups often reinforced this division and usually took place after Sunday Mass. There are two reasons for this. On the one hand, the church was the spot where the whole parish was gathered, and could therefore be considered neutral ground. On the other hand, as opposed to the *festas*, no strangers were expected to be present, which meant that parish allegiance did not conflict with hamlet allegiance.

On the day of St Sebastian, however, all the youth of the parish assembles for their *festa*. Each *festa* has one or more *festeiros* or *mordomos* (people who organize it and collect funds for it) of each sex, and there is an established procedure by which these are chosen. Traditionally, the male *festeiros* of St Sebastian were young men who, having presented themselves at a military recruitment office, had been exempt from military service.

By organizing this *festa*, these young men were thanking the Saint for having liberated them from 'war' (military service is abhorred, even in periods of peace). This festa was celebrated annually until 1976, when the priest (who ironically is a great devotee of St Sebastian) decided to put in the position of *festeiro* a person of his own choice. As the people did not feel that he was entitled to choose the *festeiros*, they simply did not participate in or contribute financially towards the *festa*.

The result of this action was that the *festa* was practically unattended, and the priest had to shoulder most of the expenses himself. For some years the *festa* did not take place at all because each subsequent year the priest insisted on directing it himself. This gesture angered people, as he had also summarily abolished other traditional *festas*, and in particular the *festa* of St Michael in September, of which the parish priest was traditionally the organizer. They feel he is hypocritical in that he opposes all *festas* except that of his chosen saint, St Sebastian. Indeed this attitude is a clear example of how the priest is torn between the religious beliefs of the church hierarchy and those of what he calls 'popular religion'.

The exceptionally high rates of emigration during the 1960s and the early 1970s meant that many young men left the parish before they were married. Concomitantly, the number of young men who saw their future as farmers was rapidly diminishing. Those who proceeded into further education integrated themselves into town life (for there are no high schools in rural areas) and later, if they managed to enter a university, into city life. Those who could not afford an education and did not manage to emigrate took up paid employment which, as a rule, took them away from hamlet society and from agricultural work. This process was further facilitated by the ready availability of transport. Young people became progressively more likely to find the kinds of entertainment and social life which they desired in the towns and elsewhere in the borough. Courtship was now separated from agricultural activities and even from the yearly cycle—the *festas*, which had previously punctuated the whole year, were now concentrated in the summer and around Christmas, when the emigrants return on holiday, displaying their wealth and offering their marital proposals.

Interestingly, this process does not seem to have altered significantly the pattern of high hamlet endogamy verified above. A young emigrant who marries in his parish of origin is bound to prefer to a stranger a girl who is familiar with his parental household and kin and with his interests, in a way that only hamlet neighbours can be.

Since the end of the 1970s, however, young people have seldom succeeded in emigrating and they therefore once more share the experience of communal action which, during the 1960s and early 1970s seemed doomed. Since 1981, and in spite of the priest, whose advice has been repeatedly and pointedly overlooked, the *festa* of St Sebastian in Paço has again been taking place annually. This is certainly a sign of the revival of peer groups. Nevertheless, an irreversible change has occurred: the experience of community is less specific in both senses particularized above. First, due to facility of transport and to common interests generated by the mass media, peer groups are no longer limited to hamlet residents; their boundaries are thus less closely defined. Second, education and the possibility of obtaining paid jobs in the non-agricultural sector result in greater divergence in biographical experience and outlook.

IV

Naming is a central aspect of the individual's insertion into the social group. The rules for the inheritance of surnames stipulated by the Civil Code state that the child receives after its first names the surname of the mother's father which is followed by that of the father's father. That is, the surname of the mother's father does not pass on to the second generation. The use of surnames, however, is only of secondary importance in local terms. The residents of Paço and Couto distinguish between *apelidos que se escrevem* (surnames which are written) and *apelidos que não se escrevem* (surnames which are not written). They confront legal surnames with an informal and uncodified way of naming, which they definitely prefer in everyday usage. Indeed, neighbours are often unsure of one another's legal surname.

Following an accepted practice in European ethnography, I call the second type of *apelido* a nickname. The term, however, covers two kinds of naming: kin nicknames and personal nicknames (*alcunhas*). The latter are less important in rural areas than the former. Most people do not have a personal nickname and those who do receive them are usually people of low reputation, whose position is invariably low in the local scale of stratification.

Most people are addressed and referred to by their first name followed by a gerundive clause which is applied to the kin nickname: e.g. Carminha da Valia. Kin nicknames usually have one of four origins: they derive from personal nicknames (such as *Calão*); from surnames (such as *Souza*); from first names which are not extremely common (such as *Ester* or *Herculano*); or from house names (such as *Valia*). House names always correspond to the name of the plot or field in which the house was built. As far as I could tell, the latter only seem to be used as kin nicknames when the property of one household has remained fairly undivided over a few generations.

When used as kin nicknames, all of these refer back to an ancestor who became locally renowned. As a rule these men or women were the source of most of the wealth which a particular group of kin has inherited. For example, most of the households which originated from the original *Calão* are called after his personal nickname. Only one branch of the family, which has a new and considerable source of wealth, has adopted a new name. It is worth noting that this branch changed a kin nickname which was based on a personal nickname (*Calão*) for one which is based on a surname (*Ramos*). This took place because the familiarity implicit in all other types of nickname is discouraged by the members of this household. By accepting this change, the neighbours are vindicating this family's rise in prestige.

The example of a local shop-keeper who made some money abroad sheds light on the nature of this change. His kin nickname was *Calheiros*, which referred to the parish from which one of his maternal ancestors had come. He attempted to change this, for he wanted to mark his rise in prestige. This rise, however, had not been as remarkable as he himself believed and the neighbours simply did not accept the change and went on referring to him by his kin nickname. Confronted with this failure, he changed his name legally and adopted his kin nickname as a surname. In this way he attempted to overcome what he saw as 'the people's lack of respect' *a falta de respeito do povo*.

The preference for uxorilocality and uxorivicinality makes most people assume their mother's kin nickname. Thus, the common use of a nickname tends to identify the localized kin group based on the group of sisters described above (p. 72).

Following Gilmore's suggestion that nicknames are 'a verbal representation of a collective identity' (1982: 697), nicknaming practices may be seen as representing the nature of the experience of community in each particular social group. I have suggested elsewhere (Pina-Cabral, 1984b) that, within the bounds of European ethnography, two radically distinct types of nicknaming may be found: at one extreme of the continuum, there is the typically Mediterranean practice, where the personal nickname is more significant than that of the family and where there are no household nicknames as such (cf. Campbell, 1964); at the other extreme, the situation where household names are the single most important form of naming. This continuum corresponds to a continuum in the experience of community: at one end, there is an agonistic model of community, where the experience of equality is achieved through struggle; at the other end, a consensual model of community, where the experience of equality is strongly felt as a part of group membership.

In Paço and Couto personal nicknames do occur and, although all households have a name, people are most commonly referred to by a name which applies to a group of households. This situation, therefore, may be seen as intermediary between these two models of community. Nevertheless, it evidently more closely approaches the consensual extreme, where stress is placed on equality, personal pride is less fiercely stated, the household is more highly valued than the family, and women are given a more important role to play in the decision-making process.

12. Rituals of parish unity and correct motion

The ceremonial practices which will be described in this section share the following two features: first, they are rituals of parish and hamlet unity in that they are seen to foster the common good of all *vizinhos* (neighbours) and to bring them together; second, they are characterized by a specific type of motion which the locals endow with particular significance—motion *à direita*. The practices in question are the Easter visit of the priest to most households of the parish (*visita Pascal*); the processions on ordinary feast days; the passing from household to household of images of the Holy Family; and, finally, the blessing of the graves on the days of All Saints and All Souls.

It must be remarked that by writing about rituals which stress equality and unity among the members of a parish, I am not implying that peasants are not aware of social inequality or of intra-parish strife.

Quite to the contrary, for they are both aware of these and judge them negatively as falling short of the ideal condition of society. The significance of these ceremonies is precisely that they are attempts to bring order back into this fallen world. As Christians, the *minhotos* believe that the death of Jesus Christ endowed humans with the necessary strength to counteract the forces of strife and chaos. The pivotal role played by the processional cross in three of the ceremonies is directly related to this belief.

I

As a rule, geographically speaking, *minhoto* parishes are fairly self-contained. Both Paço and Couto consist of small valleys on the southern side of the river Lima. The borders between parishes may correspond to cultivated land, but this is certainly not the norm. On the whole, woods and scrub land are at the geographical peripheries of the parishes, most often on the hill tops which divide this region of hills and valleys. The best cultivated land—usually at the bottom of a valley—tends to be found in the geographical centre of the parish. It is here that one usually finds the parish church, generally placed at the top of a small, conical hill. But, as parish residents often point out, what is important for them is not that the church should be in the precise geographical centre of the parish, but rather that it should be in the acoustic centre of the parish, in the place from which the sound of its bells can best be heard in most parts of the parish.

The significance of the church bells cannot be overstated. Due to modern means of communication such as the telephone and motor vehicles, as well as to the fact that the State has taken over many of the responsibilities which were previously seen to by neighbourly co-operation, opportunities for communal action are disappearing and the bells have lost some of their former significance. Nevertheless, to this day, they play an important public role. The bells chime regularly during the course of a normal working day, and one soon learns to recognize what these chimes mean and to direct one's day, one's week, and one's year according to these sounds. The significance attached to the bells is such that the locals believe that, when the ringing of the bells sounds 'sad' (*triste*)—perhaps due to specific atmospheric conditions—this means that a *vizinho* is going to die. Furthermore, hamlets which are outside the aural reach of the church bells are considered to be at a disadvantage and are accused of being particularly 'backward' (*atrasado*). There is one such hamlet in Paço. Although there is no evidence to prove the legend, parish residents believe that this hamlet used to be a military prison. The present residents are said to be descendants of the prisoners who, once freed, decided to remain behind and settle there. The legendary origin of the hamlet is appropriate to its position. Symbolically, a hamlet in which the church bells cannot be heard and which is placed on the periphery of the parish and separated from the other hamlets by woods is an appropriate place for convicts—social outcasts and marginals.

The woods on the peripheries of the parishes are dominated by the image of the wolf, one of the few animals in this region to be accused of actually attacking human beings and of killing even when not hungry. In local lore, the wolf is often associated with the Devil. Once, I was sitting with some people at a café in lower Paço when one of them told the following story:

> A certain male relation of my father's, a very strong man, decided to go to a parish across the hills in the middle of the night. He took with him a sturdy cudgel such as people used in old times.
>
> As he was walking along a path in the woods, he saw the wolf sitting in the middle of the path. He approached it, expecting the wolf to run away. But it didn't. So he struck out with his cudgel with all his strength so as to crush the beast. The wolf merely leaned to the side and jumped over the stick, smiling. The wolf repeated this action as many times as were necessary to exhaust completely his opponent. When he could no longer continue, the man held the stick out in front of him, not knowing what to do. The wolf grabbed it with its teeth, held it for a while, and walked away. The man had such a fright that he went home and died the following morning.

As he finished his tale, the story-teller rose from his table and walked away, leaving all the others impressed with its impact. Looking round, however, he must have realized that I had not caught its full implication, so he shouted back at me: 'It was no wolf, man, it was the Devil!'

As the periphery of the parish is characterized by antisocial forces, so the church and the cemetery at its centre are the places where the unity of the group is most strongly felt. Above all else, the Mass is a ritual of reunion, of 'communion', and although the peasants do not have very clear theological ideas, they certainly do see it as such. The church is not only the centre where this 'communion' takes place, it is also the centre of all social activities. Any matter which interests all members of the parish takes place around the church after Sunday Mass. Immediately after he finishes the service, the priest reads the notices which the government bodies in the town send to the parish. This is also the place and time chosen for meetings of the Parish Council, or for meetings of any other associations, and for the discussion of matters related to any parish-wide festivities. It is also around the church that the *festas* are held and that any political rallies take place.

The Mass is not only a reunion of the parishioners with the divinity, but also of the living with the dead. Except for the main Sunday Mass, all other daily Masses are dedicated to the memory of the soul of a particular dead parishioner whose relatives pay the priest a certain sum of money for this service. The demand for these Masses is such that the priest finds he cannot meet it with his seven weekly Masses and there is a permanent waiting list. Suffice it to say here that when the Mass is said, both the living and the dead are thought to participate in an act of communion with the divinity. The Mass is a statement of sacred unity taking place in the symbolical centre.

II

The celebration of Easter clearly reveals characteristics of a rite of passage in which Carnival is a rite of separation, Lent is a rite of transition, and the week from Easter Sunday to the first Sunday after Easter (*Pascoela*, Low Sunday) a rite of integration.

The Carnival, which locally is called *Entrudo* (from the Latin root *introitus*—to mean 'entry', presumably because it consists of the three days before Lent and hence the 'entry' into it), is a period of revelry and rowdy humour. This festivity is characterized by the symbolic enactment of the antisocial forces which permanently threaten society and which the locals associate with chaos and death.

The main actors are the local youth, who form characteristically disorderly bands and go about masked and clothed in fancy dress, playing practical jokes. Their disguises play mainly on the themes of death, sickness, old age, monstrosity, and transvestism. The antisocial nature of the festivity is also manifest in the practical jokes, which tend to be of a sadistic nature. The *mascarados* (masked ones) play tricks such as exploding small fire-crackers under people's feet to frighten them, throwing sneezing powder, scattering foul-smelling substances, using water pistols, and dropping 'water bombs' (made of plastic bags). In the past, two comic ceremonies which are now disappearing in this region were enacted. In Paço and Couto they have not been performed since the young peer groups began to weaken in the mid-1960s. The first of these is the *Serração da Velha*, which consisted of a farcical sawing in half of an old woman (this could be done either as make-believe with an old woman, or actually with a puppet representing one). The second was the *Testamento de Judas* (Judas's will) which consisted of a public denunciation by masked youths of the evil deeds of certain neighbours. The symbolism of death, of separation, and of antisocial forces is directly expressed in these ceremonies.

Lent is a period which is mainly characterized by a series of proscriptions. People are not permitted to sing, they are expected to fast, repent, confess, and prepare themselves to take the Holy Communion at Easter. *A desobriga* (literally, the release from an obligation) is the name given to the fulfilment of one's duty to confess and take Communion at least once a year. This is a religious parallel to Judas's will, an expiation for and purification of one's faults. This duty is still taken very seriously today, and the priest keeps a record of those who come to confess and take Communion, as all parishioners should ideally start the year in a state of spiritual purity.

Holy Week begins on Palm Sunday (*Domingo de Ramos*) when the priest blesses the olive branches which the neighbours bring to church. These are taken home and hung on the outside of the houses, for they are purported to ward off the evil eye (*para não empecer*). They are also placed on the seed which has been kept apart for sowing, as they are believed to help future plants to grow.

Maundy Thursday (*Quinta-Feira Santa*) is the only day of Lent during which most people fast. Foods which are eaten on this day should not include *coisas de gordura* (fatty substances), so the locals abstain from most animal products. I was told that bread made on this day by someone who has fasted will last for ever without becoming mildewed. A certain local woman who is very devout claims to have eaten from the same loaf of bread for five consecutive Maundy Thursdays. From Maundy Thursday until Easter Sunday, the church bells are silent. On the evening of Good Friday, a procession is held in which all the parishioners carry candles.

The processions which take place on Easter Sunday and Easter Monday constitute the high point of the whole season. In the morning the bells peal when the priest, with the processional cross, leaves the church on the *compasso*: the Easter visit which he, the priest, pays to most of the households of the parish, one at a time, in an order which, once established, should never be broken. The priest is preceded by a choirboy carrying a bell which establishes the pace of the procession (hence its name *compasso*, literally, with step) and a man carrying the processional cross. The priest himself usually carries a bunch of flowers, as do most others in the procession. As he passes from household to household, new people join the group while others drop away. In the past it was common for people to dance as they followed the priest.

When he arrives at a house, the priest usually finds that it has been specially decorated to receive him. He enters the sitting-room, where there is always a table upon which are spread the best foodstuffs the household can afford (the *mesa folarenga*). Easter is 'the time for sweets', so these are provided in abundance. The priest proffers his stole for the inhabitants to kiss, and addresses them with the greetings of the season: 'Boas Festas, Aleluia.' He then sprinkles the house with holy water and lets every member of the household kiss the processional cross. The priest receives a gift (usually in cash, as nowadays they discourage the practice of offering goods), after which the procession moves on to another household. When, in this way, it reaches the end of the hamlet, the procession stops for refreshment which the young people of the hamlet have organized, with cash and goods collected from all the *vizinhos*. There is eating and drinking accompanied by music and fireworks whose purpose is to advertise that this hamlet is rejoicing in its cohesion and new life.

Then the procession moves to the next hamlet. On Easter Sunday it passes through the hamlets of the lower half of the parish (*meia de baixo*), and on Easter Monday those of the upper half (*meia de cima*).

The priest does not enter households in which there are uncastrated male animals (such as pigs, rams, and stallions), for these are considered to be impure. He also does not enter households whose head couple are not married or do not attend church. In this way the parishioners consciously prevent impurity and disorder from entering the 'path of the cross' (*caminho da Cruz*) which unites all the *vizinho* households at this most holy of moments.

The order in which the household visits are made is of particular interest. When the procession leaves a household it does not arbitrarily go to any other household: rather, it proceeds towards the next household *à direita*. The various meanings which the locals attach to this type of motion will become clearer in the process of this discussion. It could be translated as 'to the right (hand)', 'by the right (hand)', or 'on the right (hand)'. None of these translations covers the full meaning of the original. The last seems most appropriate, however, since most uses of the term do not imply movement away towards the right, but movement along the right side of a given path.

If a new household comes into being, it is added to the chain at its approximate geographical placing. If a household dies out or cannot be visited for one of the reasons stated above, it is simply skipped. The important thing is that the procession should not deviate from what the parish residents call 'the path of the *compasso*' (*o caminho do compasso*) or 'the path of the cross' (*o caminho da Cruz*), which is pre-established and is generated in theory by this movement 'on the right'. The movement of the Easter procession between hamlets is also conceived of in the same terms.

The following description of the 1980 Easter visit published by a *vizinho* of Paço in one of the town's two newspapers gives an idea of the atmosphere of boundless joy which is associated with this ritual:

On Sunday the Easter visit took place in the lower half of the parish, and on Monday in the upper half . . . On both Sunday and Monday, in most hamlets of the parish, fireworks were exploded, celebrating the happy and traditional feast of Easter, which is so very *minhota* and Portuguese in spirit. There was no shortage of decorated *folarengo* tables. There were many speeches of commemoration and a great deal of handclapping. The happiness which was experienced during these days brought together young and old in a joyous carefree intimacy.

Perhaps the most outstanding feature of Easter is the mood which takes hold of the local inhabitants. Quarrels are postponed; parsimony, which is such an important feature of local everday life, is thrown overboard; houses are open to all visitors; people greet each other with cries of *Aleluia* and *Boas Festas* (literally, happy feasts). 'Easter is the prettiest season of the year', an old woman told me. During Easter Sunday and Monday, friends eat at each other's houses, sweets and relishes are consumed without second thoughts, and the whole parish, including all individual homes, is decorated with a profusion of flowers. Easter, then, is a rite of integration, a commemoration of rebirth in community and purity.

Figure 6 is a map of the movement of the procession in Paço in terms of hamlets. The movements in Couto and other neighbouring parishes are, to all intents and purposes, the same. Smaller hamlets have been excluded for the sake of simplicity, although they follow much the same pattern.

Looking at Figure 6, we soon realize that, topographically, the movement of the cross between hamlets forms a roughly anticlockwise motion. To make sense of the local residents' statement that they move 'on the right' from household to household and from hamlet to hamlet,

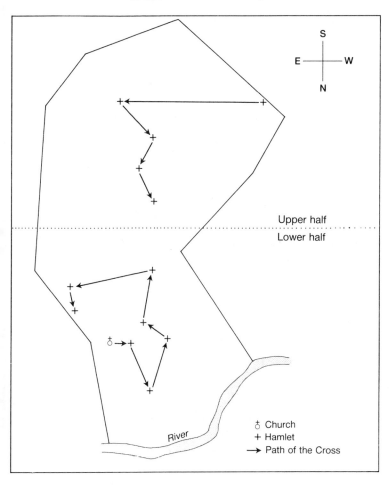

Figure 6. Path of the cross at Easter in Paço.

we have to presume what they do not explicitly state: that unless they constantly direct themselves in relation to a central point, the movement which we observe on the map could not be said to be 'on the right'. Furthermore, a second look at Figure 6 tells us that (predictably enough) this central point must be somewhere in the region of the church. (In the map, the central position of the church may seem less obvious in relation to the movement from hamlet to hamlet in the upper half of the parish. *In loco*, however, this becomes immediately apparent because of the Y-shaped valley which runs along the central part of the parish.)

In general terms, therefore, it could be argued that, when they follow the path of the cross, the neighbours are performing a rotation, that is the 'action of moving round a centre or turning round an axis'. But we must be careful not to interpret this to mean that they are performing a circular motion. The informants were careful to point out that 'it does not matter where the procession ends so long as it follows the path of the cross.'

III

This injunction for movement on the right applies to all processions. On feast days, the priest, accompanied by various symbols of religious power (figures of saints, the consecrated Host, the processional cross) and followed by a large crowd of parishioners, emerges from the church in procession. In the case of pilgrimages, they go to a shrine usually situated on the outskirts of the parish to pray for a special 'favour' or to carry out an annual celebration to the patron saint of that shrine. In normal processions, however, they come out of the church only to re-enter it at the end of a topographically anticlockwise route which encompasses the church and the *cruzeiro* (a large stone cross erected on a square or public place which is never very far from the church, cf. Figure 7).

In the nineteenth century, processions could be extended. This was particularly true of the so-called *cercos* (literally, encirclements or enclosures) of the day of St Sebastian which were practised throughout Minho. These were processions which followed the borders of the whole parish, thus securing it against antisocial forces. In 1872 the Archbishop of Braga banned these *cercos* on the grounds that they were reportedly an occasion for 'profane gatherings' (Pires de Lima, 1948, III: 235). The pressure exerted by the clergy to abolish or shorten the processions is still evident today. In 1979 in Couto the parishioners were enraged because the priest—without whom there cannot be a religious procession—refused to walk the extra hundred yards to the *cruzeiro* and simply walked round the church.

The *minhotos* argue that 'even a child knows' without having to enquire, the direction which any procession will take, as it always moves 'on the right'. If we look at Figure 7, which plots out the path of processions on ordinary feast days in Paço and Couto, we can see that,

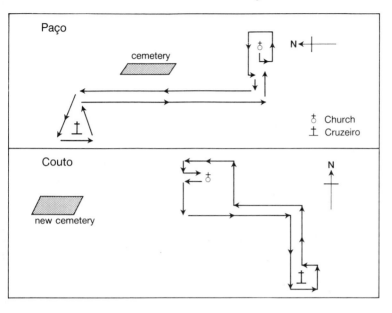

Figure 7. Present-day typical routes of processions.

when the procession emerges from the church, it turns to the left. How then can the people say that it is moving *à direita*? (I repeat, this expression can be used to mean 'on the right', 'by the right', or 'to the right'.) They can only be said to be moving *à direita* if the church is not considered as part of the movement but as a central point of reference. The church is not in the path of the cross or in the path of the processions. These start from the church because that is where the powerful symbols of sacred power, which protect the *vizinhos*, are normally kept. Furthermore, although in this case the motion is in appearance more circular than in the case of the Easter procession, I must remark that I found no evidence that the villagers see it in this way. In fact, the contrary was the case since they use the same injunction here as they do with regard to the path of the cross at Easter: 'it does not matter where the procession finishes, so long as it moves on the right.'

IV

The Easter cross is not the only object which passes from household to household along the 'path of the *compasso*'. In 1974 the priest of Paço and Couto instituted a practice whereby two images of the Holy Family (one for the upper half and another for the lower half) are continuously passed from household to household in the same order as the cross at Easter. This practice is also adhered to in most other parishes of this region, its particular popularity depending largely on the local influence of the priest. In these parishes the system is only half-heartedly followed, but in the parish immediately to the west of Paço it is carefully maintained. Whenever anyone dies the image is taken by the person who has it directly to the mourner's house, where it remains until the end of the funeral rites.

The image is mounted on a money-box. Each *vizinho* household which receives it keeps it next to a lighted oil lamp, places some money in the box beneath it, and recites daily a sequence of Ave Marias and Paternosters in front of it. Should any member of the household desire to ask a special 'favour' from the Holy Family, he or she will do so then. The female household head is in charge of the image from the moment it enters the house. After three days, it is her task to take the image to the neighbours 'on the right'. When each image has made its way round its half-parish it is taken back to the church where the priest empties the contents of the money-box and where it is kept for a few days without any particular ceremony until it starts its movement again.

This system is a good example of the policy which the Church so often follows in relation to the peasant worldview. The cult of the Holy Family is not a local cult with any significant tradition. Its success over recent years is connected with the penetration into rural areas, largely via clerical influence, of the bourgeois attitude which stresses close kinship links as the most elementary form of social identification—the *familia*—in opposition to the peasant conception of the elementary form of social identification as based on joint participation in a household—the *casa*.

By appropriating the peasant concept of a unity of all households along the chain created by the path of the cross at Easter, the priests are deliberately attempting to encourage a change from the peasant conception of the 'household' to that of the 'family', as supported by the bourgeoisie. The church's appropriation of the path of the cross, however, does not imply a compromise but rather an attempt at substituting one conception of the elementary social unit for another— the supercilious attitude of priests towards the maintenance of the correct and 'traditional' paths of the cross clearly exemplifies this (cf. Pina-Cabral, 1981a).

V

Two of the most important parish-wide festivities are the feasts of All Saints (*Todos os Santos*) and All Souls (*Dia dos Finados* or *Dia dos Fiéis Defuntos*) which are celebrated on 1 and 2 November, respectively. The focal points of these festivities are the visits to the cemetery on each of these days. These visits take place in the afternoon and they are absolutely identical, the festivity of All Saints merely being attended by a greater number of people.

After the priest says the Mass (in the afternoon), he announces that 'now, we are going to *sufragar* the souls in purgatory.' (*Sufragar* means 'to vote for', 'to side with', and 'to pray or give alms to the dead'—Taylor, 1958.) He dons his cape and the whole congregation leaves the church through the main door, preceded by the processional cross which is accompanied by two large candles, one on each side. As in all other parish-wide processions (baptismal and funeral processions too) the men go in front and the women behind. The procession goes straight to the cemetery, the cleaning of which has been seen to on the previous day by the Parish Council. During the morning of the day of All Saints, all the female household heads have sent representatives to prepare the graves. Each grave is decorated with candles, oil lamps, flowers, and a little bowl of holy water with a flower in it.

All households send at least one representative on each of these visits. Individuals who were born in another parish or whose parents came from another parish usually attend the first ceremony in their parish of residence and the second in that of their parents. Some people come from afar to be present for at least one of these ceremonies, particularly those whose family graves might otherwise have been left unattended. This visit represents a claim to the rights of neighbourhood. All *vizinho* households must be represented and, if they are not, this means that they abdicate their claims to being accepted as neighbours.

The cemetery is divided in two by the main path which begins at the gate. The two sides are then subdivided into three sections each, by two parallel paths which are perpendicular to the main one. When the priest arrives at the cemetery he recites prayers for the *sufrágio* of the souls in the first section to the right of the gate. He then asperges this section with holy water and moves on to the next section on the right side of the main path where he enacts the same gestures. In this way he goes round the cemetery in an anticlockwise direction from section to section till he arrives at the last section on the left of the gate, from which he leaves. He is said to move *à direita*.

While the priest goes about this routine there is complete silence, but people are in continuous motion. No grave must ever be left unattended by a representative of the family. When the priest blesses the graves in one section all the participating members of the families whose graves are in that section must be there. As soon as he moves to another section, however, representatives are sent to other graves. The visit to a grave at this moment is taken to be a form of 'respect' for the household of the grave one visits. The visit consists of the sprinkling of the grave with holy water by means of the flower which is dipped in it and a quiet muttering of a prayer (usually an Ave Maria and a Paternoster). This visit is taken to mean willingness on behalf of the family of the visitor to engage in or to reinstate a relationship of friendly co-operation. By the time the priest leaves the cemetery, this silent movement is at its peak. It then slowly dwindles as people begin to leave.

The high point of this ceremony is the priest's blessing of the sections of the cemetery. At that moment he is bringing together all the *vizinhos*, dead and alive. It is interesting to note that the word *sufragar* which describes these prayers for the dead can also mean 'to vote for' or 'to side with'. Thus, the living *vizinhos* are sharing their fate and identity with the deceased, with all other *vizinhos*, and especially with those with whom they have a close relationship. Once again, therefore, parish residents are using this motion *à direita* as a means of symbolizing the unity in equality and mutual support which is the ideal of neighbourhood as seen through the perspective of the subsistence prototype (cf. Harris, 1982: 56).

VI

In the late 1960s and early 1970s, paved roads were built in these parishes, which allow motor cars to reach practically all hamlets. Until then, paths were used along which only the sturdy, primitive ox carts could move. A strong distinction, however, was made and is maintained between paths (*caminhos*) and smaller tracks (*carreiros*). Theoretically, the Easter cross should always go along the paths and never along the tracks. Movement along these paths, which join the hamlets to one another and to the church, is conceived of as a motion *a direito* ('straight'—notice the masculine form which distinguishes this expression from *à direita*). Processions, baptisms, weddings, and funerals should not make detours (*desvios*), that is, they should not go along the tracks but only along the paths. In the case of baptismal parties, if they do not follow the correct route, the child's future life will be filled with detours and troubles. In the case of funeral processions, the soul of the deceased would not find its way to the church and cemetery, and would therefore be incapable of entering purgatory. It would thus remain among the living, much to the displeasure of the latter. Finally, most communal activities, such as the collection of money for *festas*, the priest's collection of tithes, the processions, and the pilgrimages had a prescribed route along these *caminhos direitos* (literally, right or straight paths).

Now it is no mere coincidence that the word for 'right' is the same as the word for 'straight'. Hertz argues that

there is nothing to authorise the statement that the Indo-European word for the right first had an exclusively physical connotation; and more recently formed words such as *droit* . . . before being applied to one side of the body, expressed the idea of a force which goes straight to its object, by ways which are normal and certain, in opposition to ways which are tortuous, oblique and abortive. (in Needham, 1973: 11-12)

Furthermore, the same word is used in Portuguese, as in most other Romance languages, for 'right', 'title', 'prerogative', 'law', and 'jurisprudence'. This word is derived from the Latin word *directus* meaning 'straight' or 'direct', which is the participle of the verb *dirigere* meaning 'to direct, drive or guide' (Corominas, 1980).

Both motions *a direito* and *à direita* are seen to be orderly, direct, certain, and right in a moral as well as a pragmatic sense. Moreover, the association of the right side with correct, sacred, male and good, and of the left with wrong, profane, female and evil, with which we are so familiar, is also evident here. (The word for the left is *esquerdo*, etymologically derived from the Basque *esku oker*, meaning 'bent hand, deformed hand', Corominas, 1980.) 'To marry with the left hand', for example, means to take a lover. The rising dough, during the process of bread-making, which is associated with pregnancy, takes its place on the left side of the *maceira*, while the bottle with vinegar (which represents the male aspect) is on the right side.

In this area of Minho most parish churches have only three altars; the most frequent disposition is for an image of the Virgin to be on the altar on the right (God's left, the heraldic sinister) and for an image of the Passion of Christ or of St Sebastian to be on the left altar (God's right). One should enter or leave any place with one's right foot to avoid misfortune. Finally, left-handed people are not feared or especially disliked but left-handedness is strongly discouraged in children and the word used to refer to a left-handed person (*canhôto*) can be used to mean both a clumsy person or gesture and to refer to the Devil. (It can also mean a thick log, which is considered a clumsy thing.)

It is noteworthy that there are no prescriptions or prohibitions associated with movement 'on the left'. This is not because such motions would be too dangerous (for there would be prohibitions against them), but because they are merely inconsequential: moving 'on the left' is like moving in any direction other than 'on the right'. It is seen as purely undirected, arbitrary motion.

When asked about the nature of motion 'on the right', my informants repeatedly stressed three metaphors. First, they compared it to the movement of motor vehicles on the roads; in Portugal these move forward on the right side of the road, *pela direita* (by the right). According to local residents, the movement of traffic is like that of the processions, it has a 'compulsory direction' (*sentido obrigatório*). They pointed out that, when cars did not move in an orderly fashion on the right side of the road, this often led to accidents and death.

Second, the locals are aware that most types of beans (*Phaseolus*) grow upwards around stalks in a genetically determined fashion which plant physiologists call 'positive', that is a helical, upward, anticlockwise movement (Baillaud, 1962). According to my informants the beans' motion 'on the right' was also a 'compulsory direction' which is 'given by Nature' (*dotado pela Natureza*). To them this is a demonstration of the inherent value of motion 'on the right': in its patterns of growth, Nature is in accordance with them.

Finally, they compared the route of the path of the cross at Easter with a screw, which also twists in a helical or spiral anticlockwise fashion.

Another expression used by the locals to describe movement 'on the right' is 'on the side of the hand which sows' (*à mão de semear*). The two expressions are used interchangeably. The interest of this second phrase lies in that it gives us an indication of the way in which the *minhotos* value this type of movement. While sowing is not the only task which is performed by the right hand, it is nevertheless noteworthy for the fact that it must be performed with the right hand. This, the *minhotos* argue, is because the right hand is considered strong and auspicious and therefore suited to carry out such an important gesture as the life-giving act of sowing.

In everyday language, however, this expression has a further meaning: one says that something is *à mão de semear* if it is within easy reach, whatever its position in relation to the speaker. When they classify the movement of the processional cross as 'on the side of the hand which sows', the locals, therefore, are not only claiming that it moves 'on the right' but also that it is the normal, easy, predictable movement to make, and that, like sowing, it is potentially a life-giving act.

VII

We have dealt with a complex variety of concepts and practices which are all linked yet are not outwardly systematized. Formally speaking, the motion *à direita* (on the right) is polythetic, for there is not one feature which is shared by all the examples which I have cited; nevertheless, we can observe a set of features which would appear to be central to the peasants' use of this concept.

Most movements described can be classified as forms of rotation, that is, they are movements 'round a centre'. As such they can be said to postulate a centre, for they presume its existence. At the same time, however, we have evidence to show that this rotation is not conceived of as circular: as with the curling of the beans and the twisting of the screw, in the movement of the processional cross the beginning and the end do not meet. Formally speaking, therefore, we can describe the *minhotos'* prototype of motion *à direita* by comparing it to the images of the anticlockwise helix or spiral moving round a central axis.

Yet greater consistence may be found when we come to specify the values which are attached to all the forms of motion described here. The right hand is associated with order, strength, control, sacredness, and life-giving powers. As these peasants point out, motion 'on the right (hand)', therefore, is a 'compulsory direction', that is, it is the correct motion in the sense that it is socially beneficial; like the 'compulsory direction' of cars, it guards against accidents and misfortune.

At Easter, the neighbours are all united in a chain of purity which is created by this life-giving motion. They are united by means of the cross which, as the priest of these parishes once claimed in a sermon, 'is the flag of the Christians', a symbol of their reception of the life-giving grace of God. Finally, *vizinhos* are united around the social and spiritual centre of their world, which is the church. This spiritual, life-giving unity is the foundation for the experience of community which unites all neighbours. It is on the basis of this spiritual unity that the neighbours can claim that 'here, we are all equal' (*aqui, somos todos iguais*), even though they are quite aware of the differences in wealth, power, and prestige which divide their society.

This 'sameness', which is joyfully experienced by *minhotos* at Easter, and poignantly so on the days of All Saints and All Souls, is matched by a still wider recognition of spiritual 'sameness'. Although the church is seen as the centre of the parish, in its architectural features it does not express the symbolism of the centre, for it is turned towards the east. The east-west symbolism manifests itself in the ordering of the community during religious services, with the women on the west near the door and the consecrated Host, Christ Himself, in the tabernacle on the east.[2] In this way the *minhotos* express a larger experience of community, one which is centred on Christ 'the light of the world' and which unites all Christianity.

13. Friendship and respect

> Mãos que aceitais e não dais,
> Quebradas sejais.
>
> *Minhoto* proverb[3]

The rituals of unity described in the previous section depend on a conception of the parish as a community created by the interrelationship of independent households with equal standing. In fact, this 'obsession with equality' of *minhoto* peasant communities is not limited to ritual circumstances but spills over into daily life. Wealthy families go to great pains to play down their affluence and attitudes of domination and arrogance are openly discouraged by all. As has been the case with many other European ethnographers, my first attempts at acquiring information about differences in wealth, prestige, and local influence in Paço and Couto were confronted by the standard assertion that 'here, we are all equal' (*aqui somos todos iguais*). This seemed inconsistent with the obvious differences of wealth which exist between neighbours. In time, however, I came to understand that this concern with equality is not a superficial and hypocritical recognition of defeat; on the contrary, it is a deeply felt awareness of the identity of all neighbours (*vizinhos*) as members of a parish or a hamlet; a recognition that they are all deemed

---

[2] Most Western churches have been thus orientated ever since the fifth century. (Cf. *New Catholic Encyclopedia* (1967), s.v. orientation of churches; and Hastings, 1918-30: s.v. points of the compass.) This practice has become lax in the Roman Catholic Church since the Second Vatican Council.

[3] 'Hands who accept and do not give,/Broken may you be.'

eligible to compete with one another for a set of communally defined goals.[4]

The theme of 'egalitarianism' is recurrent in southern European and Mediterranean ethnography. J. Davis criticizes its use by anthropologists, saying that 'given the lack of ethnographic detail, it is an open question whether or not the obsession with equality is a secondary phenomenon; thwarted in their attempts to gain dominance, men settle for the next best—"we are all equal": at least they can resist each others' assertions of dominance' (1977: 99). This is tantamount to arguing that cognitive processes have a 'secondary' role in social life—a view which I cannot share. Furthermore, Davis fails to understand that the 'egalitarian' approach to social life is not a matter for each man to decide, but one which is deeply enmeshed in the fabric of a culture.

'Egalitarianism', however, need not mean the same thing in all societies. Albeit pervasive throughout Western Europe, the concern with equality is nevertheless experienced differently according to the type of experience of community of the social group considered. Finally, the belief that 'we are all equal' does not imply a blindness to the existence of actual wealth differences—the example of the Alto Minho clearly demonstrates this.

This chapter will deal with the interrelation between this 'egalitarian' approach and the differences in actual wealth and prestige which characterize peasant society. It was argued above that local society is broadly divided into status groups. Within these, status differences may also exist. For the bourgeoisie, prestige is openly related to material wealth and occupation. This explains the profound concern with appearance, dress, and forms of speech which is a hallmark of Portuguese provincial society. The prestige of moral worth (reputation) is recognized, but it is seen as a luxury. The acquisition and demonstration of prestige based on wealth and social power (status) is the basic measure of success among the provincial bourgeoisie and those who attempt to emulate its life-style.

On the other hand, peasants place a greater stress on equality between individual members of the same status group. For them, the open expression of status differences within the context of neighbourly society is felt as antisocial and thus undesirable. Therefore, among peasants, prestige differences tend to be phrased in the idiom of moral worth, that is, reputation.

[4] A rephrasing of G. M. Foster's statement that 'Every society designates those of its members who are deemed eligible to compete with each other for desired goals, i.e., who are conceptual equals as far as the goal is concerned' (1972: 170).

I

'Equality' may be perceived at different levels and it may also be manipulated. All Christians are equal in some basic sense. Yet this recognition has little practical value. The perception of the 'equality' of the *vizinhos* which is based on a particular experience of community at parish and hamlet levels is far more real. But even this assertion of the 'equality' of *vizinhos* has to be qualified. Landless peasants are placed in an ambiguous position for, in an individual sense, they are *vizinhos*, yet since they do not form permanent households (*casas*), they are not *vizinhos* in the widest sense of the term.

In their everyday conversation the residents of Paço and Couto divide society into three large, sharply defined status groups which are ranked in a scale of ascending prestige. At the bottom, landless peasants, the urban proletariat, but particularly beggars and gypsies are seen as having no relation with the land; as such, they are accused of not knowing how or not wanting to 'work' (*não sabem*, or *não querem trabalhar*). In the middle, the peasantry define themselves in terms of their direct link with the land; theirs is a 'hard life', working the soil. At the top, the *senhores* (the wealthy urban strata) who are said not to 'work', since the concept of 'working' (*trabalhar*) for a peasant applies only to physical labour.

This social division of labour is characterized by a judgement of prestige. Peasant life is not romantically idealized, for 'the work of the land is a dirty thing' (*o trabalho da terra é coisa suja*). *Os senhores* are thought to be unsuited to work. Should one of them insist on working the land, this is appreciated by the peasants, for it 'gives them respect' (*dar respeito*). Nothwithstanding, physical labour is seen as a 'humiliation' or as 'humbling' (*humilhação*) for the urban person. The pride demonstrated by a peasant who feels he has managed to become a member of the bourgeoisie (symbolized in Portugal by a careful manicure) is the other side of the coin of this peasant feeling of status inferiority beside the urban élite.

Even though the 'egalitarianism' of the peasant worldview only applies fully to landed peasants, its maintenance in the face of the wide variations in wealth and prestige which exist within this group must still be explained. Peasants do not deny the existence of differences in wealth, but they prefer not to conceive of their society in terms of these. Thus, they play down all expressions of the permanent existence of any form of stratification. A good example of this is the explanation which is so often given for the existence of poor people and particularly of peasants who have recently lost their land. For their *vizinhos*, these people are poor only because they are lazy and incapable of controlling their desires.

Having asked a local man who the poor people in the parish were, I was told in all seriousness, that 'they are the drunkards.' Rather than a complex set of vested interests, it is man's sinfulness, his incapacity to control his affects, which local residents choose as an explanation for why society does not achieve the ideal perfection of absolute equality. Finally, this process of thought leads to the circuitous logic that a fully responsible member of peasant society cannot fail to have a proper relation with the land, because those who do not have such a relation, are thought not to be fully responsible. This strong link to the land is both what defines a peasant in his own eyes and what most visibly distinguishes the peasant worldview from its urban counterparts.

Visible manifestations of wealth are strongly discouraged among peasants, for they are perceived as antisocial in nature. For example, neighbours are watchful of one another's eating habits. Members of wealthier families confessed to me that their children were taught to be secretive about what they ate at home from a very early age. They do this so as to avoid being called *lambões* (greedy). Similarly, the wealthiest man in Paço continues to dress in old, peasant clothes and wooden clogs so as to avoid his neighbours' 'envy'. Other examples could be cited, such as that of the wealthy upland household which, in the 1940s, would keep secret the fact that the members had time to clean their house thoroughly. Rather, they had to preserve the outward appearances of a normal daily routine so that the neighbours would not think they were too wealthy, thus withdrawing their co-operation and behaving in a jealous and hostile fashion.

Besides self-imposed restrictions, neighbours also enforce restrictions on outward demonstrations of status. For example, a local man who had emigrated to Canada was given an enormous pool-side parasol as part of a promotion in that country. On his return to Paço he had the strange idea of placing it in his yard, thus redefining it—it was no longer a farm-yard but a bourgeois garden. His neighbours answered this provocation with angry ridicule which followed the best of burlesque traditions, so that the beloved yellow parasol was finally torn to pieces.

When questioned about the reasons for their self-imposed restriction on 'visible markers of identity', local residents always give the same explanation: they behave in this way so as to prevent the neighbours from thinking that they are presuming to be different, to be 'rich', or to be bourgeois (*a tomar ares de que é rico* or *de que é senhor*). They do not want neighbours to think this of them because 'the worst evil of this parish is "envy".' A man once told me that 'there are people who are truly envious. These are people who, even if they had all they wanted, and their neighbours were dying of hunger, would not give anything away. Other people, on the contrary, will give away anything they have. But most don't. That is "envy".' He was implying that those who do not give away their property are 'envious'. 'Envy', therefore, is the awareness of wealth differentiation and of its potential capacity to give rise to conflict between neighbours, a conflict which would destroy ideal co-operation and friendly relations.

Parish residents constantly repeat that 'neighbours should be friends,' that is, there should be no open conflicts at the levels of parish and hamlet. An integral aspect of the experience of community which characterizes hamlet life is that relations of neighbourliness are thought of in terms of 'friendship'. This is an important corollary to the subsistence prototype.

'Friendship' (*amizade*), as seen by the *minhotos*, may be characterized as a relationship of co-operation based on equality and 'voluntary' or 'binary' reciprocity.[5] From an early age children are encouraged to develop and maintain friendships. This is a particularly important feature in the education of young boys for, at a later date, it is men who are mainly responsible for the creation and maintenance of inter-household relations. This is a major characteristic of the sexual division of labour which has already been referred to. Female sociability, particularly after marriage, tends to be classified as 'gossip' (*má língua*, literally, evil or bad tongue), while male 'friendships' are encouraged as forms of co-operation essential both to men themselves and to the household. As there are no other forms of institutionalized co-operation at hamlet or parish levels, friendship is the only means of obtaining this.

But friendship has a still larger significance since, as relations of dominance and dependance between *vizinhos* are not openly acknowledged, one's very social identity is defined by it. As local residents put it, 'tell me whom you associate with and I will tell you who are are' (cf. Pitt-Rivers, 1965: 35). A man must have friends or he cannot avoid being cheated, forgotten or simply dismissed.

[5] Pitt-Rivers (1971: 137) utilizes the term 'voluntary reciprocity' to mean reciprocity based on reciprocal service and 'dictated by the mutual agreement of the parties, as opposed to the prescribed reciprocity of ranks.' As I understand it, Marshall Sahlins employs the term 'binary reciprocity' in a similar sense (1972: 194).

II

The essential feature of friendships is that they engender mutual in-debtedness. When a friend asks you for a favour (*favor*) you can afford to help him for you know that, should you in turn ask for something, he will help you. This is what the locals call *confiança* (trust). But *confiança*, they stress, must be tempered by 'respect' (*respeito*) or it leads to abuse.

Reciprocity between friends involves both ceremonial and practical duties. When asked about the former, informants answer that they carry out these duties 'to give respect' (*dar respeito*) to their friends, and that 'these are favours which must be paid back.' The safe continuation of the system of reciprocal co-operation between friends depends on the maintenance of these ceremonial demonstrations of respect; villagers take the fulfilment of these duties as signs of willingness to engage in a relationship of friendship.

These duties consist of joint feasting at Easter and Christmas, of 'kissing the cross' at one's friends' houses at Easter, of attending and helping with baptisms and weddings, but most of all they relate to assistance and attendance at funerals and commemorative masses, to paying for masses for the souls of 'the dead' (*os mortos*) of one's friends' households, and to visiting friends' graves on the days of All Souls and All Saints.

'Respect' implies a form of social contract, inasmuch as others can be said to grant it to you only when they follow the agreed norms of correct and morally acceptable behaviour, but it is only deserved by you if you also follow these same rules. Friends, therefore, should ideally be equally 'respectable'.

Respect, however, can be seen to have two separate meanings. There is one sense in which to 'respect' someone is to acknowledge his or her social identity. In this way different people deserve different types of respect. A man may be respectful towards his father as well as his servant, even although he behaves differently towards each. In this sense one may equally 'fail to grant the respect owed' (*faltar ao respeito a*) either to a servant or a father, if one does not behave towards this person in the way that he or she feels is deserved. Here respect is relative.

But there is a sense in which respect is absolute. One must 'respect' or 'give respect' (*dar respeito*) to people to whom one is indebted. Thus, children should respect their parents, servants their masters, and status inferiors their status superiors. This form of respect is not reciprocated and thus respect turns into prestige. This is why a prestigious man is said to be *respeitado* or *de respeito*.

When peasants use 'respect' in its absolute sense (to mean prestige), they usually stress moral qualities rather than wealth and occupation. The emphasis, therefore, is on reputation and not on status, which is consistent with their conception of all *vizinhos* as status equals. In spite of this, however, wealth differences are clearly related to respectability. In both Paço and Couto, the most 'respected' (*respeitadas*) households are all at least reasonably wealthy, and the least 'respected' are those of people who have drifted from the Middle Wealth group to that of the landless peasantry.

The observable link between respect and wealth is no mere coincidence. Wealthy people are in a better position to observe desirable norms of behaviour and to demand that others follow these forms in relation to them. Concomitantly, as one owes respect to people to whom one is indebted, wealthy households are in a better position to grant 'favours' which cannot easily be repaid, and therefore to accumulate respect. For example, when a poor man needs a cow he may ask a wealthier man to buy it for him and, eventually, when the cow is sold, to share the profits. Strictly speaking, this system is beneficial (even if unevenly so) to both parties. Once the contract is established, however, the poor man is morally indebted (*agradecido*, thankful) to the wealthy man for his 'favour', that is, for having chosen to accept his services rather than those of another poor man (cf. Bourdieu, 1980: 213). Other such 'favours' are lending money, letting a house or a field, and lending foodstuffs and agricultural products during periods of dire need.

To reciprocate these 'favours', it is not sufficient to return what was borrowed (be it a cow, money, or the use of a field), because the favour does not consist of a gift of goods, but of the choice of bestowing the favour upon one person above another. As opposed to the ceremonial favours described above, which are 'favours which must be paid back', these latter favours cannot be 'paid in kind' but must be paid with 'respect'. The former are based on symmetrical reciprocity while the latter are based on asymmetrical reciprocity. Wealthy households, who do not require favours of this kind, therefore increase their prestige.

A shrewd use of the economically advantageous activities open to the locals (particularly emigration) may lead to an increase in the fortunes of a household. Emigrants who return with large gains give rise to a type of household which is wealthy but not yet 'respected'. Upon return from abroad, emigrants and their households go through a period of conspicuous consumption and public demonstration of their economic power. Typically, the members of these households are very sensitive to issues of precedence and they are willing to shout down and 'disrespect' (*desrespeitar*) anyone, even members of the urban élite, at the smallest provocation. They drive their cars along the small streets and winding roads of this hilly region with a complete and often fatal disregard for traffic laws and elementary safety. This behaviour is profoundly resented, not only because it offends the conventions of peasant behaviour, but also because it implies a new claim for 'respect'. By behaving thus, an emigrant is attempting brutally to break with his past position, so that he can move up the unstated, local scale of prestige. Once this is achieved, he can once more accept the normal standards of his community, and it is interesting to note that two or three years after their return to the parish, emigrants generally abandon all this exuberant behaviour. As soon as an emigrant has established his rise in prestige, it is in his own interests to draw less attention to his wealth, in order not to perpetuate feelings of enmity and jealousy among his neighbours, on whom he is once again dependent for co-operation.

III

Kinship links do not play a major role in the relations of co-operation which are established between households. Outside what I have called the localized kin group, households develop links of co-operation and 'friendliness' with particular neighbours. These associations between households usually last for as long as friends are the heads of their households. Friends work and enjoy themselves together. They are called upon at moments of emergency, or for the loan of implements or assistance in the fields during labour-intensive activities. When they go on pilgrimages, to fairs, to *festas*, and for visits to the big cities or the seaside, it is also among friendly households that men and women look for companionship. At baptisms, weddings and funerals, it is to these *casas* that they turn for assistance. Finally, cattle-breeding arrangements are often made with friendly neighbours.

Although relations of 'friendship' are conceptually dyadic, 'friendly' households within hamlets tend to form groups, so that in fact the dyadic relations become subsumed under an unstated form of group allegiance. Once one starts to study the composition of these informal groups of households, one discovers that they tend to include few kinsmen and that the wealth differentials between the households involved are quite significant. In fact, these groups are usually centred around one wealthy household of local prominence, and are also comprised of peasants of average wealth, share-croppers, and even, on the fringes, landless peasants. When they look for marriage partners, wealthy peasants prefer households of equal wealth and prestige. When they look for 'friends', however, they seem markedly to avoid their equals.

An important function of these groups of friendly households is to provide extra labour. During the last two decades, many mechanical labour-saving devices have been introduced, which have considerably reduced labour requirements. Nevertheless, the procuring of extra labour remains a problem which confronts wealthy households. This is particularly true as the introduction of labour-saving devices has been accompanied by a radical reduction in the number of landless labourers and agricultural servants and by an equally radical increase in the salaries earned by these people.

Three methods of acquiring extra labour during peak seasons are open to the local residents; *a vindos*, *a jornal*, and *a favor*. *A vindos* is a system which is no longer practised in Paço and Couto but which survived until approximately the mid-1960s in the upper hamlets of both parishes and which is still employed in certain mountain parishes. This system operates by the co-operation of four or five households for the duration of the entire agricultural year (from Easter to St Michael's Day in September). Labour-intensive tasks are then planned in such a way that all households are equally satisfied. Help, therefore, is not asked for; all know when their assistance is required by the others. (I suspect the etymology of this dialectal word lies precisely here. *A vindos* would then mean, literally, 'by those who come' to one's house.) Similarly, no 'favours' are exchanged since help is strictly paid for in kind.

The *a jornal* system refers to the hiring of labour for a certain wage. The word *jornal* means the labourers' daily wage. This was sometimes paid in products in the past, but now most labourers insist on cash.

Finally, *a favor* is the system which nowadays assumes the greatest significance. Here, the household asks its 'friends' to provide the help required, and it is then expected to reciprocate in labour or in goods and services. (Cash is not used, for it would transform what is seen as a 'favour' into a form of 'employment'.) The reciprocation is proportional to the labour employed but it is not pre-established. People are very conscious of the need to be generous in this, since future help depends on friendly goodwill.

During all communal tasks, the receiving household behaves as a host and all labourers, be they *a jornal* or a *favor*, eat together at the same table, where a good meal is always served. Members of the receiving household are expected to participate in the work, not only to direct the proceedings but also as a token of 'respect' to those who work. These events also provide an occasion for much singing and dancing. Until the mid-1960s, wealthier peasants, who had large groups of people working for them, always made sure that there was someone present with an accordion or a guitar so that everyone could dance and sing during and after the completion of the work. To this day, the jovial atmosphere of these labouring parties is thought to be one of the most 'beautiful' (*bonito*) aspects of peasant life.

The full significance of the *a favor* system does not become clear until one realizes that poor peasants do not require labour from wealthy ones, that most peasants of average wealth employ less labour than they give, and that wealthy peasants can seldom afford, during the peak season, to dispose of the labour resources of their households. In other words, most labour *a favor* is not exchanged for other labour, as the locals would have us believe, but is paid for by other means. In the hamlet where I lived during most of my fieldwork and where I participated in the labour *a favor* system, most payments took place either in goods or in the loan of agricultural implements and facilities, the latter being particularly important. Poor peasants, who cannot afford to buy many of the implements required for agriculture, are dependent on wealthy peasants for the loan of these. Poor peasants often made their wine in the wine-press of the people for whom they provided labour *a favor*. Cattle were lent by the wealthier household to make a pair to enable the poorer household to plough the land. Finally, the poor peasants were also allowed to put their maize or rye in with that of rich farmers who hired mechanized threshers.

As these services are conceptually symmetrical favours, the reciprocation is not treated properly as a payment but as a counter-gift or a counter-'favour'. It is, therefore, informal and temporally irregular. The labour *a favor* can be either the 'favour' or the counter-'favour', and as a matter of fact this distinction is often blurred, as both the labour and the 'favours' are part of a system of reciprocity between two households which, in most cases, is of long standing.

These 'friendships', therefore, which are ceremoniously symmetrical, and which are predominantly based on a system of labour exchange which is outwardly conceived in terms of symmetrical reciprocity, can be seen to enclose a system of asymmetrical reciprocity between poor households, households of average wealth, and wealthy households.

IV

'Friendships' equally conceal a form of low-level patronage, inasmuch as wealthy peasants tend to function as brokers between the parish world and the urban élite. A full discussion of patronage at borough level, due to its complexity and its interrelation with the élite of the cities, would require an independent treatment and cannot find a place here. In general terms, during Salazar's regime, direct patron-client relations between the peasantry and the bourgeoisie tended to be weak. The virtual absence of electoral politics and what Forman and Reigelhaupt (1979) call the 'homogeneity of the élite sector' meant that the emphasis was placed on administrative processes of decision-making rather than on political processes. Local bosses, whose contact with the rural population was minimal, tended to appear in the towns. In a nearby town, a businessman who held the Presidency of the Municipality for the greater part of this period, based his power on two main factors. First, he had an absolute control over all bureaucratic (and even most commercial) employment at town and borough level. Second, he had an alliance with an old aristocratic family which had some land holdings in the borough and members in influential positions among the northern élite based in Oporto. With various vicissitudes, this alliance operated as the only legitimate source of local power right up to 1975, when its power was checked.

Apart from the power of the priest, which will be discussed below, the only officially recognized institution to operate at parish level is the Parish Council. Throughout Salazar's regime, the Council held very little real power and had practically no independent economic resources. As intermediaries between the parish and the town bureaucrats, the Presidents of the Council held a certain amount of prominence. The priest, together with local wealthy households, controlled this institution.

Wealthy peasant households, such as those of the Gomes family, acquire access to borough–and district-level sources of power by means of male children, whom they educate and attempt to raise to bourgeois status. These men either enter the priesthood or take up bureaucratic posts, but they always keep in contact with their rural relations. The Portuguese bourgeois tradition of spending the summer holidays 'in the village' (*na aldeia*) finds its roots in this system.

1. A returned emigrant with his tractor. A shrine to the souls in purgatory can be seen in the background

2. The procession at the *festa* of a rural parish

3. The Easter visit. The meal at one of the hamlets in Paço

4. Votive offerings in the Chapel of Utelinda da Barca

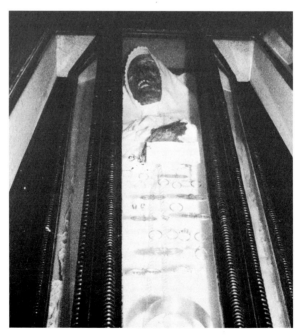

5. Incorrupt body of Utelinda da Barca

Until the 1960s, when their importance declined, seminaries were the main recruiting grounds for a type of provincial intelligentsia which formed the backbone of Salazar's power in the rural areas. Wealthy peasant families prided themselves on having a priest or an educated ex-seminarist amid their relations. Since then, due to the wider accessibility of lay education, to emigration which has brought disposable money into the rural areas, and to the decrease in the prestige and power of the priesthood, the children of wealthy peasants have started to prefer lay education as a means of access to bureaucracy.

In the years which followed the political upheavals of the 1974 Revolution, political mobilization of the rural population in this area by the parties has been effected via the links already existing between wealthy peasant households and members of the provincial bourgeoisie. The local power of these households, which was being eroded by the improvement in fortune which emigration had brought in the 1960s and 1970s, has been somewhat reinforced by the renewed significance of the Parish Council, whose budgets have been greatly increased.

Via their children, siblings, or cousins who are placed in bureaucratic, commercial, or religious positions, wealthy peasants succeed in functioning as brokers to their poorer friends. This allows them to hand out asymmetrical favours, which increases their prestige and the dependence of their neighbours on them. In turn, this dependence assures easy access to labour *a favor* and other forms of local co-operation.

Finally, sexual exploitation by the male heads of wealthy households is frequently encountered. In numerous cases reported to me, this behaviour was directed not only at landless peasant women, but also at the wives of neighbours who had emigrated, and the daughters of poor neighbours. According to local residents, this behaviour is no longer quite as common as it used to be, because 'previously, there was a greater respect for the rich' (*antes havia mais respeito pelos ricos*). Here 'respect' implies domination; it is being used to refer to a form of prestige which is different from that implicit in most other uses of the term *respeito*, for it implies a differentiation based on wealth and power and not on moral worth. Once again we see that the division between prestige based on reputation and prestige based on status is ambiguous and that, behind the apparent concern with 'equality' and symmetrical reciprocity between neighbours, there is an awareness of the actual existence of stratification and of asymmetrical reciprocity at hamlet level. The latter, while still being a form of reciprocity, may be seen in the context of this society, primarily as a form of appropriation of surplus labour and therefore as a 'gentle, hidden exploitation', to use Bourdieu's term (1977: 192). The element of hidden violence which Bourdieu encountered behind such types of exploitation is clear when we consider that, under the banners of 'respect', 'friendship', and 'neighbourliness', wealthy peasants find licence for sexual abuse.

The relations of friendship between poor and wealthy households, however, should be interpreted neither simply as forms of exploitation, nor as simple forms of reciprocity, for they are both at all times.

V

The surge in emigration of the 1960s and 1970s, as well as the increased penetration of local society by State structures, the capitalist sector of the economy, and the mass media, brought about a radical change in working conditions, in the ownership of land, and, consequently, in peasant social differentiation. Many of those who previously had no land could now buy it; those who had been dependent upon wealthy *casas* for wages and favours could now rely on non-agricultural incomes for their livelihood; wealthy farmers were forced to reduce their demands for extra-household labour. This radical change in agricultural working conditions was accompanied by an alteration in the structure of social relations at local level. In Paço and Couto, the national revolution of 1974 which ended Salazar's regime corresponded to a kind of coming out into the open of a situation that had already been in practice since 1969: the marked wealth differentiation of peasant society had crumbled, giving way to new conditions for the ideology of egalitarianism to bloom. Politically speaking, the changes were not very significant at parish level: in Paço, the new President of the Parish Council belongs to a different branch of the family of the deposed one (the Gomes family). But the social relations of labour changed. The forms of 'hidden exploitation' discussed above became less easy to enforce. The symbols of social differentiation became even less permissible. Until 1970, a wealthy farmer did a 'favour' to the landless peasant by allowing him to earn some money by working for him or fattening his cow; he 'gave the work' (*dáva trabalho*). Since then, the situation has been reversed. It is now the labourer that 'gives his work' (*dá o seu trabalho*); he does a good turn to the farmer by working for him instead of another.

In 1978, when I started fieldwork, the egalitarian euphoria resulting from the generous remittances of emigrants was only beginning to cool down. One of the few signs of this was that emigration had become implausible for the young, and the capitalist sector of the economy was not expanding. Since then, the economic situation has steadily deteriorated and there has been a significant decrease in standards of living, which had risen so rapidly during the 1960s and early 1970s. The economic marginalization of peasant agriculture in the 1970s did not imply its social and cognitive marginalization: for the residents of Paço and Couto, to have land and to work it remain the ultimate means of obtaining social security and belonging.

14. Votive offerings and reciprocity with saints

In the previous section I described the relations between neighbours as favouring conceptually a system of symmetrical reciprocity, in the belief that concepts of exchange are integral parts of a worldview and that an understanding of their operation is central to our knowledge of each particular cultural reality. Presently, I shall demonstrate that relations of reciprocity are not limited to humans but that they also extend to relations with the saints,[6] and furthermore that different social groups at different periods in time have adopted divergent systems of exchange with divine beings.

In the past, the nature of these relations has been approached by social anthropologists mostly in terms of their similarity to patron-client relationships (Cutileiro, 1971: 271; Christian, 1972: 44; Foster, 1974; Campbell, 1964: 342). This analogy, however, presents some problems, since secular patronage is by no means uniform and differs from area to area and from period to period. Moreover, although secular patronage played a relatively small role in popular life throughout Salazar's regime, divine patronage was still eagerly procured. I shall look at the relations between humans and saints as though they are based on culturally specific concepts of exchange, which in turn may also be reflected in patron-client relations. This is not necessarily the case, however, for specific systems of patronage are strongly related to the nature of the State, a factor which is largely beyond the control of the rural populations with which this study is primarily concerned.

The most visible evidence of the existence of such relations of exchange between human beings and specific saints are votive offerings.

[6] Throughout, the term 'saint' will be used generically to refer to beings who are the recipients of these offerings that is, the souls in purgatory, the saints, Christ and the Virgin.

These are presented to the saint as thanksgiving for his participation in particular human affairs. These *votos* or *promessas* play a central role in the popular religion of the whole of the north-west of the Iberian peninsula. Traditionally, they have been called ex-votos, which means 'according to what was promised': the believer promises to make a specific offering if the saint meets the specific demand. If the saint, then, makes the 'gift', the human must not fail to pay the counter-gift.

These ex-votos are offered at shrines or churches which are dedicated to a specific saint. Most offerings are exhibited publicly and they are accumulated, hanging on walls or heaped inside display cabinets. The administrators of these shrines or churches are not allowed, without permission from the bishop, to sell or dispose of any ex-votos, with the exception of those which are given in money. In Minho, the accepted practice is for permission to be granted regularly so that the church or shrine may transform these gifts into money. Another means of deriving economic benefit from these pieces is to sell them to other believers. Although most priests deny that this takes place, it is in fact extremely frequent. The sales are usually effected by the sacristan—it is difficult to know whether there is any connivance between the sacristans and the priests. In the sanctuary of Fátima, which receives immense numbers of such gifts, wax pieces are burnt in public. This practice, which previously was not common elsewhere, has now spread to one or two other shrines.

In general terms, these ex-votos are emblems of a successful exchange between the divine being and the individual. For this reason one should not make too strict a distinction between propitiatory offerings (which attempt to please or placate the saint) and thanksgiving offerings. Although the majority of *votos* are votive, that is, thanksgiving offerings, one does find some that were given before the demand of the believer was answered, as a sort of enticement to the saint. The terms ex-voto or votive offering, which I have adopted must, therefore, be understood here in a loose sense to mean a human gift which balances a divine or saintly gift. This classification of votive offerings as 'gifts' is part of the local vocabulary, which uses the same terms to refer to both reciprocal relations among humans and between humans and saints: one 'pays a favour' (*paga um favor*) both to a friend and to a saint.

The objects and actions which may be encountered in use as ex-votos are bewilderingly diverse. No clear-cut classification, therefore, can be made. Tradition carries a great deal of weight, and people do not necessarily apply standards of clarity and integrity to their daily lives. For this reason, they are quite capable of utilizing types of ex-votos which do not best portray their conception of the relationship between saints and men. Nevertheless, in spite of this form of cultural inertia, in Minho there have been broad changes in the types of votive offerings used over the past two centuries and, at the same time, different social strata tend to use different ex-votos. For this reason I feel it worthwhile to make a loose classification into three types which correspond largely to arbitrary divisions in a continuum which extends from a peasant worldview to an élite and 'modern' one.

II

The first type of ex-voto to be examined is at the popular extreme. The most common representatives of this type are the wax figurines present in large quantities in all sanctuaries and shrines of northern Portugal and Galicia. These represent the object, animal, person, or part of the body which has benefited from the action of the saint. They are usually smaller than life-size representations, although life-size ones are also found. Finally, they are either three-dimensional or in high-relief.

The significance of these gifts was underlined by Th. Homolle in his description of similar ex-votos found in Greek and Roman temples. He says that 'ne pouvant offrir le membre lui-même, on en offrait l'image' (Homolle, 1896: 375). The author is thus claiming that there is a metaphorical equivalence between the object affected by the divine being—the saint's gift—and the object given to him—the believer's counter-gift.

The fact that *minhoto* peasants use the same vocabulary to describe the exchange of gifts between friends and between humans and saints suggests that the basis of the exchange with the saint is a form of reciprocity. We have already distinguished between symmetrical and asymmetrical reciprocity. There is a sense in which the relationship between the saint and the human is always necessarily asymmetrical. It stands to reason that the only fully symmetrical counter-gifts to the healing of an arm, for example, would be for the believer to heal the saint's arm or alternatively for his own arm to be cut off and given to the saint, just as Abraham was prepared to sacrifice God's greatest gift, his son. These alternatives, however are clearly not feasible. In practice, therefore, human counter-gifts inevitably lead to an asymmetrical relationship. However, the exchange is symbolically symmetrical, for the counter-gift is made to represent, to stand for, the gift. As in the case of the *a favor* system of acquisition of labour described above, an asymmetrical system of exchange is clothed in the guise of a symmetrical form of reciprocity. By stressing both equality of participation and mutual benefit, this system of exchange leads to an experience of community between humans and saints, such as is ideally present among *vizinhos* and among friends.

This concern is also evident in the attitudes of peasants to saints. Typically, peasants approach saints with a familiarity which is completely foreign to urban people. This is evinced, for example, in the tales and anecdotes describing the adventures of St Peter and Jesus. They are extremely abundant, and play a prominent role in everyday entertainment. They are usually comical, although they always take a moralistic turn at the end. Other examples are the rough treatment received by images of St Antony when the saint is late in providing a marriageable girl with a husband, or the lack of awe and piety which characterizes peasant attitudes towards the relics of saints. Saints are seen as potentially powerful partners whose favour it is useful to have on one's side. The first type of ex-voto described here is a manifestation of the existence and nature of the partnership between humans and saints.

Another kind of gift may be classified within this first type. In the case of the figurines, the equivalence between the gift and the counter-gift is signified by a metaphor. However, the hair of a victim, the dress or bouquet of a bride, the clothes of a child, the crutches of a paralytic, the spectacles of the formerly blind, the huge candles of the same weight or size as the believer, are all metonymic representations of the object or person affected by the saint's action. Not all of the votive offerings in this category are objects. When a soldier who has returned unscathed from the colonial wars crawls around the saint's shrine as he had done somewhere in Africa under the enemy's fire, he is also entering into a symmetrical exchange with the saint: he 'pays back' (as he would put it) for the safety afforded by the saint, by metonymically re-enacting the danger.

In Minho and Galicia, another kind of ex-voto may be found, which was common in the rest of the peninsula until the middle of the nineteenth century, but which is employed only in this region now. This consists of dressing in mourning for a year, or of being carried in a procession inside a coffin wrapped in a shroud. The peasants argue that these practices are compensations to the saint for the saint's abdication of his or her claims to a soul. By performing a false mourning or a false burial, the believers are offering the saint a metonymical representation of their own death. These too, therefore, are symbolic forms of symmetrical reciprocity.

The study of these counter-gifts would be incomplete without a glance at the nature of the original gifts themselves, that is, the 'miracles' or 'favours'. The precise nature of the concept of 'miracle' (*milagre*) is something which has fascinated some of the best minds in European thought; I cannot hope to further this discussion here in any significant way. All I will attempt to do is to classify the changes in the uses of the concept 'miracle' which accompany the changes in the uses of different votive offerings in Minho.

Basically, the concept of 'miracle' presupposes the action of a divine being upon 'this world' (*neste mundo* or alternatively *na terra*). Apart from this basic point, very few other characteristics seem to be shared by different uses of the term. Most learned definitions stress the fact that 'miracles' are 'prodigies' or 'signs of God', and that they break 'the laws of nature'. But these definitions are not satisfactory when we attempt to deal with the peasant use of the concept. St Augustine pointed to this problem when he claimed that 'we say all portents are contrary to nature (*contra naturam*), but we are deceived. For how can that be against nature which is effected by the will of God, the Lord and Maker of all nature?' (quoted in Keller, 1969: 20). Modern scientistic thinking tends to see as absolute the probability of regularity in the eventuation of the world. For the peasants of today, as for St Augustine, philosophical doubt regarding the certainty of the fact, for instance, that the sun will rise on the following day, is a truly lived phenomenon. The sun has risen today because God wanted it to; therefore, if God does not want it to, it will not rise tomorrow.

I think a clear example of this can be seen in the caption of an ex-voto quoted by Rocha Peixoto, in which the believer thanks the Virgin 'for having broken only one leg instead of both' (1906: 201). Considering that his leg was broken because the Virgin allowed it to be, it follows that he must thank her for his not having broken both legs. For the peasants of Minho, therefore, a miracle need not be a prodigy which contradicts 'the laws of nature'. Rather, it is much more loosely defined and much more frequent in occurrence. A 'miracle' can be any event which corresponds to the previously expressed desires of the individual, particularly if these were expressed in the past by means of prayers, promises, and vows.

All forms of reciprocity create a sense of sharing of interests between the partners involved. Different kinds of reciprocity, however, do this in different ways. For the moment we shall deal only with symmetrical reciprocity. This type, while bringing about and maintaining a sharing of interests between equals, does not effect a fusion of interests—throughout the exchange the partners remain separate. In fact, Sahlins (1972: 70) has even argued that the exchange fosters this separation since the obligation to 'pay back' is an essential part of these systems. The rationale behind this ruling is that no partner should benefit from the exchange more than the other, thus implying that they are both equal and separate.

In the case of the first type of ex-voto, by symbolically returning what they had received, the peasants are marking a relationship of co-operation (sharing of interests) between two separate spheres: 'this world' (*este mundo*) and the 'other world' (*o outro mundo*). Each vow is a type of covenant with the divinity, which is why there is such a stress on the dutiful return of the gift of the saint.

Peasants fear that 'the saint may avenge himself' (*o Santo vinga-se*). He can do this by causing other misfortunes, such as an accident; annulling his gift by causing the return of the cured disease; and, finally, preventing the soul of the guilty person from following the normal process of integration into 'the other world' after death. Such a soul remains an *alma penada* (soul in pain), of which more will be said later. It is nevertheless noteworthy that it is not only duties based on a form of symmetrical reciprocity which involves humans and saints, that lead to this punishment if they are not honoured; the souls of those who, at death, leave behind unpaid debts, also remain *penadas*. Symmetrical reciprocity is a central organizing principle in the peasant worldview.

III

Ex-votos not only bear witness to the existence of a relationship of reciprocity; they are also forms of validation of the saint's power. They are hung in public places as testimonies to the past occurrence of divine influence on human affairs. All shrines have their *casa dos milagres* where the faithful may 'season' their faith in the 'proof' of previous demonstrations of the saint's power.

The votive offerings dealt with so far do have a validatory value, but this is a particularly salient feature of the next type: votive paintings and public forms of self-mortification. The former are small painted panels which depict the 'miracle'. As such, they can still be said to correspond to a representation of the gift of the saint. But their role as instruments of symmetrical reciprocity is now subordinated to their role as instruments of validation, as their captions demonstrate. They pay the saint back mainly by confirming his or her power. This implies a change in attitude towards the exchange. While they can still be used as instruments of symmetrical reciprocity, these painted panels may also be used in the context of asymmetrical reciprocity for, if the believer's counter-gift is predominantly that of validating the saint's power, it is intrinsically different from the saint's original gift. A similar argument can be made in relation to public forms of self-mortification, which are payments 'in pain' for the pain that was prevented or stopped, but the purpose of which is mostly forcefully to publicize the saint's gift.

Two types of asymmetrical reciprocity, to which I apply terms coined by Marshall Sahlins, may be distinguished: 'redistribution' and 'generalized reciprocity'. Votive paintings, when they are used in the context of asymmetrical reciprocity, correspond to 'redistribution', that is, a system of reciprocity whereby, on the one hand, gifts flow towards a centre and, on the other hand, other gifts are redistributed downwards. The believer's counter-gift consists predominantly in demonstrating to the world that the saint is *miraculoso* (miraculous). This is thought to increase the saint's prestige and to please him. The captions themselves clearly reveal this intention:

For the memory of the faithful, he had this painting made and put it in His Home for the fervour *doserictamus* [*sic*]. (In Rocha Peixoto, 1906: 204)

So as to immortalize this stupendous prodigy, he had this picture made. (In Rocha Peixato, 1906: 195)

In contrast to symmetrical reciprocity, 'redistribution' presupposes the existence of a group of people unified in a hierarchical or pyramidal relation. Between peasant *vizinhos*, relations of status inequality are not openly acknowledged. Between individual peasants and members of the urban élite, however, relationships are quite openly asymmetrical and hierarchical. The second type of ex-voto is evidence of relations between human beings and saints which more closely approximate those between individual peasants and members of the urban bourgeoisie than those between fellow neighbours. Similarly, in this second type of votive offering, the literate definition of a miracle as an act which contradicts the 'law of nature' is already becoming apparent. The miracle is no longer merely the event by which the saint favours an individual; it is also an event which stands out as somewhat abnormal.

The practice of offering votive paintings seems to have accompanied the development of the bourgeoisie in the Peninsula. The paintings were infrequent before the end of the seventeenth century, and they reached their apogee by the first half of the nineteenth century. At this time, we find votive paintings offered by educated people and also some painted by very distinguished artists. But by the middle of the nineteenth century the bourgeoisie, which was now in power, had moved far from its popular roots, and this type of votive offering, which still implies a vestigial form of symmetrical reciprocity, no longer appealed to its religious feelings. By that time also, the upper bourgeoisie had entered into a close alliance with the Church, and for the Church, with its strong stress on a pyramidal structure, the model of 'redistribution' was the only acceptable one. With decreasing strength, this practice was maintained by the popular strata until the first quarter of the twentieth century.

The offering of votive paintings completely disappeared with the advent of photography, and its accessibility to a wide public at cheap rates. The photographs used for votive purposes, however, differ from the paintings in that they distance themselves even further from the ideal symmetry between gift and counter-gift which characterizes the first type of votive offering. The photographs no longer represent the miracle itself, but rather the person who benefited from its effects or who had prayed for it. Their validatory value has now completely superseded their value as representations of the miracle. Concomitantly, the Church has begun to oppose acts of public self-mortification and has attempted to transform what were public and quite violent manifestations of gratitude into private and subtler manifestations.

In these cases of asymmetrical reciprocity the believer can never fully pay back the original gift of the saint: he is necessarily placing himself in the position of an inferior and as such can only assure the continuation of the relationship (its reciprocal aspect) if there is a fusion of interests.

In order to understand the use of the second type of ex-voto by peasants, we have to take into account a distinction drawn by G. M. Foster (1974) in relation to the attitudes of Mexican peasants to saints: the familiarity between the individual and the saint is so real that it actually changes according to the type of relationship which they have had in the past. A distinction is made between saints to whom one always has recourse, and saints who are approached only if one is in dire need. A frequently heard complaint is that 'household saints perform no miracles.'

A person who appeals to the favours of a saint is said to *apegar-se ao santo* ('to attach onself', 'to adhere to', or 'to stick to' the saint). Peasants have, individually, a number of saints in whom they trust for the solution of their small, everyday problems—from thunderstorms to various bodily ailments. These are usually saints whose images are kept at home or in the parish church or the hamlet shrine. But proximity breeds lack of interest. Thus, for very important problems, it is felt that these local saints are not sufficiently powerful and that recourse must be had to mightier ones. These are usually the cult figures of provincial or even national sanctuaries (such as Fátima). With local saints, peasants always have a relation of symmetrical reciprocity; with the others they establish predominantly relations of asymmetrical reciprocity, characterized by the second type of votive offering.

In this second type we can also include other kinds of offerings, such as portraits of the saint, religious symbols (particularly images of the Sacred Hearts of the Virgin and Jesus), and small written notes which describe the saint's gift. All of these are purely validatory and they all imply a redistributive system of exchange.

IV

Progressively the term 'miracle' has been replaced by the terms *graça* (grace, benevolence) and *mercê* (mercy or benefit). This substitution puts a different emphasis on the exchange, stressing that, in theory, the gift of the saint is being freely given. Furthermore, the use of these terms manifests an unwillingness to use the actual word 'miracle'. These words are less forceful in their implications and they do not suggest the idea of a prodigy. The concepts of 'nature' and the 'laws of nature', which are already employed by the people who tend to offer these ex-votos, clash with the concept of a miracle.

The use of terms such as *graça* and *mercê*, however, only partially resolves the problem implicit in the concept of miracle. This becomes evident in the third type of ex-voto. These can, in fact, hardly be called votive offerings for, according to those who offer them, they are neither directly reciprocal nor directly validatory. They correspond to a conception of the relation between the believer and the divine being (saint or God himself) which is so close and direct that it does not accommodate 'payments'.

The following quotation best exemplifies the attitude of those who share such views. (It is taken from the *Jornal o Tempo*, 12 February 1981, from the column *Pergunta InterDITA* which is supposed to ask well-known people embarrassing questions.) This question was put to Dra Manuela Eanes, the wife of the President of the Republic:

Before the 7th of December, you promised to give your engagement ring to the
Senhor Santo Cristo dos Milagres dos Açores and later you kept your promise.
Was this related to the victory of your husband in the Presidential elections?

This was her reply:

A promise is an act of personal faith which must not be judged, either as to ends
in view or to motivations. It is a very intimate attitude that only concerns the
interior of each person and God. As an expression of faith and as an act of great
authenticity, a promise has nothing to do with superstitions, nor with a business
transaction with God, precisely because the dominant note is this great act of
faith.

We find here what Marshall Sahlins calls 'generalized reciprocity' or
'the solidarity extreme', where the fusion of interests is such that the
very concept of reciprocating a gift is seen as breaking the relationship,
and reciprocity is taken for granted but not specified. God's nature is
perceived as inherently 'giving' and therefore the very idea of repay-
ment is almost shocking.

The objects used in this third type of votive offering—such as objects
of great personal value, candles, and money—are not specific to it and
may be found, with different interpretations, as accompaniments to any
of the other two types of votive offering discussed above. The specificity
of this type lies in the attitude to the counter-gift and to the original
prayer. This attitude is assumed mainly by an educated urban élite
whose emergence accompanied the structural changes which took place
in Portugal during the 1960s. This élite is characterized by liberalization and a smaller emphasis on hierarchy, which is typical of present
Western European social democracies.

V

The differences in the objects offered to the saints are used here as
rough indices of the attitudes of those offering them. Our purpose is to
achieve some understanding of different attitudes to the relationship
between divine power and human life. In many ways, the above
categorization into three types corresponds to W. A. Christian's
classification (1972) of attitudes to religion in Asturias into three
categories which, although temporally defined, can all still be encountered today in conflicting coexistence. A similar coexistence was
encountered here in relation to votive offerings. The first type of ex-
voto, which stresses a kind of symmetrical reciprocity and in which the
relation between the two 'worlds' is one of co-operation and mutual

respect, may be seen to correspond to a pre-Tridentine attitude to religion, with its stress on the experience of community, a strong awareness of sacred space, and a concern with the acquisition of practical benefits for everyday life. The second type of ex-voto is characterized by a relationship of 'redistribution' and of unequal status, where the believer is at the bottom of a pyramid which is topped by God the Father, and it may be seen to correspond to post-Tridentine religion with its strong stress on purity, on individual salvation, and with an authoritarian morality imposed via the services of the Church. Finally, in the third type, we witness a relationship of close identification with the divinity where, as in most cases of 'generalized reciprocity', the very idea of reciprocation is unacceptable. This attitude, which finds its roots in the Second Vatican Council, abolishes the need for intermediaries and stresses instead the need for an interiorization of the moral principles of Christianity. One factor, however, runs through all these three types: external manifestations may change, they may be more or less visible, but the need to bring divine power to bear upon everyday life and the urge to do this by means of a system of exchange, seem to have survived all changes and to apply to all strata in Portuguese society. Finally, the kind of exchange to which people have recourse in their relations to supernatural beings reflects the notions of exchange which are so deeply ingrained at the centre of each worldview.

VI

Underlying the aspects of *minhoto* life dealt with in this chapter is an experience of community which is inextricably linked to a particular ideal image of what peasant life should be like. Spiritual and material well-being are associated with the reproduction and reinstatement of a state of affairs which approaches this ideal image. Previously, it was found that this image was built around a particular conception of the elementary social unit, the *casa*; now it has been shown that equality, friendship, co-operation and symmetrical reciprocity are the principles by which the elementary social unit should be integrated into the social whole. As such, they are integral parts of the subsistence prototype.

V

Coping with evil

The very attachment to the ideal of community and equality enshrined in the subsistence prototype means that *minhoto* peasants are well aware of how far from it their social life is in effect. For them, this failure is not only manifest in the existence of social conflict and inequality, but it is also related to most types of misfortune, which are seen as departures from an ideal state of well-being. Moral evil and the evil of misfortune are deeply interconnected, for they are both aspects of the same thing—they are shortcomings in the ideal life desired by the group. Fertility, wealth, physical well-being are not sufficient, for they have to be set within a social world, one which is characterized by order and which is thus distinguishable from the animal world. By 'order' I mean the capacity to control, so as to predict and to fit reality to a set of shared goals.

Thus, the problem of explaining how people believe in the efficacy of 'magic' is a false one. Wittgenstein, commenting on Frazer, says: 'Burning in effigy. Kissing the picture of a loved one. This is obviously *not* based on a belief that it will have a definite effect on the object which the picture represents. It aims at some satisfaction and it achieves it. Or rather, it does not *aim* at anything; we act in this way and then feel satisfied' (1982: 4e). When people ask for rain just before it is bound to come, they are not committing an 'error', they are rather addressing the unitary nature of their image of life. They do not simply require rain, they require a 'blessed' rain; one that comes in due course and for a certain duration.

Indeed, the Christian concept of 'blessing' is perfectly apposite here. Blessings may be *invocative*, when God's favour is asked for someone or for the good use of something, or *constitutive*, when someone or something is dedicated to holy service. They are usually accompanied by a purificatory gesture: the sprinkling of holy water. We see here too an association of moral good with material good. But the illuminating nature of the concept lies particularly in a further set of associations, that of order, correct use, holy service, and purification. Blessing, then, is an act of communication (for it may be both to God and from God) which attempts to institute the ideal life—thus the material benefits therein are inextricably associated with the spiritual benefits, for they are one. In this way, we may understand why the Catholic Church only allows its blessings to be given to non-Catholics in order for them to ask for the gift of faith or, together with it, health. A non-Catholic cannot ask for a material benefit as he lacks its essential correlate, the spiritual benefit of faith.

15. Envy

I

This chapter deals with the way the *minhotos* perceive the existence of evil in their midst and the means they use to cope with it. I have already referred to conflict between households. This may be very bitter and last for a long time without coming out into the open. People are not eager to express openly their enmity to others. Thus they often employ sly acts of aggression for which they cannot easily be blamed. For example, some residents of Paço and Couto have been known to pick green grapes off the pergolas every time they pass an enemy's field so that his harvest will be reduced; they may throw stones from their field to the next man's; or they may deflect the course of the water which the enemy uses for irrigation. There is a name for this: *desgaste*, that is, to wear away one's enemy's patience. In most cases these enmities are mutual, although sometimes a *vizinho* may remain unaware for quite a while of precisely who 'wishes him evil' (*quer mal*).

A person whose economic position or whose prestige has increased considerably over a short period of time often takes this opportunity to bring such a conflict into the open. Returned emigrants, and particularly their wives who often remained behind and possibly suffered economic hardships or personal slights during the husband's absence, are known to engage in this sort of action. They are called *justiceiras* because they take the smallest complaint to court. Their newly found wealth allows them to arrange for witnesses and, if necessary, to bribe the court officials, lawyers, police, and preferably (if possible) the judges. In this way, they harm their enemies while being able to claim that they were justified in doing so.

Conflict between informal groups of friends, as described in the last section, is also common. Conflict between households often takes this form, particularly when the fight is between wealthy peasant households who form the core of different groups of friends. These groups of friends are especially useful when the case is taken to court, for it is among the households of one's friends that one looks for witnesses, for economic support, and for contacts with bureaucrats and officials.

In order to explain the existence of conflict in their midst, as well as that of many other types of misfortune, the *minhotos* invariably refer to the concept of 'envy' (*inveja*). Considering the strength of feeling attached to it, as well as the frequency with which it is invoked, it could be argued that this is one of the central concepts of the peasant worldview.

II

According to an informant, the following is the thought process of an 'envious' person: 'I worked as hard as or even harder than him. I was very parsimonious. Why did I not earn as much as he did?' But it is not only 'losers' who are accused of 'envy' because 'envy is the worst crime of this parish. People are very envious, they couldn't be more so. If you live well, they look at you askance; if you live badly, they say "he lost everything, he is a bad manager".' Envious people 'are all evil inside. They have the poison hidden in them.' 'Envy', then, is harmful and is related to awareness of differences in wealth and fortune. Typically, rich people are accused of not being generous, of 'wanting everything for themselves', and thus of being 'envious', while the 'envy' of poor people manifests itself in their wanting what belongs to others. Concomitantly, there is a vague awareness that the accusation that others are 'envious' presupposes the recognition of a real reason for this 'envy'. Everyone has an uneasy feeling about 'envy'; it is a shortcoming which befalls the whole society. People may say that they do not know whether or not they suffer from it, but they cannot positively claim not to.

We must be wary of interpreting what the rural *minhotos* call 'envy' (*inveja*) by resorting to the English or the Portuguese bourgeois concept of envy as an emotion. Envy as an emotion is only one aspect of the term *inveja* as used by the inhabitants of Paço and Couto. Indeed, this was something which made it difficult for me at first to understand the concept. 'Envy' for a *minhoto* is a principle of evil, an uncontrollable and unpredictable force existing in society, a basic reason why humans cannot create the perfect society in this fallen world. In opposition to envy as an emotion, it does not exist purely within the person who experiences it, but rather as a relationship between the person who generates it and the person who suffers its effects.

As opposed to other regions of northern Iberia, where misfortune caused by envy is predominantly blamed on outsiders (cf. Cátedra

Tomás, 1976), in the Alto Minho it is generally blamed on other residents of one's hamlet. Until recently, it was common for members of households to recite the rosary together in the evening. Each group of ten Ave Marias was accompanied by one Paternoster, which was always dedicated to a specific cause. In Paço and Couto, most households used to dedicate one of these to 'the enemy near the door', i.e., the *inveja* of their neighbours.

This expression is particularly interesting because it demonstrates a connection between *inveja* and the Devil—*o Inimigo* (the Enemy). This connection is further supported by the well-known proverb which claims that 'the Devil is the father of envy.' Furthermore, the reason why women turn into witches is also said to be *inveja*; and, if a woman is accused of being a witch, she should not be antagonized because witches kill those whom they 'envy'. Indeed, it is not only witches who do this, but also women who 'wish evil' on others.

The existence of *inveja*—an emotion *and* a force—is a concept which the bourgeoisie finds increasingly difficult to understand. The priest of Paço and Couto was encouraged, in a conversation with some of his colleagues, to attempt to show his parishioners that their conception of 'envy' was incorrect.

My observation was that he found it impossible to do so for two reasons: first, as a native of the region, he himself could not fully understand envy as an emotion only, and was therefore incapable of creating a consistent distinction between it and *inveja*; second, as the term used for both concepts is the same, the peasants simply claimed that he did not know what he was talking about for 'can't one see all about the effect of the envy of these malicious people?' They argue that 'envy' is one of the major causes of misfortune; if misfortune occurs, surely 'envy' must exist.

As a profoundly death-dealing, antisocial force, *inveja* is a dangerous tool to use. Although it is more harmful to its victims, its effects are also felt by those who are 'envious'. Thus, local residents argue that 'envious' people are usually thin, sinewy, and wan. While healthy people are said to *medrar* (thrive), 'envious people have a poison in them.' Similar symptoms may be seen in people who, although not suffering from *inveja*, remain with a very strong desire or craving unsatisfied. Such people, usually children, are said to be *augados*. In both instances, people who lack control over their desires suffer, as a result, from a serious diminution in their life force, possibly even leading to death.

'Envy' operates in many different ways. We have already commented on its relationship to inequality and on how this leads to actions of conflict, usually of an underhand type: *o desgaste*. A second way in which 'envy' may manifest itself is in gossip: *falar mal* or *dizer mal* (to speak or say evil) or *má língua* (evil tongue).

Women in particular are said to be 'gossip-mongers'. Because of the 'evil will' which is caused by their *invejedade*, they are believed to have recourse to gossip as a means of harming other people. (The word *invejedade* is specific to local parlance and is best translated as 'enviousness'. It can be used as a synonym for *inveja* in the sense of envy as an emotion but not in the sense of envy as a spiritual force. While using it, people are not fully aware that they are making a distinction.)

A third way in which envy may be expressed is by means of *feitiço* (sorcery). Although neighbours seldom admit to having been party to its use, evidence that this means of harming others is utilized can occasionally be found in the form of remains of the ritual actions involved.

The word *feitiço* applies to preparations and incantations which are believed to have a definite and negative or evil effect on the future course of events. As such it is practically impossible to acquire definite information about it, for neighbours do not want to be known for having knowledge which might be used in this antisocial way. Most of the information required for the practice of feitiço is acquired from the *Book of St Cyprian*, a renowned treatise on sorcery, yet no one admits to owning a copy, for it would automatically imply that they had the intention of using it.

Love potions have great local currency. They are used extensively by young unmarried women and married women alike, both to win the love of young men and to preserve that of their husbands. When men claim that women *enfeitiçam* (bewitch), they mean it both metaphorically and literally.

A young man of Couto returned from France suffering from pains in his stomach. Recalling that a young woman whom he had dated had given him an item of food which she had put aside especially for him—and perhaps feeling guilty for having deserted her—he decided that with it she had given him *feitiço*. He went to a white witch who confirmed the diagnosis and administered a purgative. This made him feel better and furthermore 'proved' his suspicions because his faeces contained hairs, a sign that he had eaten *feitiço*. The purgative used is available at the town pharmacies at a very low cost and many people take it without consulting a white witch.

Feitiço may be used to attack a neighbour's cow, hay, produce, and even health. One of the most common means of casting a *feitiço* is by lighting a *defumadouro*, a broken piece of earthenware on which various herbs purported to have special powers are burnt. When performed with a piece of clothing which belongs to the proposed victim and which has been in contact with his flesh, it is supposed to have dire effects. This is particularly true if one lights a *defumadouro* at a crossroads, if one casts the ashes into the sea, or if one lights it at the *Horas Abertas* (open hours), which are midnight, noon, and sunset, when the bells chime for prayers at the end of the working day (*Trindades*). Crossroads, the sea, and 'open hours' all have in common the fact that they are seen as openings to outside forces and influences. The *feitiço* thus cast is therefore believed to be lost beyond recovery. This is particularly important, for the way to invalidate a *feitiço* is to recover it and to cast it into the sea. *Defumadouros* may also be used as counter-*feitiço*. If, however, the original *feitiço* had been a *defumadouro* which had been lit at a crossroads or thrown into the sea, the likelihood of recovering it would be nil, and it would be impossible to stop its effects.

Not all *feitiço* is effective, for 'it may not take.' *Vizinhos* who suspect a neighbour, therefore, use a small amulet which can be bought at fairs and which is hung around the neck. This is called an Agnus Dei and it consists of a heart made of two parts so as to form a locket which contains a piece of blessed wax inside. (A woman once told me she was not certain but thought that the thing inside was a piece of the Host.) By using these charms, people are enclosing themselves within the life-giving, protective powers of Christ and are thus avoiding the effects of evil; as they put it: 'the Devil does not accompany whoever wears this thing.'

Finally, 'envy' may be manifested in *pragas* (curses), which may at times also be referred to as *feitiço*. A curse is the expression of the desire for a specific misfortune to befall another person. As opposed to *feitiços*, curses must be handled with extreme care for they can easily fall back on the person who casts them and their power increases according to the conditions under which they are cast. Peasants say: 'A justified curse, I wouldn't wish it on my dog's tail,' for such curses are thought to be certain to take effect.

Although the motivation for curses is still 'envy', there is a sense in which they are moral, particularly as, if one casts a curse on an innocent person, the curse will be returned. The most efficient *pragas* are those which are cast during Mass. In the period between the elevation of the chalice and the Host the person must say: 'I bind so-and-so by his (or her) feet and hands.' An informant once told me that to do this 'is the greatest sin, because that moment represents the time when Our Lord shed all his blood for us. These are very dangerous things.' When using *feitiços*, the *minhotos* are manipulating an evil force as a means of causing damage to their neighbours. However, in using *pragas*, they are laying hold of a basically good force for their own lowly desires. This explains why curses work only when they are justified, why they misfire when they are unjust, and why they are more powerful when issuing from people whose power over the victim is morally vindicated, such as priests and parents.

III

Perhaps the most important manifestation of 'envy', however, is the evil eye. The expression *mau olhado* (evil gaze) is not the most common means of referring to this concept. The residents of Paço and Couto prefer the verb *tolher* which describes the action of the evil eye on the victim, and which otherwise means 'to hinder, hamper, impede, bar, restrain, prevent, paralyse, or cramp' (Taylor, 1958). The distinction between the evil eye and *inveja*, furthermore, is not clear-cut. This is something which other ethnographers of northern Iberia have pointed out (e.g. Cátedra Tomás, 1976: 12). Lisón Tolosana distinguishes between the evil eye and other means of causing harm by envy (1973: 830). I shall not do so, however, for the *minhotos* use the same terms to refer to both phenomena. Apart from *tolher*, other words used to refer to the capacity of others to harm people by causing sickness, general misfortune, and accidents are again *feitiço*, *bruxedo* (the action of witches), *mal d'inveja* (envy's sickness), *enguiço* (evil eye, bad luck, mishap). Finally, the word *inveja* itself competes with the word *tolher* to mean harm caused by 'envy' transmitted mainly via the eyes. People who *tolhem* are thought to have such a 'strong gaze' that if they look at clothing which is hung outside for bleaching, the cloth will tear.

Once again most accusations of *inveja* or *tolher* are directed at neighbours and especially at neighbours in the same hamlet. Furthermore, women are accused of this more frequently than men, although the latter are not exempt from blame for causing misfortune in this way.[1] Nevertheless, it is claimed that female 'envy' is more powerful

---

[1] This calls our attention once again to the different assignation of gender roles to that found in the south of the Iberian peninsula, where only women can cause misfortune through envy. (Cf. Pitt-Rivers, 1971: 183, and Cutileiro, 1971: 276).

than that of men. This stress on the association of 'envy' with femaleness explains why male genitalia and articles of clothing which are specifically male (such as hats and trousers) are particularly endowed with the power to protect from the evil eye and other *coisas más*. This is one reason, for example, why men's trousers may be put on the cradle of an unbaptized child as an alternative to scissors.

The following story illustrates the form which most accusations take, and how the neighbours view this dreadful force. A woman of the hamlet in which I lived had a milch-cow. This cow was pregnant and, as is to be expected, stopped lactating as the time approached for the calf to be born. The day before the milk dried up, a certain female neighbour had come to ask this woman whether she would give her some milk. The woman, however, had to refuse since she was already providing three other persons with milk, and she would have none left for her own household's consumption. When the cow stopped lactating quite abruptly, she immediately decided that this was due to the *inveja* of the female neighbour. On hearing this, I pointed out to her that in any case the cow was due to stop producing milk at any moment. She answered that this was true, but that the milk might well have lasted a few days longer. In any event, she said, the milk had dried up abruptly, which need not necessarily have happened.

The female neighbour who was accused of having *tolhido* the cow is famed for her evil eye. She is an old and poor woman who is particularly bitter and quarrelsome. The residents of the hamlet are afraid of her. When the *vizinhos* go to the fair on Wednesdays with their produce, they always avoid her. If they happen to see her before departing, they are immediately convinced that they may as well remain at home because their produce will not sell at good prices, if indeed it sells at all.

When I questioned the veracity of the claim that this poor woman had the evil eye, I was told that there was no element of doubt in this, for it had been tested. Two women were planting potatoes one day when the 'envious' neighbour approached them. She leaned against a wall chatting to them as they continued with their task. The women say that she praised their seed potatoes saying: 'God willing, the harvest will be plentiful because your seed potatoes are very good.' They did not trust her and, when she left, they stuck two sticks in the ground to mark the area which had been planted in her presence. At harvest time they were only too pleased to discover that that area had produced less than other parts of the field.

It is interesting to note that this woman's position within the hamlet is rather ambiguous. She and her husband are poor but they have some land of their own, and their son is doing well in France. Although her sisters are unmarried landless labourers, she managed to marry a man with a little land. She also does not suffer gladly the small but systematic acts of exploitation and high-handedness of wealthier neighbours, about which she always complains loudly. Finally, her hamlet is roughly divided into three large groups of friends which are centred around three wealthier households; she and her husband, however, managed to remain on the periphery of two of these without ever taking sides.

Whatever the actual reasons for this woman's reputation are, her hamlet neighbours blame it on her 'envy'. One informant told me that perhaps she was born that way, others denied this, saying that she acquired it.

The capacity to *tolher* may be something which a person acquires quite innocently before birth, if the expectant mother turns back during the elevation of the Host, or if her cravings for food remain unsatisfied. Although these two forms of behaviour are metaphorically related to 'envy' (see p. 106 above) they are not directly so and the result is that some people may be feared for their gaze even though they may not be accused of experiencing actual *inveja*. The *minhotos* do not have a special name for this type of congenital evil eye.

People who acquire a reputation for suffering from the congenital evil eye are not necessarily looked down upon for it. Among them, the proportion of men to women is greater than among those who are accused of *tolher* due to malice, where women are predominant. Furthermore, in my experience, the majority of those who are said to have the congenital evil eye are wealthy people. This contrasts with the otherwise dominant imputation of the evil eye to poor people. Those of whom I heard, and with whose life histories I was acquainted, were people who had undergone a very rapid increase in prestige and wealth, often due to a successful marriage.

Ultimately, however, the blame for misfortune on 'envy' was reasserted, since *minhotos* claim that there are means whereby people with the congenital evil eye can avoid causing harm. Thus, if a person who suffers from this 'disease' actually does harm somebody, it is completely his fault for not having 'purified' his vision in the morning, for example by looking through a piece of glass immediately upon waking up. This lapse his neighbours then attribute to 'envy'.

IV

The gaze which transmits 'envy', is said to be 'evil' (*mau* or *ruim*) for it causes misfortune. We have already referred to the fact that gossip is named 'evil tongue' (*má língua*). Similarly, in the Alto Minho, people sometimes refer to the 'evil air' (*mau ar* or *ar ruim*). The residents of Paço and Couto are very imprecise in their use of this last expression. In general terms it may be said that this 'air' is the vehicle by which evil can be transmitted. A man whose sexual potency had waned after being attacked by witches, consulted a white witch who performed on him a ceremony which was described to me as 'cutting the air' (*cortar o ar*). (The verb 'to cut' is often used to describe an attempt to separate an evil force or a disease from a person.) Unbaptized children are very susceptible to attacks from this 'evil air', particularly if they are out during the 'open hours'.

All evil is ultimately related to the Devil. The Devil himself may appear in various guises, usually as an animal (a sow with piglets or a wolf). Other apparitions, such as a man the size of a tree, or a woman whom no one recognizes and who appears on different stretches of the road and then disappears on others, are also somehow related to the Devil. These apparitions are labelled *coisas más* or *coisas ruins* (evil things) as are all other antisocial phenomena which give rise to misfortune, such as gossip, the evil eye, the evil air, witches, werewolves, ghosts, and souls in pain.

Different *coisas más* demand different counteractive measures, yet the distinction between therapeutic and prophylactic measures is not always clear. Moreover, not all attempts at protecting oneself and one's household from these forces are of a mystical nature; people also take practical measures to avoid them. For example, if a certain stretch of road is known to be haunted. One avoids using it at night; if a neighbour is known to have the evil eye, one raises the wall of one's farmyard; finally, if the sight of women in mourning causes the market day to be unsuccessful (because of their supposed 'envy') one leaves home before sunrise so as to avoid them.

Therapeutic measures, as a rule, demand the intervention of a specialist, be it a priest or a white witch. We shall discuss these later. Prophylactic measures are usually individual decisions and the person has recourse to a store of symbols and practices which are common knowledge.

To protect oneself against the evil eye, witches, or *feitiço*, one may use a *figa* (clenched fist with the thumb clasped between the fore and middle fingers) made with the left hand, or a flowering *alho porro* (leek) which has been stolen during St John's night. One may also use a seal of Solomon, a horseshoe with the points turned upwards, a branch of an olive tree or one of shepherd's purse (*bucho*). If these branches were blessed on Palm Sunday, their efficacy in frightening away the *coisas más* is even greater.

Many other prophylactic and therapeutic instruments are objects which form part of orthodox Catholic ceremonial and which refer either to the Passion of Christ or to his transubstantiation in the Eucharist. This is the case of the Agnus Dei pendants described above, of the fragments of altar stone, the keys to the tabernacle, and the tassels of the maniple.

There is one symbol, however, which towers above all others, due to its power and to the frequency with which it is encountered: the sign of the cross. If they are confronted with any surprise or sudden cause for anxiety, fear, or awe, the peasants always 'make the sign of the cross' and may even exclaim: 'Cruzes, Cristo!' (literally, Crosses, Christ!). In the Alto Minho, one often finds crosses on hill or mountain tops; next to the churches, at the centre of the parish, are the *cruzeiros*; along the ascent to shrines, a sequence of crosses commemorating the Passion of Christ is almost always encountered; crosses are placed on top of churches; and finally, along the road, wherever anyone has met a sudden death, there will be a stone or iron cross to commemorate this and to help the deceased through the struggles of the afterlife. Most of these are Latin crosses, whose vertical axis is longer than the horizontal one, and they are direct references to the Holy Cross (*O Santo Lenho*).

But Latin crosses by no means form the majority of crosses that may be found in this area. The equilateral (Greek) cross is seldom placed in institutionally recognized surroundings, yet it is generally far more frequent. It is roughly painted or scratched on walls, roadsides, stables, granaries, chairs, tables, tools, doors, doorways, trees, water tanks, corners of houses, ovens, etc. When the bread is rising it is marked with an equilateral cross, and the portion of dough which is left over for the next batch of bread is also protected in this way.

The adoption of the equilateral cross is not simply a reference to Christ's death, for people mix orthodox Christian symbolism with what the church would consider to be 'pagan' beliefs. The use of the cross with one meaning does not imply the negation of others. The function of these equilateral crosses is to scare away *coisa má*. The crosses may be placed at strategic points so as to forestall the potential attack of these antisocial forces, but many which are found at odd places on walls and in streets were painted or scratched there on the spur of the moment by some person gripped by fear (usually at night).

The following dream, recounted to me by a local man, clarifies the use which locals make of the equilateral cross. In the dream, he found himself near a disused chapel. There he saw a strange, tall, bearded, and very frightening man. He tried to make the sign of the cross or to draw a cross on a wall but he did not succeed in doing so. He could not speak either. When he woke up in a cold sweat, he found that in his sleep he had pressed the side of one hand against the palm of the other so as to form a cross.

The cross is also used to represent human presence. A person who cannot sign his name draws a cross on the page. When a person wants to indicate to another that he has been at a certain spot, he draws a cross. When the Portuguese sailors in the fifteenth and sixteenth centuries discovered a new country, they erected a cross. In this way they were taking possession of the land and, at the same time, consecrating it. By virtue of this consecration, however, they were, so to speak, 'creating a new land' (Éliade, 1961: 32). Similarly, the *minhotos* who use the sign of the cross are consecrating their world. As Éliade points out, '*if the world is to be lived in*, it must be *founded*—and no world can come to birth in the chaos of homogeneity and relativity of profane space. This discovery or projection of a fixed point—the centre—is equivalent to the creation of the world' (1961: 22).

In a less metaphysical tone, and employing the happy expression of the priest of Paço and Couto, we may argue that peasants utilize the Cross as the 'flag of the Christians', that is, as a means of demarcating sanctified or blessed space, in opposition to an unsanctified, chaotic space. Moreover, once again the failure to distinguish clearly between moral and practical good and evil is evident: sanctified space is also socially beneficial space. In one sense, all inhabited—and even most uninhabited—land in Minho is permanently sanctified, thanks to the Easter procession which was described above, and to the sacred symbols such as crosses, chapels, and shrines placed at strategic spots throughout the landscape. But a battle is continually being waged between the forces of good and evil. Furthermore, sanctified space has gaps in it such as crossroads, or the 'open hours'. Mostly, however, these gaps are due to man's ineradicably evil nature, the major evidence of which is 'envy'.

The *minhotos* attempt to close these gaps by having recourse to Christ's redeeming death which, in any case, was the condition for the existence of a socially beneficial space in this fallen world. At the moment of His death, Christ endowed humanity with God's grace and therefore made it possible for humans to be Christians and to avail themselves of the powers of the social and individual, spiritual and physical life which the grace of God allows.

As we have seen, fertility and all other manifestations of physical life are desired but are also feared, for they lead to social chaos. It is by controlling physical life that the peasant can achieve that greater ideal: reproduction in purity, controlled fertility, life in its widest sense. The cross creates the socially beneficial space wherein that process may occur.

V

In his cross-cultural statistical study of belief in the evil eye, J. M. Roberts comes to the conclusion that 'social inequality is probably a precondition to any elaboration of the evil eye' (1976: 261). While this may certainly be the case, the concern with 'envy' and the evil eye encountered in the Alto Minho is strongly dependent on the existence of an egalitarian ideology. Maria Cátedra makes a similar point when she claims that among the Vaqueiros of Asturias, it seems as if 'the eyes'— envy—come into play when those who should be equal are found to be different. In other words, ' "the eyes" appear to be a characteristic of a group which, ideologically, tends towards economic, social and sexual equality in an attempt to reinforce it' (1976: 43). A person who accepts that another is his rightful superior does not envy him. This explains why accusations of 'envy' do not fall on bourgeois people, since peasants accept the existence of differences between themselves and members of the bourgeoisie as part of the natural order of things. Peasant society is riddled with 'envy' because it sees itself as egalitarian while at the same time being obliged to admit that it does not achieve this ideal.

16. Bruxos

In spite of all preventative measures, misfortune is unavoidable. Things do go wrong, and people require means of coping with this. I shall not repeat here Evans-Pritchard's famous example of the Azande granary (1937: 69–70). Suffice it to say that even when people know *how* things went wrong, they often still require an explanation as to *why* they did so. That is, a moral explanation for misfortune—such as is provided by 'envy'—is required. In this section, I shall consider some of the therapeutic means which *minhotos* use in order to explain and cope with evil. Central to these is the figure of the white witch, to which people in the borough of Ponte da Barca usually refer by the depreciatory term of *bruxa*.

I

Over the past fifty years, previously unavailable technical means of coping with sickness and accidents have become accessible to the rural population. Weak as they are, health services are already available and veterinary surgeons and agricultural technicians are starting to make an imprint on local society as providing useful means of coping with specific types of misfortune. Furthermore, misfortune in the form of social conflict also has a technical solution—the courts of law. In less isolated areas of this province (such as the parishes described here), the use of courts of law as a means of resolving social conflict is disliked but is nevertheless a time–honoured practice (cf. Coutinho, n.d.). Other specialists have been available to rural *minhotos* for an even longer time, such as the pharmacist, the (untrained) midwife, the bone-setter, and the *entendidos das vacas* (literally, those who understand cows). Before the Second World War, blacksmiths were also held to have a special ability to cure wounds. Finally, saints and their ex-votos also have an important position as assistants in times of misfortune.

Confronted with specific misfortune, peasants usually have recourse to more than one of these. For example, if a child falls ill, its parents take it to the doctor; modify the doctor's prescription according to the advice of the pharmacist; promise an ex-voto to a saint; and finally, consult a white witch to know whether the neighbours are casting the evil eye or whether the child is *augado*.

Two attitudes explain this multiplication of specialists. First, although the practical means of curing the disease may be readily available (as, for example, in the case of a local infection) peasants believe that the cure may still not take effect if the moral reasons for the ailment are not dealt with (such as, for example, *feitiço*). Second, as was argued with regard to the concept of 'miracle', *minhoto* peasants do not share the scientistic, mechanistic views of cause and effect of the 'educated' bourgeoisie. There is no conception of necessity in the outcome of events, no concept of 'laws of nature'. This is particularly true of complex chains of events, the precise mechanism of which peasants do not fully command. The medication prescribed by both doctors and white witches has a chance of being successful, but neither of them has an absolute control over future events and therefore neither is fully reliable. By using more than one approach in attempting to resolve a specific misfortune, peasants expect their chances of success to increase.

Certain specialists, however, are more efficient at solving certain types of problems than others. If you suspect your child of being *augado*, you do not go to the priest who denies the existence of such things, but rather to a white witch. Peasants distinguish between, on the one hand, *doenças de cá* (literally, sicknesses of here) or *doenças de médico* (doctor's sicknesses), and, on the other hand, *doenças da lá* (literally, sicknesses of there), or *doenças que não são de médico* (sicknesses which are not for the doctor).

Some physical sicknesses are straightforward and the person does not feel it necessary to accompany medical treatment by other procedures. But if the illness is serious or prolonged, if it requires surgical intervention, or if the doctor fails to diagnose immediately the true nature of the disease, then even 'doctor's sicknesses' are seen to require supernatural intervention.

Supernatural illnesses are usually, though not always, what we would call psychological ailments. Their symptoms may be the onset of visions, trembling, trances, aches and pains, poltergeist phenomena, odd behaviour, withdrawal from social life, manic behaviour, and disturbing dreams. It must furthermore be pointed out that this distinction between *doenças de cá* (natural sicknesses) and *doenças de lá* (supernatural sicknesses) may already be a response to bourgeois thought patterns, since doctors are not only often inept at dealing with mental patients, but are also sometimes hostile to them. Doctors are usually city people for whom the vocabulary used by peasants to describe mental problems is not only completely opaque but also distasteful. The same is not the case with pharmacists, who are members of the provincial bourgeoisie and who, despite outwardly rejecting peasant beliefs, are fully conversant with them. They have a control of the peasant vocabulary of disease and they exploit it to their own benefit. For example, pharmacists sell purgatives against *feitiço* under the counter, although there is no official reason for this. By doing so, they demonstrate their familiarity with the peasant worldview, which demands that matters related to *feitiço* should be dealt with in utmost secrecy.

In the words of the young doctors of the health centre of Ponte da Barca, their greatest local enemies are the church, because of its opposition to family planning, and the pharmacists, because they sabotage the doctors' prescriptions. The peasants have a vested interest in showing pharmacists respect because, while the doctors are usually temporary residents, the former reside locally and peasants will have to continue dealing with them. Furthermore, the pharmacist is more convincing, for he exploits his acquaintance with the peasant language of disease. Even though they systematically side with the attitudes of the bourgeoisie of the big cities against the peasant worldview, the provincial bourgeoisie is caught between two worlds. Their acquaintance with the peasant worldview allows them to make use of its vocabulary when this benefits their interests. Indeed, what is true here of pharmacists can also be argued for all of the town's tradesmen, lawyers, and bureaucrats.

There are some specialists among the peasants, such as the bone-setters, water-diviners and 'those who have a way with cows' who have no supernatural aura about them. (The latter have updated their techniques to such an extent that their services are at times almost indistinguishable from those of veterinary surgeons.) They possess a 'gift' (*dom*) which is seen as possibly emanating from God, but which has no utilization outside its sphere of action. Their popularity does not appear to have suffered from competition with more scientific alternatives.

II

Although changes in their attitudes and the images they present have taken place in the recent past, white witches remain central figures in peasant life. The impression I gained from my fieldwork experience is that the number of white witches, and the frequency with which they are consulted, is increasing. Nevertheless, such changes are, of course, impossible to assess with any degree of precision.

The word *bruxa* covers a whole range of meanings. Primarily, this word refers to a witch proper, in the sense of 'a woman regarded as having supernatural or magical power and knowledge, usually through a compact with the devil or a minor evil spirit' (*Chambers's Dictionary*). However, when peasants say 'so-and-so went to the *bruxa* yesterday,' they do not mean a witch in this first sense, but rather a person endowed with supernatural powers to annul the effects of antisocial forces and, at times, to counter-attack these. This person may be a diviner, a sorcerer, a faith-healer, a medium, an exorcist, or even a certain type of priest. Even though people fear and talk derisively of such specialists, they certainly do not confuse them with witches in the proper sense of the word. Furthermore, they are quite certain about the fact that witches proper are all females, while white witches may be either male or female.

This ambiguity is by no means limited to northern Portugal. The fact that a distinction between white witches and witches proper is drawn, but that this distinction is ambiguous, has been reported by a number of Iberian ethnographic writers (Caro Baroja, 1961: 317–18; Pitt-Rivers, 1971: 195; Lisón Tolosana, 1971b: 322; Christian, 1972: 192; Cátedra Tomás, 1976: 40). A further example of this ambiguity may be seen in the use of the word *feiticeira* which means 'a person who makes *feitiço*' (Morais, 1952). A peculiar inversion takes place in local parlance between this and the word *bruxa*. When the locals want to express the difference between witches proper and white witches, they call the former *feiticeiras* and the latter *bruxos/as*. At other times the words may be used as synonyms but with the qualification that *feiticeira* is always applied to a woman and is far more heinous in its implications. When the word is used to describe a female white witch, it implies a specific desire to denigrate her character. A woman of Paço to whom I suggested jokingly that she should adopt the métier of *bruxa*, for it would yield better profits than agriculture, answered that she would never do that because 'the neighbours would call me *feiticeira*.'

Yet the women whom I heard being accused of being witches proper were not white witches and vice versa. The affinity between these two figures, which the locals express by means of this lexical ambiguity, must therefore be searched for at a deeper level of signification. This is particularly the case since I was never told that white witches who acted in a singularly antisocial fashion would become witches proper, and since priests themselves can be white witches.

The clandestine way in which peasants enshroud their consultations with white witches may hint at a possible explanation. When a peasant requires the services of a white witch, public transport is avoided to prevent the destination of the trip becoming apparent. Taxis or the motor cars of close relatives and friends are used. People often leave their hamlets at night and return after dark on the following day.

A partial explanation for this secrecy is that the powers of white witches may be used in an antisocial fashion to attack and to attempt to influence their *vizinhos*. But this does not explain why, for example, the purgatives which help in the expulsion of *feitiço* should be bought and sold in secrecy despite theirs being purely protective measures. Indeed, one of the favourite topics of local gossip concerns other people's consultation of white witches. To consult a white witch slightly lowers one's prestige, and the local gossips, who themselves frequent white witches, are permanently engaged in publicizing the visits of their neighbours. The explanation given for the secrecy of one's own visits and for the concern with publicizing those of others is that 'those who consult witches most frequently are said to cause the greatest harm themselves.' No one will ever admit to visiting a white witch more frequently than the other *vizinhos*. As the white witch deals mainly with the unfortunate effects of antisocial forces, the person who makes use of her services is in effect accusing his neighbours of giving vent to these forces. Since local society should ideally be free of these, to acknowledge openly that one has to protect oneself against them is tantamount to saying that one is participating openly in the interplay of these forces. This is particularly true as many of the means used by white witches as protection against evil can also be used to cause evil.

White witches, then, even when they operate with powers overtly based on the life-giving grace of God, are regarded as signs of the existence of the evil, death-dealing, antisocial forces in the midst of human society. As such, analogically speaking, they are seen to signify female greed and envy: the prototypes of human moral weakness. This explains the lexical ambiguity between two personages who are outwardly so readily distinguishable—white witches and witches proper.

III

There are many different types of white witches. On the whole, they may be divided primarily into two categories: (1) those who, basing themselves mainly on traditional sources of knowledge, have a local clientele usually consisting of poor, rural people; (2) the new type of white witch who is urban, bourgeois, often educated, and bases his or her work on many different kinds of information. I cannot specify precisely when this second type first appeared. It would seem, however, that its original impact dates from the mid-1960s, when so many ideological and economic changes took place in Portugal. In the Alto Minho, this second type has practically replaced the older type of white witch. Furthermore, they are progressively taking over many of the attributes and functions which had belonged to priests and which the 'modernization' of the priesthood since the 1960s has prevented them from exercising.

These new white witches rely heavily on a network of intermediaries who bring them their clients. These are either unmarried women with an eye for business or taxi-drivers with whom the white witch has a special arrangement. It is essential for the image of the new *bruxos* that they should reside in cities or large urban centres (unless they are priests) for they constantly stress that they are not 'just any old country bumpkin' (*qualquer labrêgo*) but educated people with status. Moreover, their geographic distance from their clients' homes allows them not to have to worry about preserving a reputation because, when they have exhausted a particular rural area, they can look for their clientele elsewhere. In fact, the taxi-driver of Paço once said that he changes the *bruxo* he recommends to his co-parishioners regularly so that the novelty does not wear off.

White witches of the first type are becoming very rare. These are called *mulheres de virtude* (women of virtue), *entendidas* (those who under-stand), *habilidosas* (skilful ones), *curiosas* (curious ones), and finally, *bruxas*. These were women who had two primary functions: to divine and to heal. Their images and attributes varied considerably, however, ranging from the midwife with some magical knowledge to the special-ist with a large clientele, who lived exclusively by the profits of her trade.

Most accounts of the actions of white witches of the old type which I obtained were based on visits which had taken place over twenty years ago. These women gathered their knowledge from all possible sources and the result was a welter of information which even at times included sound medical advice. Their one outstanding source of esoteric knowledge, however, was the *Book of St Cyprian*. There they learnt how to divine with playing-cards, which appears to have been their principal means of acquiring knowledge about the past and the future.

A few of these women have survived the competition with the new type of *bruxos/as*. Outstanding cases in the region of Ponte da Barca are, for example, a woman in a parish across the river from Paço and Couto who specializes in love-potions, or a woman in a nearby town who throws the cards (*deita as cartas*) and, in a state of trance, predicts the client's future.

The following is a description of a consultation of a white witch by a *vizinha* of Paço, which took place in the early 1960s. This woman's husband was going to take his driving test and his success was absolutely essential, for it was hoped that by becoming a taxi-driver he would succeed in paying off his debts. She left early in the morning, accompanied by her sister, and spent the whole morning walking across the hills. They reached the house of the white witch at about noon. The latter already had a large group of clients waiting. Eventually, the *bruxa* received the two women, who had brought with them a handkerchief belonging to the husband in question, as white witches often ask for a piece of clothing belonging to the person about whom information is wanted. The *bruxa* held this cloth in one hand and threw the cards. Having done so she reached for a crucifix and muttered some prayers. Then she told the woman that her husband would pass the driving test, but that he would have to go to Brazil as he would not make much money locally. (The client remembers this consultation very clearly precisely because this prediction turned out to be correct: her husband was forced to leave her and their two young children for ten years to work in Brazil.) Before returning to Paço, they offered the white witch some money for 'she does not charge anything, but it is customary to thank her.'

I visited a man in a nearby borough who has a great reputation, particularly as a diviner. Whether it is true or not, this man's story is singularly interesting. His clients believe that he had died but that, during the wake, he suddenly 'returned'. Unfortunately, the story runs, an old friend of his was just at that moment asperging the pseudo-corpse with holy water, as it is customary for visitors to do during the wake. When the friend saw the 'corpse' rise, he was so shocked that he had a heart attack and died on the spot. Thanks to his trip through the 'other world', this man is supposed to have particular divining powers. His was the only case of this kind which came to my attention. I do not, therefore, know whether it corresponds to a new trend or to an older one. In all other aspects he behaved like a *bruxo* of the old type, for he was poor and uneducated and asked for no fee, only accepting a 'gift'.

The power to divine roughly divides the white witches of renown from the simple local women who have acquired some knowledge of healing techniques and prayers—*curiosas* (curious ones) or *rezadeiras* (those who say prayers). These prayers are often dedicated to specific saints and are accompanied by cures utilizing local herbs and products which are purported to have power: olive oil, blessed olive branches, bay, shepherd's purse, spurge-flax or daphne (*trovisco*), eucalyptus leaves, garlic, and rosemary. Objects blessed by the priest (such as tree branches, candles, water and oil) are also endowed with special powers, as are objects which accompany the Eucharist (the altar stone, the fringes of the stole and maniple, the keys to the tabernacle). Some of these women also specialize in the burning of substances which accompanies both the casting of *feitiço* and counter-*feitiço* and in the making of amulets against *feitiço* and the evil eye, for the use of both humans and animals.

Before the advent of the new type of white witch, the only other competitor to the *bruxas* was the priest. Priests used to exorcize and heal by prayer. Already before the 1960s, some priests were particularly renowned for their aptitude for these tasks. Nowadays, however, most priests refuse to perform them and this role has been taken over both by the new type of white witch and by specific priests who specialize in this field. The local residents refer to the latter too as *bruxos*. Their role and position will be discussed in the next chapter.

The new type of white witch depends largely on urban status symbols, on church symbolism, on medical jargon, and on esoteric knowledge of the literary type—astrology, spiritualism, parapsychology. Most of all, he or she relies on a whole new type of literature, mainly from Brazil, which has flooded the Portuguese market particularly since the 1974 Revolution, when the censorship of books was lifted. These white witches approach their activities with a surprising professionalism: most of them have visiting cards and they even advertise in newspapers. Finally, among them there is a higher percentage of men than women, which is another interesting divergence from the old type of white witch.

The increasing prestige of technology and science over the past few decades has been accompanied by a growing feeling of powerlessness among those who do not possess these resources. The new type of *bruxo* exploits this feeling; he uses bourgeois status and symbols of learning as a means of enhancing his own prestige and impressing the peasants with his power. Notwithstanding, the essential ideas and the ceremonies and ritual tools utilized are very similar to those of the traditional white witch. It is more the style than the ritual essence that has altered. This is, in a sense, to be expected, for otherwise they would cease to appeal to the peasantry altogether.

The fact that they charge a 'fee' for their 'consultations', which is at least as high as that of a medical doctor, and which they justify by claiming that they are professionally trained, is one of the most important innovations. They are, in this way, claiming adherence to an urban world. White witches of the old type, who are placed within the cultural sphere of the subsistence prototype, still rely on the old system of not receiving a fee but allowing their clients to believe that, if they are 'thanked', their services might be more effective. According to them the reason for this is to prevent clients from accusing them of being *comedores* (literally, eaters), that is, of wanting personal gain over and above the welfare of clients. Nevertheless, although they attempt to dispel this image, white witches of the old type are regarded as being potentially greedy and thus of being *comedores*. Because they deal with the dark side of humanity, they are viewed with suspicion and mistrust. In this they are similar to urban undertakers who are disliked for their messy task, even though it is so essential for the community which they serve. The insistence on paying something even to the old type of *bruxa* is not primarily an indication of the clients' 'thankfulness' but rather a demonstration of mistrust: the clients believe that if they did not pay, the white witch might be offended and his or her services would either be of no avail or perhaps would even be turned against the client.

White witches are consulted for many varied reasons. Some cases are prolonged and involve repeated consultations. Most, however, are quite simple. The owners of a shop in Paço were told by a *bruxa* in Oporto (who claims she has a 'degree in spiritualism') that their shop was avoided by clients because it had been attacked by *feitiço*. The *bruxa* came to the shop and performed exorcisms and a *defumadouro*. She divined the place where the *feitiço* was hidden. This *feitiço* consisted of some nondescript floor dust which she said should be cast into the sea. A *vizinho* of Couto consulted a white witch because he dreamt of a deceased friend telling him that he too was going to die soon; another wanted to know whether her husband was unfaithful; a third wanted to confirm her suspicion that a certain man had stolen money from her house; finally, one wanted to discover what was wrong with her ailing child.

The choice of white witch depends on the gravity of the complaint. For a small problem, peasants consult a nearby *bruxa*: for a more important problem they are willing to spend more money and to consult one of the new type of powerful *bruxos* in the cities. Most clients of white witches are women who do not often leave their boroughs of residence and who seldom have reason to visit the cities. A visit to the white witch is regarded by them as a treat which they anticipate with impatience. The success of the urban *bruxos* is not unrelated to the new prosperity of peasants in the past twenty years, which makes such journeys possible. Previously, peasants would not have been able to avail themselves of the services of such costly *bruxos*. They were forced to make do with the local *entendidas*.

IV

When a *minhoto* peasant wants to convince someone of the quality of a white witch, the aspect of his or her powers which is most likely to be stressed is the fact that the white witch can have access to information which other people would not normally possess. The terms *curiosas* and *entendidas* are indices of this search for the acquisition of esoteric knowledge. This is an aspect which the *bruxos* themselves are always keen to stress. Many white witches, however, go further, for they can know what other people would not be able to know at all: they can *adivinhar* (divine). The accounts given to me of past consultations of white witches always centred around their extraordinary capacity for revealing things which they had not been told. Indeed, this is the single most important reason why the majority of people consult *bruxos*. The medicine prescribed by white witches is seldom very significant and, in fact, I was surprised to discover that informants were not always very interested in it. Rather, they were fascinated by the fact that some *bruxos* can feel in their own bodies where one's sickness is located, while others can 'see' beyond normal human powers.

It is by demonstrating knowledge about the past life of a client that the *bruxo* usually validates his claims about the future. As he passes from the easily predictable to the more particular aspects of a client's life, the *bruxo* is directed by the responses of the client to his divination. What surprised me most in the sessions I attended was how the clients actively participated with the *bruxo* in extracting from their general statements a specific answer to their problems. The *bruxo*'s propositions acted largely as mnemonic devices or as a means for lateral thinking. As David Parkin put it in relation to African diviners, 'the style and narrative theme of divinatory speech is a parallel example of problem-specifying being problem-solving' (1979: 147). In the more complex cases, the solution only emerges slowly in the process of various consultations with a number of *bruxos*. In other cases, however, an answer which satisfied the client was found without much delay. To a woman who complained that her husband, who worked in Lisbon, did not want to return home, for example, a *bruxa* explained that her husband's lover had cast a *feitiço* into the sea; it was therefore irretrievable. The solution did not please her; it did however prove satisfactory as an answer, for it gave her the possibility of coping, without a complete loss of self-esteem, with the fact that her husband had abandoned her.

As sorcerers, *bruxos* provide the *minhotos* with the possibility of acting beyond normal human powers; as exorcists, they protect them from supernatural powers. The *minhoto* who consults a white witch is attempting to borrow powers which are normally outside his reach so as to counter the evil forces which besiege his world. But this is perhaps not the main task of white witches. Through divination the locals succeed in placing misfortune within a cognitive framework and therefore in transforming its utter meaninglessness into a reality which they can comprehend.

17. Priests

I

In coping with evil and in organizing their lives in a way which they hope will bring about social and material well-being, the *minhotos* rely primarily upon the Catholic Church, its rituals and its representatives. The primary mediator between human society and the divinity is the priest and as such he has a major role to play in local society. In contrast with other areas of Portugal, the influence which the Church and the clergy have traditionally exerted both among the rural and the urban populations of Minho is, nowadays, still considerable, although it is undergoing change.

The village priest is, so to speak, the pedestal of the ecclesiastical hierarchy. Each parish has a church and a priest. Although nowadays it is common for priests to take on more than one parish, in this area they seldom have more than three. The size of the parishes may vary considerably (they range from just over 100 to 3,500 inhabitants). Even when they are responsible for more than two parishes, priests seldom have more than 3,000 souls to care for, that is, between 600 and 700 households. This means that they usually get to know the majority of their adult parishioners reasonably well, especially since, once a priest finds a parish he likes, he tends to remain there until his death. This means that it is common to find priests that have been in the same parish for twenty-five to thirty-five years. The links between the *minhoto* rural priest and his parish tend to be further reinforced by the fact that the great majority of priests are natives either of the borough or even of the very parish where they work.

On the whole, rural priests are children of wealthy peasants, since to keep a son in a seminary was thought to be costly even though the Church subsidized most of the boy's education. The prestige of wealthy households was enhanced by the fact that they had priests in the family. Today, however, the religious vocation is less attractive; few households still have priests and the pressure on young people to adopt an ecclesiastical career is no longer what it used to be. The following figures may provide an idea of what is called 'the crisis of vocations': in 1957 Braga had 298 senior seminarists; in 1967 it had 214; and in 1977 it only had 52 (Silva, 1979: 40).

Most of the priests one encounters today started their careers before the great changes of the past twenty years. They were sent to the seminary when they were approximately thirteen and returned home only for major feasts and summer holidays; the rest of their lives, until they were ordained in their early twenties, was spent under highly regimented conditions. Few priests nowadays would disagree that until the mid-1960s the atmosphere in seminaries was oppressive and furthermore that it was designed to give the pupils a feeling of personal and institutional pride which was accompanied by what was then already an out-moded education.

Although on the whole the system of inheritance in the rural Alto Minho tends to favour the child who marries and remains at home 'looking after the parents', other children also have rights to inheritance. This means that a priest inherits the same amount as those of his siblings who did not remain at home. Moreover, in this region, where there is no special concern with preserving the male line, one encounters couples whose sole male offspring becomes a priest.

Each parish has its vicarage (*residência*), adjoining the churchyard. Even when the priest lives near land which he inherited from his parents, this is usually handed over to a share-cropper, as it is considered incorrect for a priest to dedicate himself to manual labour and particularly agricultural labour. The priest is an ex-officio member of the bourgeoisie, and is thus not 'equal' to other parish residents. As 'the work of the land is dirty,' agricultural labour would lower his status.

A large number of rural priests also work as high-school teachers in nearby towns. With two sources of income, they usually manage to maintain what, locally, is a good standard of living. The salary of a priest who dedicates himself only to parish work is, however, meagre. If he does not have any other source of income, he may find it difficult to live up to the expectations which peasants and bourgeois alike have of him.

A rural priest is paid for the services he performs (baptisms, weddings, funerals, masses). At harvest time he receives a kind of tithe (*côngrua*) from each household, which is still paid in kind (but does not correspond to a tenth of the product). Whenever there are *festas* or any other religious activities the priest also receives a fee. If he is a good orator, he is in constant demand to preach at other parishes' *festas*, for people are very eager to hear what they consider a 'good' sermon—that is, one which is vividly pronounced, with much gesticulation and emphasis on keywords, one which is full of resounding analogies with few analytic terms.

It is also customary for priests to be paid to go to other parishes to hear confessions. People are very suspicious of their local priest's capacity to keep confessional secrecy. They therefore invariably prefer to confess to outside priests. A few days before each major *festa*, a parish priest calls four or five colleagues to come and confess a large number of parishioners, who take this opportunity to purify themselves of their sins with a reasonably good chance of disinterested secrecy.

A rural priest is not only responsible to his congregation but also to the ecclesiastical authorities he represents. Over the past twenty years, with the opening of tarred roads and new transport facilities, contacts among priests at a regional level have increased considerably.

It is in their different symbolic and ritual expressions that the peasant and bourgeois worldviews are most visibly distinguishable to local residents themselves. In the person of the rural priest, who is the most important mediator between the divinity and humans, both for the bourgeoisie and the peasantry, the confrontation between the two worldviews is most acute and may even assume the characteristics of a conflict. Confronted with this situation, priests react differently according to their particular personalities and conditions. In general, however, we can propose a classification of three types of priest, according to the strategies they adopt towards this confrontation: (1) the 'modern' priest; (2) the 'old-fashioned' priest; (3) the *bruxo* priest. This typology, of course, is not absolute as it merely refers to general trends.

At present, most *minhoto* priests may be categorized as belonging to the first type. These are priests who have already been influenced by the Second Vatican Council. As the effect of the Council in Portugal was not as strong as it was elsewhere in Europe, the 'modernity' of these priests should not be over-stressed. Notwithstanding, they evince the tendency to foster the secularization of the ecclesiastical profession, which accompanied the liberalization of religious and ideological attitudes which took place in the 1960s and 1970s among the national bourgeoisie.

'Modern' priests avoid the use of ecclesiastical robes and dress in a way which does not distinguish them from other reasonably prosperous members of the bourgeoisie. They drive cars, and most of their time is spent teaching humanities at the local high schools. Their vicarages are renovated or even rebuilt according to urban ideas. They have icono-clastic tendencies; the cleaning-up operations in the churches for which they are responsible have led to the destruction and loss of a great deal of the local artistic patrimony, and with it the religious value of these churches for the parishioners.

In their reactions to the peasant worldview, these priests are charac-terized by two principal attitudes: their opposition to any manifestations of a local or communal character and their loudly proclaimed abhorrence of 'superstitions'. The concept of religious activity which is at the root of these two attitudes is, in itself, age-old. The secularization of the clergy which has taken place over the past twenty years has merely exacerbated it. Already S. Martinho de Dume, in his sixth-century pastoral letter *De Castigatione Rusticorum*, protested against what today are called 'pagan superstitions'. And throughout the Middle Ages, the Church continued to feel the need to oppose its concept of religion against what it saw as popular deviations. All forms of worship which, theologically or geographically, stress the specificity and independence of a local community, are detrimental to the church. If it is to remain Catholic (that is, universal) and united, the Church must insist that all forms of worship must be strictly dictated and authorized by the ec-clesiastical hierarchy and that they must not be locally specific. The analogy between the Church and the Body of Christ is here very signifi-cant: the body cannot operate if its limbs move independently of one another.

Among 'modern' priests this attitude is accompanied by a singularly strong need to separate and distinguish the profane and sacred elements in everyday life. The secularization of the clergy referred to above is a corollary to this attitude. Confronted with the penetration of science into its traditional sphere of influence and concomitantly an increasing separation from State power, the Church was forced to adopt an attitude separating the sacred from the profane. On the contrary, for the *minhoto* peasant, to whom 'miracles' take place every day, the sacred and the profane are closely integrated. He lives permanently within sanctified space, for he systematically protects his environment with sacred sym-bols. This is parallel to the peasant familiarity with saints which was described above.

The second type of priest, the 'old-fashioned' one, is becoming less common today. Their homes are more unkempt and have a rustic character; their churches have not been cleaned up and they may even not be in possession of a loud speaker (an instrument which has come to dominate *minhoto* religious life). These priests still often dress in religious robes and, within certain limits, they are prepared to participate in locally specific religious activities. This does not mean that they would confess to believing in 'superstitions', but rather that they are more willing to compromise with their parishioners.

The third type I call *bruxo* priests because the people also refer to them as *bruxos*. These priests are willing to participate in the forms of symbolic behaviour which were described in the previous chapter and which the Church is repudiating with increasing intensity. While 'modern' priests complement their salary by means of high-school teaching, *bruxo* priests receive from their clients gifts in goods and cash.

Some of these men achieve such fame that people from all over north-western Portugal come to consult them. One such *bruxo* priest, who died in 1979, was consulted by so many people that, on weekends, he was at times obliged to attend ten people at once, and queues of cars formed at the entrance of his rustic mountain hamlet. Because they are priests, these persons are more respected than other white witches. They are not numerous, but they are by no means disappearing.

It is significant that *bruxo* priests tend to be priests of isolated mountain parishes: places where the influence of the capitalist sector of the economy and the pressure of urban values have not yet been felt as markedly as in more easily accessible parishes. In these isolated places the priest is more dependent on the opinions and attitudes of the population than in areas where the strength of the urban ruling class is easily experienced. As J. Riegelhaupt demonstrated in her study of a parish near Sintra (1973), priests of more accessible parishes may even go so far as openly to take advantage of the power of the influential members of the urban élite to impose upon their parishioners innovations in their religious life which they would otherwise reject. Since 1974, a few cases where the conflict between the priest and his parishioners assumed alarming proportions have made their way into the national press.

When I asked 'modern' priests why their colleagues work as white witches, I invariably received the reply that this is the only way in which they can make a 'decent' living since they work in poor and remote parishes. Thus, not having other economic means, these priests are forced to adopt peasant beliefs and practice as a means of acquiring both the prestige and the economic power which are necessary for the maintenance of their image as priests. It is perhaps also for this very reason that their 'modern' colleagues, who are normally so harsh on 'superstitions', appeared to be benevolent and understanding in their judgement of these men.

II

The role of the rural priest in borough life is by no means limited to religious activities. Throughout the nineteenth century and the first half of the twentieth, the parish priest was one of the few people in his parish, if not the only one, who had received a formal education—limited as it may have been in the first half of the nineteenth century. His intimate knowledge of and contact with the rural population, accompanied by the 'respect' which was granted to him by the bourgeoisie and the peasantry alike, meant that he was in an ideal position to act as an intermediary or mediator between these two groups. This role was particularly important during Salazar's regime, since direct patronage links between the urban élite which controlled the institutions of the State at borough level and the individual peasants were relatively weak.

The attack on the temporal power of the Church by the bourgeois governments in the first quarter of the nineteenth century was based on the legislation of Mouzinho da Silveira. These laws were not antagonistic to parish priests, quite the contrary. Until the Republican Revolution of 1910, the secular clergy received salaries from and were appointed by the government. Such a situation led to an alliance between the ruling classes and the secular clergy (Oliveira Marques, 1972, II: 24).

In the 1840s, the legislation of Costa Cabral continued this tradition, in that it depended on the support of the secular clergy for its success at grass-roots level. The priests were in charge of collecting the census on the basis of which the new system of taxation was to operate; priests were essential for the implementation of the health laws, as they collected the tax on burials and were legally obliged to report on failure to comply with the laws; finally, they were charged with organizing elections at parish level. Failure to fulfil these duties was punished harshly.

In 1846, however, the *minhoto* peasantry revolted against the Costa Cabral legislation in what is known as the Maria da Fonte Revolution. The position of the secular clergy during the hostilities which immediately followed this revolt was most interesting, for it pointed to their role as intermediaries. While, on the one hand, they had been influential in attempting to implement the laws which proved to be so odious to the rural population, on the other hand, it was among the secular clergy that the people found the leaders who eventually directed its revolt.

The alliance of the clergy and the ruling classes seems to have survived throughout the rest of the nineteenth century. In 1890, for example, the population census which the government organized was carried out largely by means of the rural priests, and the parish priests were then ex-officio members of the Parish Council. The reading of the minutes of the Council of Paço, for example, shows that only after the 1974 Revolution, with the exception of a short Republican interlude in 1911–25 did the Council finally become independent of ecclesiastical control, even though, since 1910, priests have no longer been on the government's payroll.

The present incumbent of both Paço and Couto did not share in his predecessors' prestige and good fortune. In the early 1960s the power and influence of the Church all over Portugal started to wane. At national level, the opening to foreign capital, the progressive liberalization of the economy which followed the onset of the African wars of independence, the widening of educational facilities, and the enormous increase in emigration, all led to an atmosphere of liberalism which progressively corroded the alliance between the Church and the State. At the same time, there was a noticeable decrease in the prestige of the secular clergy. During the first years of the decade of the 1960s, there was an inversion in the trend of entrance to seminaries. The priesthood no longer proved to be an attractive proposition for the young.

The present priest of Paço and Couto may be classified as 'modern'. His increased opposition to the peasant worldview and his summary abolition of a series of rites and practices which the peasants cannot see as 'pagan archaisms', has alienated much of the support of his parishioners. His political power has been weakened considerably, particularly since 1974. In the elections which followed the Revolution, his parishioners did not feel obliged to vote for the party for which he so actively canvassed (the right-wing party, CDS).

Nevertheless, the political influence of the Church in this area remains considerable and its support of right-wing and centre parties must be taken into account in the interpretation of popular voting patterns in the Alto Minho. In 1976, rural priests were key figures in the movement against the Communist Party, which involved the burning of its headquarters in various boroughs in this district.

The power of the clergy, however, is being eroded. The new borough élite is starting to form stronger patronage links with influential peasant families, and formal education is no longer a monopoly of the clergy. Finally, these two factors allow the peasantry far more direct access to bureaucratic institutions, thus bypassing the mediation and authority of the clergy.

III

It is not only in the secular field that the power and influence of the rural priest are being undermined, but also in relation to spiritual matters. The conflict between local religious attitudes ('popular religion') and the 'religion of the priests' (*a religião dos padres*) has a long history in the Iberian peninsula. One of the principal characteristics which Iberian anthropologists have imputed to this 'popular religion' is its profound association with territorial identity. Similarly during the course of this work, an association between peasant religious attitudes and the experience of community at local level was repeatedly encountered.

The areas of conflict between the Church and the peasantry are varied and wide-ranging. In 1979, the new Bishop of Viana published a pastoral letter dedicated to the subject of popular *festas*—celebrations of a popular, public nature which are attached to a particular sociogeographic unit. Thus, hamlets can have *festas*, as can parishes, boroughs, and districts. Hamlet *festas* in the Alto Minho are infrequent. Most *festas* are held at parish or borough level. They are held on special occasions, usually saints' days. Although they are celebrations of sociogeographic identity they are also attended by people from nearby parishes, boroughs, and districts. They share with pilgrimages to specific saints' shrines (*romarias*—the two categories often merge) the fact that they are occasions for both secular entertainment and rejoicing and for religious celebration. For the *minhoto* the two aspects are closely interwoven. The central moment of each *festa* is the procession. Firecrackers are exploded and the celebrations usually extend throughout the day and late into the night. *Festas* are an occasion for loud music, dancing, and the consumption of relishes and large quantities of wine.

The letter of the Bishop to his priests centred around the need to distinguish more clearly between the 'profane' and the 'sacred' elements of *festas*. According to him the profane element is not consistent with, and distracts popular attention from the sacred nature of the celebration. He advised the priests to attempt to control the organization of *festas* so as to be able to discourage this profane element. The priest of Paço and Couto had been acting along these lines for a long time and was greatly encouraged by this circular.

This attitude of the ecclesiastical authorities is not a recent phenomenon. Nevertheless, the concern of the clergy to sever the profane from the sacred has increased recently, causing great resentment among the peasantry, for whom the *festas* are pivotal moments of community life.

Another area of disagreement is the age-old opposition of the Church to 'popular canonization'. The Church does not oppose all cults that are popular in origin.[2] It does, however, regard these forms of worship with suspicion and is vigorously opposed to all those cults which it has not officially recognized. The case in point may be a relic, such as the incorruptible body of someone whom the people believe to be a saint; it may be a living person whom the people also believe to be a saint; finally, it may be a cult surrounding a certain image which is particularly 'miraculous' or, for instance, a rock upon which the Virgin Mary may have descended.

The objects, persons, or places around which these popular cults develop are, for the *minhotos*, highly efficient means for the control and acquisition of supernatural power. Through them the *minhoto* obtains benefits of a spiritual as well as a temporal nature. The objects present themselves to the peasant as means of acting temporally upon the world. They are, therefore, items of ownership which can be 'stolen' or criminally damaged. The history of S. Torcato, whose body belongs to the parish of the same name near Guimarães, is a good example of the 'possessiveness' of the inhabitants of a specific socio-geographic unit (Santos Silva, 1979). The Chapter of Guimarães wanted to transport this relic to the town, as it yields large profits in the guise of ex-votos. They attempted unsuccessfully to do so forcibly in 1501, 1597, 1637, and finally 1805. At each of these four attempts the people of the parish rose up in arms and succeeded in preserving control over 'their' saint. A similar event which took place in 1976 in Ponte de Barca is reported below.

Although these cults jeopardize its control over worship, they are useful to the Church as a means of preserving popular religious fervour, which the cults encourage through their immediacy and proximity to the peasants. This explains the ambiguous attitude of the ecclesiastical authorities who vigorously oppose local cults when they are beginning,

---

[2] I use the word 'cult' here in the sense of the set of activities which surround the worship of a specific supernatural entity.

but who attempt to co-opt them when their expansion is such that it can no longer be checked. The behaviour of the Chapter of Guimarães is a good example of this attitude, for the canons did not only attempt to control the body and the profits it yielded, but they also changed the popular legend so as to make of this unknown man a martyr bishop. R. Hertz, writing at the beginning of this century on the Alpine cult of St Besse, puts forward a similar point of view when he argues that, for the ecclesiastical authorities of Ivrée,

it became necessary to *detach the sanctity from the Hill* and to concentrate it on the body of the saint: the large stone [which was at the origin of the cult] was to remain rooted in the same spot, the body, however, real or invented, is mobile and could well be used as a vehicle for beneficial energy, should it one day please these powerful masters to 'enrich' their sacred treasure with it. (1928: 168).

Finally, the opposition of the Church to 'superstitions' indicates a similar attempt by the hierarchy to control religious behaviour at popular level. To the peasants, the opposition of most priests to 'superstitions' presents a problem. Due to their special powers, priests are capable of operating not only as celebrants of rituals which directly enhance 'community' (such as processions and the Mass), but also as celebrants of rituals of a therapeutic nature, which counteract evil forces: particularly as healers and exorcists. Priests possess something which peasants themselves do not: esoteric knowledge and sacramental power. For the peasants, these two aspects of a priest's calling are deeply interlinked; the priest's sacramental power is derived from his ordination, which in turn is given to him only after he successfully carries out 'very intensive studies' in the seminary. The esoteric knowledge thus acquired is associated with literacy, and particularly literacy in Latin. Latin as an expression of this special knowledge is in itself a most powerful spiritual tool. A famous *bruxo* priest specializing in diseases caused by 'envy', heals by reciting prayers from the *Rituale Romanum*.

As esoteric knowledge, literacy, and sacramental power are closely interrelated, the great stress on the education and knowledge of priests can thus be understood, irrespective of its disproportionate relationship to reality. The clergy fosters this image consciously and surrounds itself with symbols of knowledge: all vicarages have an 'office', where one always encounters what is by local standards a large number of books (sometimes even in languages which the priests themselves cannot read) and a typewriter. The telephone—a symbol of the priest's position as an intermediary with the urban élite—is also in this room, where the priest receives his parishioners.

It has already been remarked that the dominant characteristic of white witches is that they have access to information which other people do not possess. Similarly, the *minhotos* associate the spiritual power of priests with their control of esoteric knowledge. The priest's spiritual power is not independent from his temporal power, as the latter is also based on his literacy, and the rural *minhotos* do not distinguish between mind and spirit.

The parishioners need this spiritual power. Previously, the 'old-fashioned' priest, despite perhaps not being fully in accordance with peasant beliefs, was nevertheless willing to compromise with them. If he were approached at nightfall (for these things are always done in secrecy) by some woman asking him to 'close the body' of a relative of hers who was *tolhida* or possessed by a 'soul in pain', an 'old-fashioned' priest would be sure to agree to use the keys of the tabernacle and to recite some Latin prayers for the sick woman. A 'modern' priest would react quite differently—as indeed the priest who recounted this event to me did react. The woman received an instant sermon on the subject of 'superstition', and most probably she found that she could not trust the priest's discretion.

'Modern' priests refuse to use their instruments of grace for the purpose of obtaining practical benefits, and furthermore, they do not believe that such a use would bring about the desired effects. Most of them accept the theoretical possibility of faith-healing, of possession by the Devil, and perhaps even of communication with the dead; in practical terms, however, they refuse to interpret specific instances of psychological or psychosomatic deviation in this way. The increasing distaste of 'modern' priests for such explanations means that they refuse to act in ways which, twenty years ago, would have been accepted as fully legitimate. It is partly to this refusal by the priests to operate as exorcists and healers that the new type of white witch owes his or her outstanding success. It is significant that these new *bruxos* should so openly borrow the tools of Catholic worship and, in addition, that they should so often be *bruxo* priests or claim to be ex-priests.

It was argued above, when dealing with votive offerings, that since the 1960s a new attitude to the relationship between believers and the divinity has developed, which accompanied the liberalization of attitudes among the urban classes. In W. A. Christian's terms, 'this approach erases the need for divine intermediaries and questions the continued use of shrines and generalized devotions' (1972: p. xiii).

This attitude is consistent with the development of bourgeois ideology, but not with that of the peasantry. The isolation and cultural homogeneity of the rural communities have been greatly eroded, which means that consensus is more difficult to achieve, and that even the individual experience of community has weakened. Borough and district *festas* are becoming more important, while those of parishes and hamlets, which were attached to a direct sense of communal fate, have lost some of their previous glamour.

This tendency leads to an experience of anomie at hamlet and parish levels, particularly as the attachment to the basic values of the peasant worldview did not weaken. There is a growing awareness of the existence of antisocial and destructive forces, which explains why the recourse to *bruxos* is, if anything, on the increase.

This experience of anomie is manifest at yet another level, in the belief that people are no longer as happy or healthy as they used to be. Not only has the individual experience of community been reduced, but the nature of subsistence itself has been altered. As the parishioners became dependent on external sources of income and came to participate more actively in the capitalist labour market, there was a rise in standards of living, with an increasing demand for a variety of products which cannot always be produced locally. Wealthier peasant households partly succeeded in keeping up with this development, as far as edible products were concerned, by widening the range of the produce grown. Average and poor peasants, however, could only keep up with these changes at the risk of upsetting the careful balance which the traditional mixed farming system demands. Thus, they were forced to rely increasingly on consumer products.

The belief that 'in the old times' (*antes* or *antigamente*) men used to be stronger and live longer than they do today is not new to this society or specific to it—the myth of the Golden Age is a major theme of European thought. Nevertheless, this attitude has assumed interesting characteristics in this region, which I believe are profoundly connected with the process of change described immediately above. Rural *minhotos* often stress the power which they derive from the earth, and their relationship with the earth is seen as a spring of life and vitality. Their work, they argue, is the source of life for the whole nation. Their relationship with the land is regarded as the root of good health: 'natural, pure, fresh, clean' food is desirable and is that which has recently been produced by the household. According to them, the reason why many emigrants cannot withstand the life in foreign cities, and return weakened and emaciated, is that urban foodstuffs are lacking in 'strength' (*força*). Townsfolk are also said to be weaker for this same reason.

At the same time, old doctors are reputed to have been better than new ones because they used to prescribe 'natural' infusions made with local products. Modern medicine, I was told, damages the liver in order to cure the heart. Health is drawn from the land for it depends on its life force. 'My medicine,' peasants brag, 'is good maize bread and untreated wine.' There is a profound abhorrence of synthetically made wine (*vinho de martelo*, literally hammer-wine) which is supposed to damage the drinker's bowels.

As their reliance on consumer products increases, so the feeling of loss of strength becomes more pressing. This preoccupation provided a favorite topic of conversation in Paço. One Sunday, in 1977, after Mass, the male heads of most wealthy households in Paço engaged in a contest to determine which of their households was least dependent on purchased food products. The household which finally won (whose female household head is a descendent of the Gomes family) is to this day proud of it. In Couto, a contest which so strongly stressed the subsistence prototype would never have been possible, for there are far fewer families that manage to live up to its standards.

At this point it is perhaps worth summarizing what has been said so far. As intermediaries between social groups and contrasting worldviews, particular priests adopt different responses. 'Modern' priests reject peasant values, *bruxo* priests assume peasant values and distance themselves from the urban élite. If the mediation of priest has become more difficult since the 1960s, the tensions and incoherences to which it leads are not new phenomena in local society; they have merely been highlighted by the changes which are taking place. Nevertheless, priests still act as mediators, and they are still respected by both the bourgeoisie and the peasantry: neither do people abandon the churches and dismiss the priests (except in very rare cases), nor does the urban élite take too repressive an attitude towards *bruxo* priests and the new type of *bruxos*. The remainder of this chapter will be concerned with an attempt to draw out the mechanisms which in the majority of cases allow for the continuing existence of this mediation and prevent the conflict from being radicalized.

IV

Although the 'modern' priest rejects a very important area of the peasant's view of the world, the functions which he does fulfil are nevertheless central to peasant society. Thus, the Mass is still said, the Easter visit still takes place, baptisms, weddings, and funerals are still celebrated (even if not as the peasants would like them to be), and some processions and *festas* (albeit shortened and altered) remain.

Paradoxically, however, perhaps the most important factor which prevents the conflict between the priests and the parishioners from resulting in a rejection by the peasantry of the Church as an institution, is a phenomenon which has deep historical roots in the Iberian peninsula: popular anticlericalism (cf. Silverman, 1975: 170). The meaning of this term has not always been clearly specified. It must be remarked that, in this context, anticlericalism does not mean militant atheism, nor even an attitude of confrontation with the Church. Northern Portugal has never experienced anarchist anticlericalism as encountered in southern Spain, for example. Two divergent forms of anticlericalism have been present throughout its recent history: popular anticlericalism and bourgeois anticlericalism, usually adhered to by educated people and attached to masonic, republican, or socialist movements. I shall deal here only with the first of these.

In its most typically rural and *minhoto* expression, anticlericalism is an aversion either to the person of a particular priest or to all priests as a group. It does not usually imply a disbelief in the power of priests as a whole, but is rather an expression of the perceived ineptitude of individual priests to fulfil the tasks which they are given. Thus, parishioners all over Minho have the habit of criticizing 'their' own priest and of regarding as examples of what priests should be like, the priests of other parishes or the previous incumbent of the post. The residents of Paço and Couto and their neighbouring parishes systematically particularize their aversion to the attitudes and opinions of priests.

This is particularly true in the case of outspoken 'modern' priests, whose destructive actions are interpreted as those of an incompetent human being, rather than as evidence of a religious attitude which is profoundly different from that of the parishioners themselves.

While for a 'modern' priest there is an intrinsic difference between his activities when he performs a baptism or funeral, or when he says the Mass, and the activities of exorcizing evil spirits or healing, for the *minhoto* peasants this distinction is not at all clear. They tend to see the priest's refusal to perform these tasks as arbitrary and based on personal idiosyncrasy.

The specific terms in which anticlerical feelings are phrased in this region are interesting in themselves. The criticisms which I heard directed at specific priests could be classified into three basic types: (1) the priest is greedy (he is *comedor*, 'egoist', 'only concerned with money', he uses the money of the parish for his own personal gain'); (2) he is incompetent ('incapable', 'inefficient', 'cannot say a sermon', 'is lazy'); (3) he is accused of sensuality (*lambão*, 'likes a drop', i.e. wine, and various references to real or imaginary lovers and illegitimate children).

It is noteworthy that the accusation of lack of chastity is not as deeply resented as the others cited above. For the locals 'a man is a man,' and cannot help having sexual desires. It is women who are able to control their sexual urges but do not want to do so. The particular interest of the terms in which these criticisms are phrased lies in the fact that they are precisely antonymic to the terms used by the *minhotos* to qualify popularly canonized saints (cf. p. 233 below).

Particular instances of behaviour of which the parishioners disapprove are explained by reference to these terms. Thus, in Paço and Couto, the priest's reluctance to bless water (which is due to his belief that holy water is used 'superstitiously' by peasants) was blamed on his 'laziness'; his refusal to exorcize people who were possessed by the soul of a dead relative was explained by saying that 'he is afraid,' or 'he can only repair machines and not people'; and his destructive attitudes towards most types of communal ritual were claimed to result from his 'only being interested in his own saint', or being 'self-seeking' (*interesseiro*), or 'wanting all the parish money for himself'.

This personalized anticlericalism is further supported by the fact that not all priests reject the peasant worldview in quite the same way. The peasant who lacks an overview of the whole of the Church as an institution does not understand that it is not 'the priests' (*os padres*) who fail to satisfy his expectations, but the Church as a hierarchical institution.

The *minhoto* peasant sees himself as destitute of both intellectual and spiritual powers. He is dependent on priests both for temporal and for spiritual functions which he himself would otherwise be incapable of performing. The destruction of the ecclesiastical apparatus is as frightening to him as it is to the clergy. Paradoxically, perhaps the most important reason why the left wing failed to gain the support of the rural population of Minho after the 1974 Revolution was its militant, atheistic anticlericalism. The peasant who blames individual priests for his own dissatisfaction with the Church does so largely because a more radical attitude, which would attack the Church as an institution, would be against his own interests.

V

The bourgeoisie takes a significantly different attitude towards the role of priests as intermediaries between the urban élite and the peasantry. For the urban élite, the obvious differences in thought between these two social groups are due to the peasantry's 'lack of education'. On the one hand, this refers to their lack of literacy and technical knowledge; on the other, it indicates the peasantry's acceptance of a whole set of conceptions which the urban élite considers superfluous and easily eradicable 'superstitions'. The meaning of this expression as used by the bourgeoisie is that of 'false ideas' (*ideias falsas*), i.e. concepts which do not correspond to reality as defined by the bourgeoisie. It is also implicit in most uses of the word that those who believe in superstitions are vaguely lacking in clarity of mind. Superstitions are not understood as integral parts of a worldview, but rather as 'pagan survivals' or 'degenerations': forms of retrogression to a pre-Christian type of thought. Thus they are not part of 'religion' but rather extrinsic additions to it. The rural priest, therefore, is seen as an 'educator' of those among whom he lives. At face value he is thought of as a vehicle of 'rationality' and not as a mediator.

Bruxo priests and other white witches present a different problem for the urban élite. Should one of these deviant priests become too famous or vociferous, he is admonished by his colleagues and his bishop. The civil authorities too may attempt to curb the activities of white witches who are becoming too renowned. Often, however, the attitude is one of apprehensive and uneasy tolerance. The attitude of the townsfolk towards 'superstitions' is by no means systematic. The provincial bourgeoisie is in constant contact with the peasantry; although they reject its worldview, they are still impressed by the power which its images hold. This explains why sometimes they react with fear to situations which outwardly they refuse to acknowledge as frightening.

The widespread belief and interest in parapsychology and herbalism among the priesthood and the provincial bourgeoisie of this region further illustrate this ambiguity of the bourgeoisie towards the peasant worldview. The priest of Paço and Couto attended two courses in parapsychology and had personally invited to the parish a famous 'herb-alist'. These 'disciplines' present in the 'scientific' and 'rational' language of the bourgeoisie what are, basically, peasant beliefs. In this way, they are ideal modes of resolving this ambiguity. The premise of parapsychology which particularly interests us here is that it accepts as 'scientifically verifiable' manifestations of the 'human mind' a whole set of phenomena explained by the peasants as manifestations of *coisas más*. The form of parapsychology expounded by a certain Father Quevedo SJ of Brazil had particular impact in Ponte da Barca. The Faculty of Philosophy of Braga (a Jesuit college) has been influential in broadcasting this interestingly Catholic version of parapsychology, which distinguishes neatly between the 'effects of the mind' and Christian, Church-approved miracles.

Similarly, herbalism is a curious means of compromising peasant beliefs about the life-giving powers of the earth and the rejection of consumer products based on the subsistence prototype, with a scientific 'rationality'. Both of these 'disciplines' provide a mediation of the cultural conflict as experienced by the rural clergy and other members of the provincial bourgeoisie.

VI

For the peasant, the roles of priests and white witches are not contradictory, as priests would have it, but they are complementary: the peasant who relies on the priests for prophylactic purposes has recourse to the white witch for therapeutic purposes. The priest represents an unambiguously positive morality, and there is no secrecy in a priest's actions as, in the eyes of the peasantry, they are fully consistent with the interests of the community as a whole. The white witch, on the contrary, is morally ambiguous, and is used for purely individual or household interests. These may well conflict with the interests of other individuals or other households. For this reason, white witches are consulted in secrecy, are regarded with suspicion, and indeed are called by the same name as witches proper who, though associated with 'envy', are more properly symbols of the existence of another threat to the social group: female sexuality.

VI

Life and death

18. Death and Burial

I

Burial practices are not uniform throughout the Alto Minho. They sometimes differ from parish to parish, reflecting the relative isolation of rural parishes on the one hand, and their divergent histories on the other. A third factor, however, may explain this: the varied impact of a new way of approaching death and burial. The Alto Minho is undergoing a process of radical change in attitudes to death and burial. What is surprising is that locally there is not a clearer awareness of this.

Since the sixth century AD, the Christian faithful have demonstrated a strong desire to be buried *ad sanctos*, that is, it was believed that spiritual benefit in the afterlife was to be derived from burial near the relics of a saint or in holy places (for a general historical discussion of death practices in Christian Europe, see Ariès, 1975 and 1977). In Minho, as there was not enough space for all within the church, only the wealthy received this preferential treatment, the majority of *vizinhos* being buried in the churchyard, in either communal or individual graves.

This meant that, when the living gathered for prayer, the dead were beneath their feet, thereby emphasizing that parish membership created a unity which reached beyond the grave.

It would seem (although my informants could not be specific) that until the twentieth century many people were buried without a coffin. Wrapped in a shroud (*mortalha*), they were carried to the grave in open communal coffins (*esquifes*).

Throughout southern Europe, during the eighteenth century, the practice of burying people in churchyards came under criticism. In Portugal such criticism was only really felt after the Napoleonic invasions and it came to be enshrined in the so-called health laws of the 1830s and especially the one of 1845. (cf. Pina-Cabral and Feijó, 1983). As Ariès comments in relation to France, it is not clear whether the indignation was due to a real concern with the fact that the unkempt condition of churchyards was a true hazard to public health or to the fact that new attitudes to death had evolved. I tend to follow Ariès in placing greater stress on the second conclusion.

The reaction of the *minhoto* peasantry to the direct attack on its burial practices which the 1845 health laws represented, was violent and it delayed the construction of cemeteries until the end of the nineteenth century. In Paço, the records of the Parish Council show that during the 1880s and 1890s, there was talk of building a cemetery which would be physically separated from the actual churchyard. In fact, the cemetery only started to be used during the second quarter of the twentieth century. That of Couto, however, was built as late as the 1970s. The utilization of cemeteries at all signifies that peasant attitudes had already begun to change.

Burial in cemeteries takes place in separate household graves. These can be bought and all average and wealthy peasant households own the graves in which they bury their dead. They are usually decorated with a marble slab on which are found small plaques where the names and dates of the deceased are engraved. Other religious symbols are usually present, such as a crucifix or a statue of the Virgin Mary. These decorations are conscious imitations of urban fashions and they bring prestige to the household. Poor households cannot have these as they do not own their graves. The right to use a grave is inherited by all the children of the original owner. In practice, however, there is usually one grave per household and people are buried in the grave of the household to which they belong or in that of their parents if they do not have a household of their own.

Two innovative aspects are noteworthy in relation to burial in cemeteries. First, cemeteries are situated apart from churches, even though they are holy ground. In the cities this may have been largely due to demographic needs. In rural areas, however, it represents a change in attitude in which the previous familiarity with the dead begins to give way to a greater separation of the realm of the living from that of the dead. The *vizinhos* no longer pray literally on top of their dead. The attempt to abolish this practice appears to have been one of the most shocking aspects of the health laws for nineteenth-century *minhoto* peasants. To this day the comments of the *almocreve* in Julio Dinis' nineteenth-century novel *A Morgadinha dos Canaviais* can still be heard: the graves do indeed look nice, like those in the cities, but the cemetery is a cold and wet place, where the dead are left alone and uncomfortable. Nowadays this is accepted as an inevitable condition; in the nineteenth century it was felt to be completely unnecessary.

Interestingly, as the peasants started to adopt urban practices and to build cemeteries, they nevertheless found it impossible to give up completely the previous sense of familiarity with the dead, which was an expression of the strong feeling of parish community. When they were built, cemeteries were placed as near to the churches as possible, in the path which the processions follow when they go around the church and the *cruzeiro* on feast days. This is, in fact, in contravention of the original health laws, which specified that the cemetery should be on the borders of inhabited zones. Furthermore, in Paço and Couto, neighbours always go to visit the dead after Mass on Sundays, thus re-establishing the link which the building of the cemetery had threatened to sever.

The second feature of cemeteries which represents a radical change in attitude is the existence of separately marked graves belonging to different households. As Ariès pointed out

le besoin de réunir à perpétuité, dans un lieu préservé et clos, les morts de la famille correspond à un sentiment nouveau qui s'est ensuite étendu à toutes les classes sociales au XIXe siècle: l'affection que lie les membres vivants de la famille est reportée sur les morts. (1975: 153)

Natalie Davis reports on the beginnings of this tendency in sixteenth- and seventeenth-century France. At that time, and particularly among Protestant families, there appeared a need to stress what she calls 'the family arrow in time and space' by means of a concern with family history, a limitation of the active kinship links, and a greater concern with the active planning of family strategies. Among Catholics this tendency was checked by a strong regard for inter-familial, communal links which were expressed in 'the traditional Catholic forms [of burial which] were connected directly or symbolically with corporate institutions hardly moribund in the sixteenth and seventeenth centuries, such as village assemblies and vestries, professional groups and craft guilds, confraternities and the like' (1977: 99–100).

In cemeteries, the *vizinhos* are not placed in an indistinguishable unity as they were in churchyards; people no longer pray for the parish dead but for 'their own dead' (*os nossos mortos*). The two tendencies, however, coexist—the pull of the community and the pull of the household. This coexistence is not a recent phenomenon and has been encountered throughout this study. Burial in separate, decorated graves in the cemetery is not only an indication of a weakening of the experience of community but equally of the notion of household which is inextricably related to it, as was argued above.

II

As has often been pointed out, death as a social phenomenon is a process and not a complete event taking place at the precise moment of physical death. As in many other societies, death for the *minhoto* peasant has an existence of its own and can be warded off, predicted, or summoned.

The *minhotos* believe that, at the approach of death, certain ominous (*agoirento*) signs appear, of which there are many. If, for instance, the church bells 'sound sad', this means a *vizinho* is going to die; if an owl alights on the roof of a house and cries out in an eerie tone in the middle of the night, this means that one of the residents is going to die; when a dog howls at night for no obvious reason, or when a fox or rabbit does not run away at one's approach—all of these are signs of imminent death.

Humans are shielded by their belonging to society—a belonging which is signalled and symbolized by baptism—from a clear perception of supernatural forces. Animals, being unprotected by baptism, are held to have a greater sensitivity to these forces: death, the presence of the Devil, the stare of the evil eye, the presence of witches or saints—all of these are often heralded by restless or abnormal behaviour in animals (cf. Christian, 1981: 75).

The dead themselves can sometimes give an indication of who is going to follow them. When a dead child's eyes, for example, cannot be closed, this means that it is 'calling for' (*a chamar*) a relative; when a person dies, the direction of his head indicates in which part of the parish—'upper' or 'lower'—the next death will occur.

Furthermore, visions of the 'procession of the dead' are encountered throughout northern Portugal and Galicia. While their particular features vary slightly, the main aspects are the same throughout this wide region. In Ponte da Barca the 'procession' consists of the *vizinhos* who are about to die or, in other accounts, who have died recently. A certain *vizinho* of Paço used to have visions of a group of people transporting a coffin. Inside the coffin lay the *vizinho* that was going to die next, and around it were those who would follow. This man believed he could not publicize the names of those he saw or he himself would die, but he used to tell people how many neighbours were due to die in the 'upper half' or in the 'lower half' of the parish during that year.

Death is a breach in the social order, not only for the alteration it induces in social relations but also because of its strong individualistic

bias (cf. Bloch and Parry, 1982: 3–5); it wrenches each member individually from the group in which, since baptism, he had been integrated. This understanding is corroborated by the belief that those who
see the 'procession' are people who were only partly baptized, their godparents not having pronounced all the words correctly during the baptismal ceremony. The balance between the social nature and the
physical or animal nature of man, in these people, favours the latter.

One interesting aspect of all 'processions of the dead' is that they are
attached to parish identity. As Lisón Tolosana has remarked of Galicia
'it must be stressed that "those of the night" [the "procession"]
scrupulously limit their nocturnal wanderings to the borders of the
parish because it has a church and cemetery' (1971b: 105). The dead
vizinhos belong to the parish community as do the living; parish community, once again, extends beyond death. This is evinced in the belief
that the night before a person's death his soul wanders about the parish
talking to his friends and visiting his fields. This occurs even if a *vizinho*
is an emigrant who is going to die away from home. A story was told to
me of a certain man who felt a presence next to his bed and his hand
being caressed during the night. A few days later he was told that a good
friend of his had died in Paris.

Death is not interpreted simply as the disappearance of the physio-
logical conditions of life; rather, it is a process which results from a
battle between the forces of life and death. There is a local concept
which illustrates this very clearly, which is the belief in *remédios da
desempata*—literally, medicine of the deciding game. The metaphor implies that there is a draw, as in a game, between life and death. When a
person is very ill, and is approaching death, the locals believe that there
is a point at which the doctors administer this medicine. If the person
has sufficient life in him he will survive; if, on the other hand, the
person is fated to die, death will immediately ensue.

III

In the Alto Minho there are four very distinct types of death to which
people's reactions vary accordingly. A person may die of old age: he has
taken Extreme Unction—a 'rite of incorporation into the other world'
(Van Gennep, 1960: 165)—and his death is therefore not problematic,
for the passsage from the living to the dead is well delineated and ritually
complete. A person may die of an illness: although in this case he may
have been able to receive Extreme Unction and to go through the rituals

of separation from the living and incorporation into the dead, this type of death creates greater problems, for it wrenches a previously able member from the midst of the living, thereby threatening the social order. To this type of death the reaction of relatives and neighbours is more violent, the wailing is stronger and the dangers which surround the period before the burial are more acute.

However, the third type, violent death, or death by accident, produces the greatest reaction from the local community. The wailing is intense, the *vizinhos* pity the deceased and the other members of his household, and all the practices attached to the fear that the dead person's soul may not have separated itself from the world of the living are strongly enforced. Finally, we have the death of children. As a rule, this is not as strongly felt as the previous two types of death. Children are not yet full participating members of society and, particularly if they are very young, their death is taken with a certain sense of resignation. Furthermore, children's 'purity', the fact that 'they had no time to sin,' also means that they have fewer links to this world and their separation from it, therefore, presents fewer problems than that of an adult.

Immediately after any kind of death, all gates and doors of the house of the deceased are thrown open to allow anyone to enter. The relatives abandon themselves to wailing, usually keeping to an inner room until the body is prepared for viewing. This is the first of three bouts of wailing, and it has the effect of calling the attention of all close neighbours who immediately come to help. A group of neighbours is quickly organized, which consists of a few women, who look after the kitchen and help to prepare the body, and a man who 'runs the burial'. All hamlet neighbours take great care in helping the bereaved household; at the moment of death, old animosities are forgotten and disputes are temporarily put aside. When two households have been enemies for a long time and one of them wishes to end the dispute, it sends a representative to work for the other household when the latter is bereaved. In practice, not all neighbours are needed and those who eventually take over the running of the household for the three days of the wake are the favoured neighbours, the 'friends'.

Usually the body is washed by a person of the same sex as the deceased with *aguardente* (a local kind of brandy made from the residue in the wine-press) which is supposed to help preserve the features. A cloth is tied to keep the jaws closed, the hair is combed, and the body is dressed in the finest available clothing of the deceased. A strong emphasis is placed on the need for the body to look 'decent', that is, to show the least possible signs of alteration. There must always be an oil lamp burning at the side of the deceased to protect him from evil influences.

Once the body is ready, the man who 'runs the funeral' calls the undertaker and any close relatives who live far away, buys food, and prepares the house for the sudden surge of people which will fill it after the second bout of wailing. Throughout the next three days the kitchen will be continuously at work, producing meals of the best quality for all who come to help with the burial, and snacks for those who come to pay their respects.

When the undertaker arrives with the coffin, he prepares the sitting-room and lays the body in the coffin. A new part of the wake begins. From now on the disorganized bustle and grief of the first few hours disappear, and everyone has a formally defined role to play. The members of the household (including the servants) initiate the second bout of wailing. They are accompanied in this by the children of the deceased, even if they now live apart, and to a lesser extent by his siblings.

The bereaved dress in black and cover themselves, even in the height of summer, as if it were the middle of winter. In this way they are protecting themselves against the bad influence generated by death. It is interesting to note that the man who 'runs the funeral' used to be called the *agasalhador*. (The verb *agasalhar* means 'to shelter', 'to wrap up', or 'to muffle up'.)

The bereaved sit wailing, accompanied by their close relatives and other visitors. Professional mourners who led the wailing were still common twenty years ago. They were called *choradeiras* (literally, those who weep). Nowadays, this task is left to the bereaved and particularly to the women, who weep themselves loudly into a frenzy. The wailing comes to regular climaxes whenever people who were close to the deceased—a relative or a friend—make their appearance, and it consists of a number of stock phrases which vary slightly according to the different types of death. On the whole, there is a concern to stress the dead person's 'goodness' and 'purity' and it is frequent to hear him or her being compared to a child or an angel, and reference being made to how unprotected the household will be now.

The visitors who continue to arrive throughout the next forty-eight hours approach the foot of the coffin and sprinkle the corpse with holy water in a practice which has the stated function of distancing the evil spirits (cf. Hertz, 1960: 63). Indeed, if the person died at home, the sprinkling with holy water and the recitation of litanies designed to frighten away the Devil would have already begun as he or she entered his or her last moments. It is believed that, if we could look through the eyes of a dying person who had not been sprinkled with holy water, we would not be able to see the light of day because the devils around him are so numerous as to obscure the light.

Following this rite, each visitor greets the members of the household individually. The visitor then leaves money for a Mass and writes his name down on a list. This practice too is a rite of separation, for each Mass that is said for a dead person helps to relieve him sooner from purgatory. By offering a Mass, visitors are helping with the process of transition of the deceased from the world of the living into the world of the dead. During all this time, prior to the Mass of the seventh day after the burial, nobody ever pronounces the name of the deceased, calling him instead *o falecido* (the deceased). Indeed, before the burial, they refer to him as 'the deceased above the earth'. (Only the bereaved maintain this practice for the whole of the period of mourning.) Visitors come and go, but the bereaved are never left alone and no one sleeps in the house before the body leaves it. Port, wine, and the local type of brandy, as well as biscuits, are served continually, and close friends, relatives, and neighbours are invited by those who 'run the burial' to take meals with the family.

It is an accepted practice for close relatives such as children, spouses, and parents, to attend the wake even when they have emigrated. At an hour's notice, the relatives leave their jobs and homes in Canada, France, Germany, Brazil, and even Australia in order to fly home. They usually arrive during the second night of the wake or the following morning, and their arrival heralds a build-up in the wailing which eventually reaches a climax by mid-morning when the priest arrives to take the body to be buried.

The bells toll during the morning to indicate that a funeral is going to take place. Thus a great number of people is present at the home of the bereaved for the prayers, most *vizinho* households who had any contact with the bereaved sending at least one representative. The audience is temporarily silent during prayers and then a procession is formed outside as the body leaves the home, to the accompaniment of the last and loudest bout of wailing by the bereaved, who are not permitted to follow the coffin, as otherwise the soul of the deceased may feel sorry for them and decide to remain behind.

The process of separation of the soul from the body and from the living, had already begun before the actual moment of physical death.

At this moment, however, the danger that this separation may not be effected properly is at its greatest and the movements of the soul must be carefully guided. This explains such practices as the prohibition on pronouncing the name of the deceased (for fear the soul answers the call). Furthermore, no fire should be taken out of the house of the bereaved during the wake, for the soul would follow it and stray. This soul would then be 'in pain' (or 'in sorrow') and it would haunt the community of the living. To prevent the soul from going astray, the priest must accompany the procession. Until recently, it was customary for the procession to stop at crossroads and for the priest to say a prayer to prevent the soul from taking the wrong turning. The present priest abolished this custom. When the coffin is being lowered into the grave, most people shift about, otherwise the soul might find them and remain with them. After the coffin is in the grave, those who have remained behind throw a clod of earth into the pit. Without this rite of separation, the soul would remain 'in pain' for, once again, it would follow the living. It must be noted that all these rituals have two symbolic functions: by pushing the soul away, the people are not only protecting themselves against being contaminated by death, they are also helping it on its way to salvation.

The danger of the soul remaining 'in pains' is especially great if the deceased has suffered violent death, in particular if he was murdered. The soul of a murdered person will sit on its homicide's back till it breaks. The only way to avoid this is to plant a cross on the spot where the death occurred. Even under normal circumstances, however, the soul of the recently deceased is dangerous, for it calls to other souls. When a funeral procession passes by, people who are lying down, even if they are sick, stand up, otherwise the soul of the deceased would collect theirs.

The funeral procession is headed by a choirboy with a handbell, rung and then quickly muffled, every third step. This boy is followed by other choirboys and adult men carrying the parish's processional cross and the banners of the confraternities to which the deceased belonged. Behind these is the priest who is followed by the coffin which is carried either by the members of a confraternity (Nossa Senhora do Carmo) who specialize in this task or by four unmarried men. The coffin is followed by the rest of the men and finally, at the tail of the procession, the women.

After the completion of the ceremony in the church, which may be more or less complicated depending upon the wealth of the bereaved, the coffin goes on to the cemetery, but many people abandon the procession here. At the cemetery, the coffin is opened once again for people to look into and is then shut and unceremoniously lowered into the grave while the people disperse.

The people who 'run the burial', as well as any who helped in the procedures, the priest or priests, the choirboys, and the staff of the confraternities which were present are given a meal after the burial. The stress on food throughout the wake and burial may be interpreted as a means of denying death and of stressing the life of those who remain behind. The importance of commensality as an expression of 'community' must also be taken into account.

Throughout the wake the bereaved must not wash themselves, comb or cut their hair or shave, neither must they change their shirts or indeed any piece of clothing. They are prohibited from singing, dancing, listening to music or to the radio, and from watching television. For this period of liminality, the bereaved also do not go to church, thus reminding themselves that they too were marked by death. Except for the prohibition on music and dance which, in Paço and Couto, is kept for the entire duration of the period of mourning, the other prohibitions are lifted after the Mass of the seventh day, which the bereaved, however, still do not attend. A second Mass is said after a month has passed and finally a third one, to mark the anniversary of the death. Throughout the next few years, the priest regularly says a Mass for the soul of the deceased, paid for with money given by the visitors who came to the wake; the rest of the money is sent to the bishop's curia, where it is allocated to priests who are not in charge of parishes (such as those in convents, seminaries, or the bishop's curia; the total number of masses ordered by the visitors to one wake may be as high as 200 or more). All of those who are close to the family make a point of attending the three principal Masses for, as an informant once put it, 'there, one sees who one's real friends are.'

Mourning is marked by the wearing of black and withdrawal from all forms of merriment. Its length varies according to one's relation to the deceased and in mountain parishes it is longer than in parishes where the urban influence has been more strongly felt. In Paço and Couto, mourning lasts two years or more for a spouse, two years for a parent, one year for siblings, grandparents, and godparents, and six months for cousins and nephews.

At present, in the Alto Minho, the process of secondary disposal of the corpse tends to be rather understated. This is one of the areas where there is a wide degree of local variation in custom. At the end of the nineteenth century, secondary disposal of bones was still a strongly attended parish ceremony (see Castelao's description for Galicia, Durán, 1976: 79), as it remains in parts of Mediterranean Europe (cf. Alexiou, 1974 and Guillebaud, 1979). The tendency towards the progressive understatement of this part of the funerary practices might be interpreted with reference to Maurice Bloch's argument. This author claims that in societies where the legitimation of power is not based on the 'canalization of the fertility of predecessors' but on the mediation of an extra-human source of power, 'there is no need to transform the corpse into a source of continuing fertility' (1982: 229) which explains the lack of secondary obsequies. The tendency towards the disappearance of these ceremonies would then accompany the weakening of the traditional authority of the household and its head (resulting, among other things, from the progressive decrease in the overall economic significance of agricultural income). A similar process took place in relation to the burial of unbaptized children who, as was stated above, are now buried silently in the cemetery and no longer within the household.

The State has stipulated a minimum period of five years during which nobody is allowed to open a grave. In practice, however, this law is not strictly followed and the disinterment often takes place after three to four years. The grave-digger is given orders to proceed by the family, at least one member of which is present at the time. The grave is opened and the bones are collected and cleaned. If there is an ossuary, they are placed there; in Paço and Couto they are carefully packed into plastic bags, which are buried at the sides of the grave.

The justification for disinterment is that the grave may be needed for some other member of the family, but my experience is that this practice is often adhered to even when no member is apparently approaching death. This acceleration of the process is due to the fact that secondary disposal marks the complete separation of the deceased from the living.

IV

Throughout this description of the death process (death, wake, and burial) we have encountered a series of rites, practices, and beliefs which stress the importance of the experience of community. The connection between death and community is something which the *minhotos* themselves repeatedly stress. Comments such as 'rich or poor, here we are all alike; we all land up in the same place,' or 'at least in this we are all the same' are standard reactions whenever the issue of death is broached or a funeral procession passes by.

This is also the significance of the 'open' state of the bereaved household, whose doors are left ajar throughout the three days of the wake. It must be noted that not all forms of 'openness' convey this message. We have already referred to the 'open hours' which are dangerous because they are vulnerable to outside influences. 'Openness' in the context of the burial, however, has to be understood in the same way as when it is used to qualify people. For example, when a *minhoto* says of someone that 'he is an open man' he means that the person in question is sociable, open to society. 'Openness', in this context, refers to an orientation towards community, which is corroborated by people's willingness to forget quarrels at death and to help bereaved *vizinhos*.

The help of those who 'run the burial', that is, the close, 'friendly' neighbours who arrived at the bereaved house at the time of the first bout of wailing, is given in a spirit of 'generalized reciprocity': a form of reciprocity where debts are not precisely balanced.

The relationship between the bereaved and the other visitors, however, is different and could be classified as a form of balanced, symmetrical, reciprocity. By attending the wake, paying for a Mass, following the funeral procession, and being present at the three Masses for the soul of the deceased, the visitors 'give respect' to the bereaved household. But these are all 'favours which must be paid back', and the bereaved keep a close watch on who was present so that they know how to behave in future.

Even though balanced reciprocity may be said to have a different significance from generalized reciprocity, on the whole both are manifestations of an awareness of community and equality. This awareness is differently stated at different levels, but is present throughout. Although this experience of community and equality at death is strongly reinforced at parish level, it is not limited to it. That death renders all men equal is not only openly stated but also depicted in the roadside images of the souls in purgatory, where the souls are represented naked or partly naked, and where all suffer alike: kings, bishops, men and women, old and young.

This having been said, it must be stressed that not everyone is given the same sort of funeral. Wakes may be distinguishable by the abundance of foodstuffs; coffins may be more or less elaborate; processions may have a larger or a smaller following of automobiles; the service in the church may include up to eight priests; and, finally, the grave may be plain, covered by a more or less elaborate marble plaque, or, in the case of wealthy landowners, it may even be a small mausoleum. Sixteenth-century French Catholics used to give out 'ostentatious "doles" to the needy' during funerals (Davis, 1977: 94). We encounter here a similar situation. 'Doles' were given as an expression of a sense of 'community', yet they were 'ostentatious', which meant that they reinforced the superiority of the donors. Similarly, the bereaved in the Alto Minho utilize the rites of community and equality attached to burials as means of stressing prestige. This is important in order to understand the local attitude to funerals and wakes—they reveal social differentiation through the expression of community. The two tendencies are inter-linked.

The story of Adam and Eve tells us that death resulted from original sin, as a necessary ending to man's physical condition. As such, therefore, death renders all men equal. Yet, ironically, physical death is a social phenomenon and as such one which exists within a fallen world: even as the naked soul enters purgatory to burn admid kings and beggars, the bereaved are participating in complex funeral arrangements, paying for expensive coffins, and erecting costly marble plaques.

19. Cults of death

> For thou wilt not leave my
> soul in Hell; neither wilt
> thou suffer thine Holy One
> to see corruption.
>
> Psalms 16 : 10

Of the various divine figures which receive worship from the peasantry of Minho, three types deserve particular attention here, not because their worship is any more widespread than that of others, but because they are singularly clear manifestations of one of the central conceptions of the peasant worldview of Minho, and perhaps also of Christianity as a whole: the opposition between physical life and death and spiritual life and death. I shall refer to the acts of worship surrounding each of these types of figures as a 'cult', and to all of these cults as 'cults of death'.

The first is that of the souls in purgatory; that is, the souls of the recently deceased burning in purgatory, waiting for the day on which they will be purified by fire of their earthly sins. The second is the cult of incorrupt bodies. These are the bodies of people who, after burial, remain incorrupt, their bodies keeping the flesh and their clothes remaining in perfect condition. Finally, we shall deal with the cult of people who are reported not to eat or drink, and therefore not to have normal bodily functions. These people are considered to be saintly and I shall refer to them as non-eaters for there is no specific established term to describe them. These cults are not at all peculiar to Portugal, and may be found throughout the Catholic, and indeed the Christian, world.

In their book, *Celebrations of Death*, Huntington and Metcalf argue that funeral rites

expresss the social order by differentiation between people of unequal status. This type of argument lends itself to extensions in many directions. Hertz himself connects it with the practice of preserving relics of individuals of high esteem, and hence the origin of ancestor cult. (1979: 73)

In my opinion, this argument, which has its value, cannot explain the internal consistency of these cults. I found that in order to cope with them, I had to go beyond this explanation. The attempt to do so forms the main argument of this section.

I

First, it is necessary to understand the local eschatological beliefs. Roman Catholicism states that the soul of a person who dies in full saintliness will be taken to heaven directly upon death. In practice, most people die with sins to their name and these have to be expiated in purgatory. Depending on the seriousness of the sins and on the religious intervention which has been effected on behalf of the deceased, the period in purgatory may be prolonged or shortened. Finally, if a person dies with 'mortal sins', if he is excommunicated, or if he has been baptized but has not availed himself of the services of the Church, his soul is taken directly to hell. Souls who have gone to purgatory can only move to heaven, never to hell. Souls which have been sent to heaven or hell can never leave these spheres.

Locally most people are thought to die with *culpas*—sins, wrongdoing, guilts, debts: this word can have all these meanings. Thus most people have to spend a greater or lesser amount of time in purgatory according to the number of their *culpas*. The problem, however, is that, although hell is often referred to, peasants seldom claim that a certain person has probably gone there. The only instances I have come across of people purportedly having gone to hell, were those in which souls that were in purgatory were specifically sent to hell by means of exorcism, because they were bothering the living. This is in direct opposition to Church belief. The idea that people go directly to hell, although held as a possibility, does not seem to be of particular interest to *minhoto* peasants. As a rule, then, after death, people's souls go to purgatory. However, we are dealing here with a very nebulous and unsystematized set of concepts. While some informants reported that souls 'in pain' (*almas penadas*) also go to purgatory, others were uncertain about this. As the Church does not believe in the existence of such souls, the eschatological framework provided by the priests has to be distorted in order to apply to them, and here we encounter a considerable amount of confusion. As Ariès has pointed out, this conception of 'souls in pains' (the French *revenants* and English ghosts) who remain to haunt the living, finds its roots in a pre-fourteenth-century Christian eschatology which saw the judgement of souls as taking place at the end of time and not soon after the person's death.

In the Alto Minho, there are two main factors which cause souls to remain 'in pain': the first and most important of these is that the soul has left *culpas* in this world. The word 'debts', understood in the wide sense, is perhaps the best translation of *culpas* in this context. For example, if a person has made a promise to a saint and has died before having been able to fulfil it, his soul is considered to be 'in pain'. Another very common and important cause is if, at the time of death, the relatives discover that there is an unaccountable absence of money. This either means that the person left business deals incomplete or that money is hidden in a secret place. The most commonly experienced *culpa*, however, is when the deceased, during his lifetime, secretly moved the landmarks that divide the plots of the various households. As there are no cadastral maps of this area, people are very fearful of this.

The second main reason for being 'in pains' is if some ritual aspect of one's burial was not properly enacted, instances of which have also already been mentioned. I have never heard of an antidote to this second problem. I presume that it is a possibility that people consider but that it is seldom, if ever, actually used to apply to specific situations. What both explanations have in common is that, on account of moral or ritual lapses in conduct, the soul of the person 'in pains' has not been able to go through the process of separation effectively. The rigour with which people follow these rites, thus avoiding dying with these *culpas* unpaid, is therefore understandable.

The cult of the souls in purgatory refers only to those souls which are not 'in pain'; souls which are going to be freed by the action of St Michael who, much against the Devil's wishes, redeems them from purgatory, due partly to the grace of God, but mainly to the intercession of the Virgin, St Antony, and Christ. When these souls go to heaven, they are thankful to those who prayed for them, and they therefore ask the saints to intercede with God for the salvation of the faithful. This is the theological and popular basis of the cult of the souls in purgatory.

The souls in purgatory, then, are liminally situated between life and death and they therefore assume both a sacred and a frightening character. Because of their very transience, they are used as mediators between this life and the next, between the powerlessness and blindness of this fallen world, and the power and omniscience of the world to come.

Public worship of the souls in purgatory has suffered greatly from bourgeois and clerical prejudice over the past decades. It has therefore practically ceased. It was, however, still practised in Paço and Couto some ten years ago. The general term to refer to this form of worship is *Encomenda das Almas* (literally, the recommendation of the souls). In Paço it was also called *alimentar as Almas* (literally, to feed the souls). The church bells chimed at 9.00 p.m. 'to the souls', just as they do when announcing a funeral. A group of men, or at other times a group of women, would then go to the top of a hill and chant the following words in a melancholy tone so that most people in the parish could hear them:

> Harken, Harken
> Life is short
> And death is certain.
> Whoever can (pray) must do so
> For the love of God.

This was an appeal to the *vizinhos* not to forget to pray with them a Paternoster, an Ave Maria, and a Gloria Pater for the souls.

Although this form of public worship has disappeared, an individual form of worship which is centred around the roadside shrines to the souls in purgatory is by no means in decline. These are little shrines, generally made of stone, which incorporate a panel depicting souls burning in purgatory, and a series of divine beings placed in an order which corresponds to their hierarchical relations. A common pattern is one in which the crucified Christ is represented centrally at the top of the panel; underneath him is the Virgin, to her left is St Antony, and, slightly lower to her right, is the archangel St Michael, pulling the souls out of the flames with his scales in his hand. Although they are now rare, I still encountered some panels depicting the Devil attempting to hinder St Michael's task. Statements by the souls are often engraved beneath the panels, typically saying: 'O passers-by, remember us who are "in pain", Paternoster, Ave Maria.' (see Plate 1.)

These shrines are constructed either by individuals as a votive offering to the souls, or by the *vizinhos* of a hamlet or parish in a communal gesture of worship. In the latter case, they are put in the charge of a household. Otherwise they are looked after by the descendants of the donor. People who pass by drop some money into a collection box or leave small offerings such as candles, flowers, corn-cobs, beans, etc. These small offerings are for the most part propitiatory, that is, they are designed to incline the souls more favourably towards the giver.

The shrines are nearly always on the roadside at the entrance to the hamlet or at crossroads. If one finds them in the middle of a hamlet, this usually means that the hamlet has grown since the time they were constructed. The liminality of the souls is the essence of their cult as it explains their worship as mediators between life and death and it also explains their positioning as guardians at the entrances to the hamlet. Furthermore, the fact that the 'recommendation of the souls' was made just past sunset, must also be interpreted in the same light.

II

I shall now deal with the cult of incorrupt bodies. As we have seen, after burial, a corpse is allowed to rest for a period of three to five years. Usually, after that time, all that remains of the deceased is a skeleton. In some cases, however, and for reasons that do not really concern us here, some bodies do not decompose (cf. Thomas, 1980: 42–4). Descriptions that I have heard of the discovery of incorruptible bodies are very similar in kind: the coffin is opened and both the person's clothing and body are found to be perfectly intact. There is, accompanying this unexpected vision of perfection, a smell of sanctity which, in the numerous and varied accounts I have read and heard, is always described as the smell of a flower, either rose, violet, or jasmine. Most of the bodies react quite badly to coming into contact with the air, and many disintegrate shortly afterwards. This, however, is not always the case.

When an incorrupt body is discovered, the people as a rule claim that it is that of a saint. The authorities and priests, however, are interested in burying it immediately, since they are loath to accept incorruptibility as a necessary sign of sanctity. Usually they are prevented from doing so by the people. This pattern has repeated itself in all recent cases that I have studied. While the body is above ground and before it has been reburied, the priest practises a ritual of 'lifting excommunication' (*Ritus absolvendi excommunicatum jam mortuum*) that consists mainly of whipping the corpse. This detail greatly surprised me until a priest guided me to a ritual in the *Rituale Romanum* where the priest is told to whip the corpse of an excommunicated person while saying a few prayers, so as to unify him or her with the body of the Church, thus allowing his or her soul to go to heaven. What the priests in this area do is perhaps very similar to all those rites of integration described by Van Gennep when he says

Whipping is an important rite in many ceremonies . . . and is equivalent to the New Guinea rite of hitting the person over the head with a club to incorporate him into the totem clan, the family, or the world of the dead. (1960: 174)

The Portuguese priests' actions may be understood if we take into account the fact that, for many centuries, the Church has held an ambivalent attitude towards incorruptibility. When a body is discovered to be incorrupt, it may either be that of a great sinner (since the formula for excommunication itself refers to incorruptibility) or that of a saint. If the body belonged to a sinner, or to an excommunicated person, then it is believed to rot immediately upon incorporation into the Mother Church, the community of the living.

There is something further to be said concerning the incorrupt bodies of sinners. Apart from the practice of the flagellation of incorrupt bodies by priests, on the assumption that they belong to sinners, I have never heard it claimed that an incorrupt body may belong to a sinner. When, in north-western Portugal, an incorrupt body is discovered and a cult does not develop, this is due to a kind of social amnesia, and not to the belief that the body was that of a sinner. Some local residents have even told me that they do not know of sinners' bodies remaining incorrupt. I presume therefore that the practice of flagellation has its roots not in the attitudes of lay people (who in fact resent it), but in the Church hierarchy.

The symbolic structure of the concept that sinners remain incorrupt is very different from that which ascribes saintliness to incorruptible bodies. The body of a sinner is incorrupt because he has left behind so many *culpas* that his body was unable to undergo the natural process of separation from the living. This is why, as soon as he is incorporated with the dead by means of lifting the excommunication, his body immediately disintegrates. He has to be seen as an extreme case of a soul 'in pains'. As with the other souls 'in pains', the rites of separation were ineffectual, only in these instances they were more so.

As a rule, when the ritual of flagellation has been completed, the priests and the authorities manage to rebury the corpse. If, however, after five more years, when the body is again disinterred, it is still intact, the pressure exerted by the people to keep it above ground is too great and the priests and authorities are forced to compromise.

I have studied in detail eight cases of this cult of incorrupt bodies, but I have references to at least twenty-one other similar cases in northwestern Portugal alone. Of the cases I have studied, two have been known for more than five centuries, while the remainder were all disinterred in the twentieth century. In the small borough of Ponte da Barca alone I discovered four cases of people known to have been incorrupt five years after the original burial and two that are exposed for public viewing in chapels in an aura of sanctity. This raises a problem: why should some be prayed to while others are not?

There are two principal answers to this problem: the first has to do with the personal characteristics of the deceased. Their lives have to conform to a pattern of sanctity. If they were known to have led morally dubious lives, they are then perhaps forgotten when they are reburied. Some bodies are forgotten because people's attention is directed to other cases that have a greater appeal. This leads us to the second answer: the sociological setting behind the cult is very significant. If two cases of a similar type are found, the second to be discovered tends to be forgotten.

Of the eight cases of incorrupt bodies I studied in detail, three belong to women. All of these are reported to have been unmarried and indeed virgins. Purity, endurance, and love are the qualities that are constantly ascribed to these women. In this they are very similar to the Virgin Mary. As in her case, preservation is seen as a particular consequence of purity. Mgr Pohle argues that 'the incorruptibility of Our Lady's raised body may also be inferred from her perpetual virginity. There is an inseparable causal connection between *incorruptio virginalis* and *incorruptio corporalis*—the one is the fruitage of the other' (quoted in Winch and Bennett, 1950: 73–4).

The male saints are characterized somewhat differently. In their case purity is not such a focal point, although two of them were priests and the others were reported to have been of unimpeachable morality. There is a similar stress on endurance of pain and suffering, and particular emphasis is laid on their material generosity. This difference is significant, for it clarifies the difference between male and female roles. While women are mainly subject to corruption in their sensual behaviour, men are subject to corruption mostly in their social and economic behaviour. On the other hand, the common stress on endurance of pain is connected with these saints' lack of concern for the basic physical needs of their fallen condition, and therefore their predominant interest in spiritual life.

Like the souls in purgatory, these incorrupt bodies are ambiguous cases. Although they cannot be said to be in a transient state as are the souls in purgatory, they are certainly in a position of liminality. The dead normally do not have a body, as this decays shortly after death, unlike the living who are characterized by their possession of a body. As having a body is a characteristic of being alive, incorrupt bodies can metaphorically be said to be simultaneously dead and live. When we take the lead suggested by Mgr Pohle in the quotation above, where he related *incorruptio virginalis* to *incorruptio corporalis*, we understand the symbolic mechanism behind this cult.

III

I shall now give a brief account of the cult of non-eaters. These are people who, due to their 'saintliness', can live in a state of permanent and total fasting. Many cases have been reported in Minho. I am acquainted in particular detail with the case of Alexandrina de Balazar. This was a girl who, at the age of fourteen, had been sexually pursued by several men. To avoid them, she jumped out of a window and as a result was crippled for life. While she was bedridden, all that she ingested was the Host every Sunday. She was reported to have 're-lived' the experience of Christ's Passion every Friday night and as a result of this she was said to have had 'an almost supernatural endurance to pain'. She died at the age of fifty-one. We find here characteristics similar to those of the cult of incorruptible bodies. This woman was a virgin and it was in order to remain 'pure' that she embarked upon this life of saintliness and suffering. It is worth noting that the other two cases of non-eaters that were encountered were also women and both of them were reported to have been sexually 'pure'.

The Bavarian case of Theresa Newman (cf. e.g. Sackville-West, 1943: 179) is similar in most respects. Why is it that these women should be

considered saintly? What in them explains people's readiness to believe
in their healing power? Once again we are confronted with an ambiguity
of definition leading to a situation of liminality. These women are alive,
but every Friday they 'die with Christ', for it is emphatically stated that
they physically experience Christ's Passion. At the same time, they do
not participate in those bodily functions that characterize humans in
this fallen world. Thus, while being alive, their bodies in effect behave
as if they were dead. It is, I believe, in this ambiguity that the symbolic
significance of this cult lies.

IV

The three cults discussed above all deal with entities that are liminal
because they lie between two worlds. This is further complicated by the
fact that life and death are used in two different senses, the physical and
the spiritual. The interplay of meaning in the use of these concepts is
central to Christianity. Cobb, from a theological perspective, has said:
'It will be clear that the New Testament and Christian antithesis is not
that of the Old Testament and Judaism, between this world and the
next, but between two kinds of life both here and there' (in Hastings,
1918-30, VIII: 19). The body, as the vehicle of physical life, is, at the
same time and through its needs and demands, the vehicle of spiritual
death, and it is with the corruption of the physical body that spiritual
purification in purgatory can take place. Physical death may lead man
back to spiritual life.

Physical life and spiritual life, then, are used as metaphors for each
other in certain circumstances, while in others they are regarded as
opposites. This complex interrelation between the two meanings is
highlighted by Bethune-Baker when he maintains that sin is

a state or condition, a particular way of living, which is described as sickness, or
even, by contrast with true life, as death. Those who are living under such conditions are 'dead'. Of this state the opposition is life, or eternal life—a particular
way of living now, characteristic of which is the knowledge of God and love of
the brethren. (1903: 77)

Although they use life and death in two different senses, Christians
seldom explicate the specific meaning it assumes in each instance. If we
attempt to do this, however, we find that there is a great contradiction
involved in the use of the same terms with differing meanings. What
characterizes physical life is that it occurs in this world, while physical

death leads into the world beyond. Spiritual life and death, however, are characterized by occurrence both here and in the beyond. The two concepts, therefore, are not exactly symmetrical.

We see, furthermore, that what characterizes physical life is the presence of a body and its needs, while what characterizes physical death is the absence of the body and its needs. Conversely, spiritual life is characterized by the negation of the body, the stress being on the state of the soul, while spiritual death is characterized by indulgence in the satisfaction of bodily needs and desires. But this does not imply that every single characteristic of the physical life/death opposition is negated in the spiritual life/death opposition. Rather, it suggests that a contradiction is present, and that this contradiction requires a mediation. Lévi-Strauss has said that 'the purpose of myth is to provide a logical model capable of overcoming a contradiction' (1963: 229). I would contend that these cults can be regarded in a manner similar to myths. The Portuguese peasant, like all Christians, lives in a fallen world, one of hardship and despair, permanently threatened by impending death. Yet he believes that there is a state of perennial life which can already be achieved in this world. To overcome this contradiction, he has recourse to entities which, because they are not clearly classifiable as dead or alive, can be used as mediators.

V

We now reach the point where we have to consider the position of Christ and the Virgin Mary in relation to this life/death symbolism. In the 1950s, the Assumption of Our Lady became a dogma of the Catholic faith. This belief, which had been widespread in the Christian Church since the sixth century, states that the Virgin died but that her body did not decay, for she was taken to heaven in bodily form. The Virgin, in her similarity to Christ, is thus believed to have been physically resurrected. They died, yet they are alive, for their death did not imply the corruption of their bodies. In this, the examples of incorrupt bodies described above are akin to Christ and the Virgin. But there is an important distinction between the two cases, for Christ and the Virgin are *incorruptible*, while the saints are merely *incorrupt*. Christ and the Virgin were immaculately conceived, that is, they never participated in spiritual death, for they did not inherit the original sin. They lived a physical life and suffered a physical death but, as they were resurrected almost immediately after their death, they are alive in heaven and their bodies are united with their souls. If their bodies did not decay, this was because, through their inherent heightened spiritual life, they managed to overcome the corruption of death.

Once more we find a situation of ambiguity, but here life has won. This is an instance of what Lévi-Strauss would call a 'helicoïdal mediation', that is, one which overcomes the original conflict which required mediation. Jesus and Mary, who are characterized by the forces of life (both spiritual and physical), confronted the evil forces of death (once more spiritual and physical); they suffered human death (here, however, only physical—even though Christ did descend into Hades), and therefore managed to achieve spiritual life for all mankind, that is, the eventual abolition of evil.

If we look at the cult of non-eaters and incorrupt bodies in the light of this, we find that they effect a similar type of mediation. They too are characterized by forces of life (i.e. their arduous struggle to achieve spirituality) and they confront the evil forces of death (both physical and spiritual). Through their own death, however, (actual in the case of incorrupt bodies and metaphorical in the case of non-eaters) they manage to bring about the victory of purity over the forces of death. This mediation is, however, no longer 'helicoïdal' in that it does not abolish the original polarity of forces, as the mediation of Christ and the Virgin had done, but merely postpones the action of the forces of death.

This second type of mediation is not specific to these two cults, for it can be said to extend to the cult of all saints, since they all mediate between the spiritual life that they acquired and the physical death to which they were subjected. The relics of saints, as signs of their existence in the world, therefore operate not only as validations of the saints' existence, but also as representations of this mediation. This would appear to be a better explanation for the use of relics in the Christian Church than the one which may be derived from Huntington and Metcalf's quotation at the beginning of this section. Their explanation, valuable as it may be in other contexts, fails to take into account the specific nature of the relics of saints within the Christian context.

The Church itself phrases the position of Christ, the Virgin, and the saints in a very similar fashion. As far as Christ is concerned, suffice it to quote from Paul's Epistle to the Romans (5: 18–19) where he says: 'For as by one man's disobedience [that is, Adam's] many were made sinners, so by the obedience of one shall many be made righteous.' It is, however, when I categorize the Virgin's mediation together with

Christ's that I am going against Roman Catholic theology. But even here I am accompanied by many theologians who openly objected to the establishment of the dogma of the assumption on the basis that it inevitably leads to an equivalence between Christ and the Virgin. When we hear Salazar speaking on this subject we see that the problem is very real. He says of Mary:

She acted as a mediatrix with the Mediator. The work of our salvation was so wrought. The Virgin expressed to her Son the desires of the human race; but the Son, deferring to the Mother, received these, and again presented to the Father the desires both of His mother and of His own; but the Father granted what was wished, first to the Son and then to the Mother. (In Winch and Bennett, 1950: 107)

It is obvious then why Winch and Bennett complain that 'the general tendency of Mariology has been to parallel the Blessed Virgin with her Son, so that every prerogative that belongs to Him should in some measure be imputed to her also' (1950: 170). For the people of northwestern Portugal, the dogma of the Assumption—which they celebrate so festively on 15 August—is so deeply ingrained that I believe I am justified in interpreting their cult of the Virgin as a form of mediation that is, in its symbolic bases, similar to the mediation of Christ.

As we have seen with regard to the broad symbolic structures of the three cults, however, the mediation performed by the saints (including incorrupt bodies and non-eaters) is a weaker version of the mediation of Christ and the Virgin. That effected by the souls in purgatory is weaker still. The latter pray for us after our prayers have saved them. But, as their liminality is based on a transition and is not a permanent state, their mediation too is short-lived.

The mediation effected by all these figures may be seen as an epitome of a wider problem which has been encountered throughout this study: the desire for physical life is countered by the need to create a bounded, ordered, righteous social world. As Hocart put it, 'ritual is not merely a quest for life, it is a social quest' (1952: 52). Through the unstable confrontation of these two opposing tendencies, the *minhoto* peasant searches for Life in the widest sense: for reproduction in purity.

In bringing to a close this perambulation through the peasant worldview of the Alto Minho, I feel I must refer back to its great cosmogonic myth: the story of Adam and Eve. All men and women are placed within a world of impending death and chaos. They all require the services of Christ's redemption—the work of the new Adam. Yet they do so differently, for as men are the sons of Adam, so women are the daughters of Eve; the most basic difference between human beings comes to represent the contradictory nature of human social life.

APPENDIX

Percentage of extended family households per age group (excluding households headed by single people)

Age-group	Paço					Couto				
	Nuclear family		Extended family		Total	Nuclear family		Extended family		Total
	Numbers	Percentage	Numbers	Percentage		Numbers	Percentage	Numbers	Percentage	
– 25	9	81.82	2	18.18	11	0	.0	1	—	1
25–9	11	50.00	11	50.00	22	6	66.67	3	33.33	9
30–4	9	60.00	6	40.00	15	10	76.92	3	23.08	13
35–9	19	70.37	8	29.63	27	12	80.00	3	20.00	15
40–4	24	70.59	10	29.41	34	16	80.00	4	20.00	20
45–9	18	85.71	3	14.29	21	16	84.21	3	15.70	19
50–4	19	67.86	9	32.14	28	12	75.00	4	25.00	16
55–9	21	72.41	8	27.59	29	9	100.00	0	.0	9
60–4	15	88.24	2	11.76	17	9	81.82	2	18.18	11
65–9	17	85.00	3	15.00	20	9	90.00	1	10.00	10
70–4	5	50.00	5	50.00	10	4	80.00	1	20.00	5
75+	12	80.00	3	20.00	15	12	85.71	2	14.29	14
?	19	82.61	4	17.39	23	23	95.83	1	4.17	24
Total	198	72.79	74	27.21	272	138	83.13	28	16.87	166

GLOSSARY

This glossary comprises only the Portuguese words which appear in the text repeatedly. Arabic figures refer the reader to main sections, while roman numerals refer to subsections.

adágios (10)—ritual prescriptions and prohibitions.
à direita (12.I, III.VI)—moving 'by or on the right (hand)'.
a direito (12.I, III.VI)—moving straight.
a favor (13.III)—labour given in exchange for labour.
a jornal (13.III)—paid agricultural labour.
alminhas (5.II)—shrine to the souls in purgatory.
alma penada (13.II; 18.III)—'soul in pain', ghost.
apelido que (não) se escreve (11.III)—patronymic versus kindred nickname.
a vindos (13.III)—labour-sharing among a limited number of households.

bicho do mato (9.V)—unsocialized human being.
bruxo/a (15.III; 16.II, III)—witch, white witch.

cabaneiro (6.IV)—person with no attachment to the land.
casa (1.II; 5.I)—house, household.
caseiro (1.II; 3.III)—share-cropper.
coisas más (15.VI)—evil things.
compasso (12.II)—Easter procession.
concelho (1.II)—borough.
confiança (13.II; 8.III)—trust.
cruzeiro (12.III)—large stone cross.
culpas (19.I)—sins, spiritual debts.

defumadouro (5.II)—ritual burning attached to *feitiço*.
deserto (9.V)—desert; backward, uncivilized region.
doença de cá, de lá (16.I)—physical versus spiritual disease.
dote (6.IV; 7.II)—dowry, expectation of eventual inheritance.

educado (9.V)—well brought up.
entendido das vacas (16.I)—local specialist on animal diseases.
estragada (8.III; 9.II)—broken down, spoilt.
ex votos, promessas (14.I–V)—votive offerings.

falar mal (9.V)—to speak foul language.
família (5.I)—family.
farta (10.IV)—full, replete.
feira (3.IV)—market.
feiticeira (16.II)—sorcerer, witch.
feitiço (15.II; 16.III)—sorcery.
festas (5.II; 11.III; 17.III)—fairs, festivities.
fogo (5.I)—fire, household.
força (10.VI)—force, strength, power, etc.
freguesia (1.II; 2.I)—parish (as a lay community).

inveja (15.II)—envy.

jornaleiro (1.II)—landless labourer, a person who works for a wage.

lambão (9.II)—greedy, glutton.
lar (5.I)—hearth, household.
lavrador (1.II)—owner farmer.
louvado (8.I; 5.III)—land assessor.
lugar (1.II)—hamlet.

maceira (5.III)—Kneading table.
malcriado (9.V)—badly brought up.
mau olhado (15.III)—evil gaze.
milagre (13.II-V)—miracle.
minhoto (1.II)—inhabitant of Minho, especially of the Alto Minho.
monstros (9.III; 10.IV)—monsters.

namoro (6.II)—courtship.

pão (5.III)—bread.
paróquia (1.II)—parish (as a religious community).
partilhas (7.I)—division of a couple's property for the purpose of inheritance.
patrão (masc.), *patroa* (fem.) (6.I; 8.III)—head of household.
praga (15.II)—curse.
produtos do ar, da terra (8.I)—things which grow well above, or in the earth.
proprietário (1.II)—wealthy landowner.
puro (5.III)—pure.
putas, putanheira (6.IV; 8.III)—whores, whorish.

respeito (13.II)—respect.

salário (6.I)—salary.
senhores (9.V)—wealthy members of the urban strata.

terra (8.I; 11.I)—earth, land, soil, homeland.
tolher (15.III)—to harm by envy.
trabalhar (13.I; 13.V)—to work (but only physical labour).

ventre (9.II)—belly, uterus.
vício (9.IV)—predisposition to evil, etc.
vila (1.II)—small town.
vizinho (1.II; 13.I)—neighbour.

BIBLIOGRAPHY

Alexiou, M. 1974. *The Ritual Lament in Greek Tradition.* Cambridge: Cambridge University Press.

Ariès, Philippe. 1975. *Essais sur l'histoire de la mort en Occident du Moyen Âge à nos jours.* Paris: Seuil.

—— 1977. *L'Homme devant la mort.* Paris: Seuil.

Bailey, F. G. 1971. 'The peasant view of the bad life', in Teodor Shanin (ed.), *Peasants and Peasant Societies.* Harmondsworth: Penguin.

Baillaud, L. 1962. 'Les mouvements d'exploration et d'enroulement des plantes volubiles', *Handbuch der pflanzenphysiologie* 17, part 2, 637-715.

Barros, Afonso, and Ribeiro Mendes, F. 1982. *Formas de produção e estatutos de trabalho na agricultura portuguesa.* Oeiras: Instituto Gulbenkian de Ciência.

Berger, P. and Luckman, T. 1966. *The Social Construction of Reality.* Harmondsworth: Penguin.

Bethune-Baker, J. F. 1903. *An Introduction to the Early History of the Christian Doctrine.* London: Methuen.

Bloch, Maurice. 1982. 'Death, women and power', in Bloch and Parry (eds.), *Death and the Regeneration of Life.*

——, and Parry, Jonathan (eds.). 1982. *Death and the Regeneration of Life.* Cambridge: Cambridge University Press.

Bourdieu, Pierre. 1962. 'Célibat et condition paysanne', *Études Rurales* 5-6, 32-135.

—— 1977. *Outline of a Theory of Practice.* Cambridge: Cambridge University Press.

—— 1980. *Le Sens pratique*, Paris: Éditions de Minuit.

Braudel, F. 1967. *Capitalism and Material Life, 1400-1800.* London: Weidenfeld and Nicolson.

Cabral, Manuel Villaverde. 1983. A economia subterrânea vem ao de cima em Portugal, *Análise Social* 76, 199-234.

Cailler-Boisvert, Colette. 1966. 'Soajo—Une communauté feminine rurale de l'Alto Minho', *Bulletin des études portugaises* ns27, 237-84.

—— 1968. 'Remarques sur le système de parenté et sur la famille au Portugal', *L'Homme* 8, 87-103.

Calhoun, C. J. 1980. Community: Toward a variable conceptualization for comparative research', *Social History* 5, 105-30.

Campbell, J. K. 1964. *Honour, Family, and Patronage.* Oxford: Clarendon Press.

Caro Baroja, J. 1961. *Las bruxas y su mundo.* Madrid: Revista de Occidente.

—— 1979. *La estación de amor.* Madrid: Taurus.

246 *Bibliography*

Carrasco, Pedro. 1963. 'The locality referent in residence terms', *American Anthropologist* 65, 133-4.

Carré Alvarellos, L. 1965. 'O lume novo e outros lumes rituás', *Actas do Congresso Internacional de Etnografia* 3, 109-126. Lisbon: Junta de Investigações do Ultramar.

Carvalho, Joaquim. 1956. A cultura castreja: sua interpretação sociológica', Supplement to *Revista Ocidente* 50.

Casselberry, S. and Valavanes, N. 1976. '"Matrilocal" Greek peasants and a reconsideration of residence terminology', *American Ethnologist* 3, 215-26.

Castelo Branco, Camilo. 1885. *Maria da Fonte.* Porto: Livraria Civilização.

Cátedra Tomás, Maria. 1976. 'Notas sobre la envidia: los "ojos malos" entre los vaqueros de Alzada', in Carmelo Lisón Tolosana (ed.), *Temas de antropologia española.* Madrid: Akal.

—— 1979. 'Vacas y Vaqueiros', in Maria Catedra Tomás and Ricardo Sanmartín Arce, *Vaqueiros y pescadores: dos modos de vida.* Madrid: Akal.

Chayanov, A. V. 1966. *The Theory of Peasant Economy*, ed. D. Thorner, R. E. F. Smith, and B. Kerblay. Homewood: Irwin.

Christian, William A. 1972. *Person and God in a Spanish Valley.* New York: Seminar Press.

—— 1981. *Local Religion in Sixteenth-Century Spain.* Princeton: Princeton University Press.

Corominas, J., and Pascual, J. A. 1980. *Diccionario crítico etimológico castellano e hispánico* (2nd edn.). Madrid: Editorial Gredos.

Costa, P. Antonio Carvalho da. 1868. *Corografia portugueza e descriçam topografica* (2nd edn.). Braga: Tipografia de Domingos Gonçalves de Gouvea.

Costa, P. Avelino de Jesus da. 1959. *O bispo D. Pedro e a organização da diocese de Braga.* Coimbra: Faculdade de Letras.

Coutinho, Luiz M. A. P. de Souza (2nd Viscount Balsemão). n.d. 'Memória sobre o estado da agricultura na província do Minho'. Biblioteca Nacional de Lisboa, F. Geral, MS 10 750.

Cruz, António. 1970. *Geografia e economia da Província do Minho nos fins do sec. XVIII.* Coimbra: Faculdade de Letras, Centro de Estudos Humanísticos.

Cunhal, Álvaro. n.d. *Contribuição para o estudo da questão agrária.* Lisboa: Avante.

Cutileiro, José. 1971. *A Portuguese Rural Society.* Oxford: Clarendon Press.

—— 1977. *Ricos e Pobres no Alentejo.* Lisboa: Sá da Costa.

Davis, John. 1977. *People of the Mediterranean.* London: Routledge and Kegan Paul.

Davis, Natalie Zemon. 1977. 'Ghosts, Kin and Progeny: Some Features of Family Life in Early Modern Greece', *Daedalus* 106, 87-114.

Descamps, Paul. 1935. *Le Portugal: la vie sociale actuelle.* Paris: Firmin-Didot.

Dias, Jorge. 1961. *Ensaios etnográficos.* Lisbon: Junta de Investigações do Ultramar.

—— 1981. *Vilarinho das Furnas* (2nd edn.). Lisbon: Imprensa Nacional, Casa da Moeda.

Douglas, Mary. 1966. *Purity and Danger*. Harmondsworth: Penguin.

Du Boulay, Juliet. 1974. *Portrait of a Greek Mountain Village*. Oxford: Clarendon Press.

Dumont, Louis. 1970. *Homo Hierarchicus*. London: Paladin.

Durán, J. A. 1976. *Historia de caciques, bandos e ideologías en la Galicia no urbana* (2nd edn.). Madrid: Siglo XXI.

Durkheim, Émile. 1932. *De la division du travail social* (2nd edn.). Paris: Alcan.

Eliade, Mircea. 1954. *The Myth of the Eternal Return*. New York: Pantheon Books.

—— 1961. *The Sacred and the Profane: the Nature of Religion*. New York: Harper and Row.

Elias, Norbert. 1978. *The Civilizing Process*, Oxford: Blackwell.

Evans-Pritchard, Edward E. 1937. *Witchcraft, Oracles, and Magic among the Azande*. Oxford: Clarendon Press.

Feijó, Rui G., Martins, H. and Pina-Cabral, João de (eds.) 1983. *Death in Portugal: Studies in Portuguese Anthropology and Modern History*. Oxford: JASO.

Floud, Roderick. 1979. *An Introduction to Quantitative Methods for Historians* (2nd edn.). London: Methuen.

Forde, Daryll (ed.). 1954. *African Worlds*. Oxford: Oxford University Press.

Forman, Shepard, and Riegelhaupt, Joyce. 1979. 'The political economy of patron-clientship: Brazil and Portugal compared', in Margolis, M. L. and Carter, W.E. (eds.), *Brazil: Anthropological Perspectives*. New York: Columbia University Press.

Fortes, M. 1970. *Time and Social Structure and Other Essays*. London: Athlone Press.

Foster, G. M. 1972. 'The anatomy of envy: a study in symbolic behaviour', *Current Anthropology* 13, 165–201.

—— 1974. 'The dyadic contract in Tzintzuntzan, II: patron-client relationship', in Dwight Heath (ed.), *Contemporary Cultures and Societies of Latin America*. New York: Random House.

Freeman, Susan Tax. 1970. *Neighbours*. Chicago: Chicago University Press.

Furtado Coelho, Eusébio. 1861. *Estatísticas do distrito de Viana do Castelo*. Lisbon, Imprensa Nacional.

Gilmore, David D. 1982. Some notes on community nicknaming in Spain, *Man* ns17, 686–700.

Goody, Jack and Tambiah, S. J. 1973. *Bridewealth and Dowry*. Cambridge: Cambridge University Press.

Guillebaud, J.-C. 1979. Article in *Le Monde*, 4 August.

Halpern Pereira, Miriam. 1971. *Livre Câmbio e Desenvolvimento Económico*. Lisbon: Edições Cosmos.

Harris, Olivia. 1982. 'The Dead and the Devils among the Bolivian Laymi', in Bloch and Parry (1982), pp. 45-74.

Hastings, J. (ed.). 1918-1930. *Encyclopedia of Religion and Ethics*. Edinburgh: T. & T. Clark.

Hertz, Robert. 1928. *Mélanges de sociologie religieuse et folklore*. Paris: Alcan.

—— 1960. *Death and the Right Hand*. London: Cohen and West.

Hocart, A. M. 1952. *The Life-Giving Myth and Other Essays*. London: Methuen.

—— 1970. *Kings and Councillors*, ed. Rodney Needham. Chicago: Chicago University Press.

Homolle, Th. 1896. 'Donarium', in Ch. Daremberg, and Edm. Saglio, (eds.), *Dictionnaire des antiquités grecques et romaines*. Paris: Hachette.

Huntington, R. and Metcalf, P. 1979. *Celebrations of Death*. Cambridge: Cambridge University Press.

Justin. 1672. *The History of Justin*, trans. Robert Codrington. London: W. Whitwood.

Kearney, Michael. 1975. 'World view theory and study', in B. J. Spiegel, (ed.), *Annual Reviews of Anthropology* 4. Palo Alto: Annual Reviews Inc.

Keller, Ernst and Marie-Luise. 1969. *Miracles in Dispute*. London: SCM.

Kenny, M. 1961. *A Spanish Tapestry*. London: Cohen and West.

Kiernan, J. 1981. 'Worldview in perspective: towards the reclamation of a disused concept', *African Studies* 40, 3-11.

Laslett, Peter (ed.). 1972. *Household and Family in Past Times*. Cambridge: Cambridge University Press.

Laslett, Peter, Oosterveen, K. and Smith, Richard (eds.). 1980. *Bastardy and its Comparative History*. London: Edward Arnold.

Lefebvre, Henri. 1971. *Au-delà du structuralisme*. Paris: Anthropos.

Lévi-Strauss, Claude. 1963. *Structural Anthropology*. New York: Basic Books.

—— 1966. *The Savage Mind*. London: Weidenfeld and Nicolson.

—— 1973. *Anthropologie Structurale II*. Paris: Plon.

Lewis, Charles T. and Short, Charles. 1962. *Latin Dictionary* (2nd edn.). Oxford: Clarendon Press.

Lisón Tolosana, Carmelo. 1971a. *Antropologia social de España*. Madrid: Siglo XXI.

—— 1971b. *Antropologia cultural de Galicia*. Madrid: Siglo XXI.

—— 1973. 'Some aspects of moral structure in Galician hamlets', *American Anthropologist* 75, 823-34.

—— 1974. *Perfiles simbolico-morales de la cultura gallega*. Madrid: Akal.

—— 1976. (ed.), *Temas de antropologia española*. Madrid: Akal.

—— 1979. *Brujería, estrutura social y simbolismo en Galicia*. Madrid: Akal.

Lopes Gomes, Francisco, 1965. *Ritos de passagem: Entre o Airó e o Cávado*. Barcelos: Museu Regional.

Maybury-Lewis, David. 1974. *Akwẽ-Shavante Society*. New York: Oxford University Press.

Morais (Silva), António. 1952. *Grande dicionário da língua portuguesa* (10th ed., revised). Lisbon: Editorial Confluência.

Mendras, Henri. 1967. *La Fin des paysans*. Paris: Sedes.

Needham, Rodney. 1973. (ed.) *Right and Left*. Chicago: Chicago University Press.

—— 1975. Polythetic classification: convergences and consequences, Man ns10, 349-69.

New Catholic Encyclopedia. 1967. Washington: McGraw-Hill.

Oliveira, Aurélio de. 1974. *A Abadia de Tibães e o seu domínio*. Porto: Faculdade de Letras.

—— 1980. 'A renda agrícola em Portugal durante o Antigo Regime', *Revista de História Económica e Social* 6, 1-56.

Oliveira, P. Miguel de. 1950. *As paróquias rurais portuguesas*. Lisbon: União Gráfica.

Oliveira Marques, A. H. 1972. *History of Portugal*. New York: Columbia University Press.

Oliviera Martins, J. P. 1925. *Portugal contemporâneo* (2nd edn.). Lisbon: Parceria António Maria Pereira.

O'Neill, Brian J. 1982 'O trabalho cooperativo no norte de Portugal', *Análise Social* 18, 7-34.

Onians, Richard Broxton. 1954. *The Origins of European Thought*. Cambridge: Cambridge University Press.

Parkin, David. 1979. 'Straightening the path from wilderness: the case of divinatory speech', *JASO* 10, 147-60.

Paz, Octávio. 1970. *Claude Lévi-Strauss: an introduction*. New York: Delta Books.

Peacock, James L. 1971. 'Class, clown and cosmology in Javanese drama: an analysis of symbolic and social action', in Pierre Maranda (ed.), *The Structural Analysis of Oral Tradition*. Philadelphia: University of Pennsylvania Press.

Pearse, Andrew. 1971. 'Metropolis and peasant: the expansion of the urban-industrial complex and the changing rural structure', in Teodor Shanin (ed.), *Peasants and Peasant Societies*. Harmondsworth: Penguin.

Pina-Cabral, João de. 1980. 'Cults of Death in Northwestern Portugal', *JASO* 11, 1-12.

—— 1981a. 'O Pároco Rural e o Conflito entre Visões do Mundo', *Estudos Contemporâneos* 3, 75-110.

—— 1981b. A Peasant Worldview in its Context'. D.Phil. thesis, Oxford.

—— 1984a. 'Female power and the inequality of wealth and motherhood in north-western Portugal', in Renée Hirschon (ed.), *Women and Property—Women as Property*. London: Croom Helm.

—— 1984b. 'Nicknames and the Experience of Community' in *Man* ns 19(1), 148-50.

Pina-Cabral, João de, and Feijó, Rui. 1983. 'Conflicting attitudes to death in modern Portugal: the question of cemeteries', *JASO* 14, 17-43.

Pintado, Xavier. 1967. Níveis e estruturas de salários comparados: os salários portugueses e os europeus', *Análise Social* 17, 57–89.

Pires de Lima, A. C. 1948. *Estudos etnológicos, filológicos e históricos*. Porto: Junta de Província do Douro Litoral.

Pires de Lima, Joaquim and Fernando. 1938. *Tradições populares de Entre-Douro-e-Minho*. Barcelos: by authors.

Pitt-Rivers, Julian A. 1965. 'Honour and social status', in J. G. Peristiany, (ed.), *Honour and Shame*. London: Weidenfeld and Nicolson.

—— 1971. *The People of the Sierra* (2nd ed.). Chicago: Chicago University Press.

—— 1973. 'The kith and the kin', in Jack Goody (ed.), *The Character of Kinship*, Cambridge: Cambridge University Press.

Redfield, Robert. 1973. *The Little Community and Peasant Society and Culture*. Chicago: Chicago University Press.

Reis, P. António. 1978. *A romanização no concelho de Ponte de Lima*. Ponte de Lima: the author.

Riegelhaupt, Joyce. 1973. 'Festas e padres: the organization of religious action in a Portuguese parish', *American Anthropologist* 75, 835–52.

Roberts, J. M. 1976. 'Belief in the evil eye in world perspective', in Clarence Maloney (ed.), *The Evil Eye*. New York: Columbia University Press.

Rocha Peixoto, A. A. 1906. 'Tabulae Votivae', *Portugalia* 2, 187–212.

Sackville-West, V. 1943. *The Eagle and the Dove*. London: Quartet Books (1969 reprint).

Sahlins, Marshall. 1972. *Stone-Age Economics*. London: Tavistock.

Sampaio, Alberto. 1979. *Estudos económicos* (2nd edn.). Lisbon: Vega.

Santos Silva, Augusto. 1979. 'S. Torcato, 1905: o povo, a religião e o poder', *Estudos Contemporâneos* 0, 15–82.

Saraiva, José Hermano. 1978. *História concisa de Portugal*. Lisbon: Europa-América.

Schlumböhn, Jürgen. 1980. 'Traditional' collectivity and 'modern' individuality', *Social History* 5, 71–103.

Schutte, G. 1980. 'Social Time and Biological Time', *Anthropos* 75, 257–65.

Scott, James C. 1976. *The Moral Economy of the Peasant*. New Haven and London: Yale University Press.

Serrão, Joel. (ed.) 1965. *Dicionário de História de Portugal*. Lisbon: Iniciativas Editoriais.

—— 1974. *A emigração portuguesa*. (2nd edn.). Lisbon: Livros Horizonte.

Shanin, Teodor. (ed.) 1971. *Peasants and Peasant Society*. Harmondsworth: Penguin.

Silius Italicus. 1934. *Punica*, trans. J. D. Duff. London: Heinemann.

Silva, António de. 1979. 'Evolução recente da sociedade-igreja', *Economia e Sociedade* 25/26, 33–41.

Silverman, Sydel. 1975. *The Three Bells of Civilization*. New York: Columbia University Press.

Taborda de Morais, A. 1940. 'Novas Áreas da Fitogeografia Portuguesa', *Boletim da Sociedade Broteriana* (2nd series) 14, 97–138.

Taylor, James L. 1958. *A Portuguese-English Dictionary* (revised ed.), London: Harrap.

Thomas, Louis-Vincent. 1980. *Le Cadavre*. Bruxelles: Éditions Complexe.

Turner, V. W. 1957. *Schism and Continuity in an African Society*. Manchester: Manchester University Press.

Valle, Carlos, 1965. 'Tradições do casamento', in *Actas do Congresso Internacional de Etnografia* 3. Lisbon: Junta de Investigações do Ultramar.

Van Gennep, Arnold. 1960. *Rites of Passage*. London: Routledge and Kegan Paul.

Viegas Guerreiro, Manuel. 1981. *Pitões das Júnias: Esboço de monografia etnográfica*. Lisboa: Serviço Nacional de Parques.

Viterbo, Joaquim de Santa Rosa. 1865. *Elucidário das palavras , termos e frases*, Lisbon: n.p.

Warner, Marina. 1978. *Alone of all her Sex*. London: Quartet Books.

Weber, Max. 1978. *Economy and Society*, 2 vols, G. Roth and Claus Wittich (eds.). Berkeley: University of California Press.

Willems, E. 1962. 'On Portuguese family structure', *International Journal of Comparative Sociology* 3, 65–79.

Winch, R. and Bennett, V. 1950. *The Assumption of Our Lady and Catholic Theology*. London: SPCK.

Wittgenstein, Ludwig. 1982. *Remarks on Frazer's* Golden Bough, bilingual edition. Rush Rhees (ed.) (2nd edn.). Retford: Brynmill Press.

NEWSPAPERS OF SPECIFIC ETHNOGRAPHIC INTEREST

O Povo da Barca, Arcos de Valdevez: Tipografia Barquense.

Notícias da Barca, Ponte da Barca: Gráfica da Barca.

PORTUGUESE STATISTICS

(All published by INE (Instituto Nacional de Estatística, Lisbon: Imprensa Nacional.)

Anuário Estatístico (yearly).

Recenseamentos da População (every decade).

Inquérito às Explorações Agrícolas, 1968.

INDEX